Philosophy and Architecture

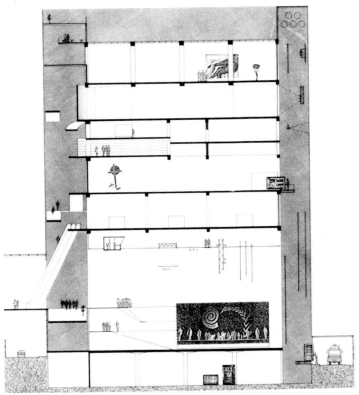

OMA, ZKM KARLSRUHE, SECTION

OMA, BIBLIOTHEQUE DE FRANCE COMPETITION, DETAIL OF MODEL

Journal of
Philosophy and the Visual Arts

Philosophy and Architecture

ACADEMY EDITIONS ·LONDON/ST MARTIN`S PRESS · NEW YORK

Front Cover: Daniel Libeskind, The Jewish Extension to the German Museum in Berlin,1990

Acknowledgements: *Half Title* & *Frontis Piece*: Illustrations courtesy of the Architects. **Andrew Benjamin** *p 6*: Illustration courtesy of the British Museum, **Jean-François Lyotard** *pp 12-15*: Translation from the French by Geoffry Bennington, published with the permision of Polity Press. Illustration from K F Schinkel Collected Architectural Designs, Academy Editions, **Sylviane Agacinski** *pp 16-21:* Translation from the French by Leslie Hill, **Geoffry Bennington** *pp 22-31:* Illustration courtesy of the Architect, **John Rajchman** *pp32-37:* Illustrations courtesy of the Architects, **Catherine Cooke** *pp38-39:* Illlustrations supplied by the author, **Moisei Ginzburg** *pp40-48:* Photographs by Catherine Cooke who also translated the text. **Gianni Vatimo** *pp 74-77:* Translation from the French by David Webb. Photograph by Andrew Benjamin, **Mark Wigley** *pp 84-95:* Illustrations supplied by the author. **Peter Eisenman** *p5 & p96* illustrations from Peter Eisenman's Wexner Center, and extract by Kurt Forster from Architectural Design Vol 59:11-12:89. Extract by the architect from an interview with Hiroshi Maruyama

First published in Great Britain in 1990 by *Journal of Philosophy & the Visual Arts*
an imprint of the
ACADEMY GROUP LTD, 7 HOLLAND STREET, LONDON W8 4NA
ISBN: 1-85490-016-1 (UK)

Published in the United States of America by
ST MARTIN'S PRESS, 175 FIFTH AVENUE, NEW YORK 10010
ISBN: 0-312-03986-7 (USA)

Printed and bound in Singapore

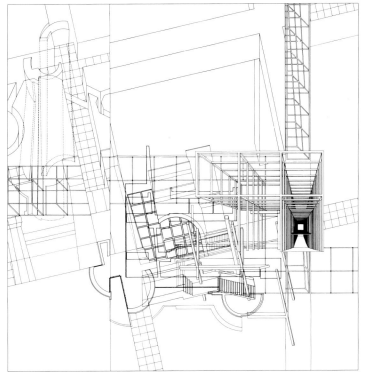

PETER EISENMAN, WEXNER CENTER, DISECTED ELEMENTS

Contents

ANDREW BENJAMIN
DISTANCING AND SPACING

THE TOWER OF BABEL, FROM AN EIGHTEENTH CENTURY ETHIOPIC MANUSCRIPT OF HYMN TEBABA TABIBAN

Even if the two poles of absolute and relative are resisted space and distance can still be said to take place between two points. Here however reciprocity is also at work since their separate existence as points is itself dependant upon space and distance. This is not intended to be a geometrical claim for the points in question function as no more than markers of that separation and, thereby, of that which

is separated. The relationship between these 'points' could be envisaged as one of radical separation, two points in chronological time; or interdependent separation, self and other; or even one to be overcome, the separation between mode and object of interpretation. In each instance distance and space are essential. How then are they to be understood? The question is one of a beginning; of developing an approach to space.[1]

The problem of reflecting on space – its becoming an object of either thought or reflection – is, that from its inception, such an act will have to involve a two-fold spacing. The first spacing is the one that can always be said to exist between thought and its object. (Even though the actual mode of existence in question remains to be clarified.) The second emerges because this primary spacing is reproduced; though now as the object itself. Spacing would seem to have been doubled, moreover this doubling would then have to function as a precondition for any attempt to think space. It is clear that just from these elementary considerations a number of complex issues have come to the fore. However at this point of departure they do not concern space as such; though they do *already* concern the possibility of any postulated 'space as such'. The initial difficulties that must be confronted are those inherent in the formulation of spacing. Even this expression is problematic for what is at stake here is not space as a given but the philosophical consequences of

tracing the preconditions of an already presupposed space. The presupposition may only ever be present in terms of a given formulation, one which can always be denied within an explanation. The possibility of a denial of distance – its having been reworked within a totality – cannot overcome the initial recognition of doubling. However as a beginning this is to do no more than offer a tentative approach. All that has been presented thus far is the inevitability of the inscription of spacing within the activity that seeks to take it (spacing) as an object. Now within the 'stakes' of spacing it could be conjectured that the two elements of central importance are distance and relation. (Though it must be added that these are not radically distinct or isolatable elements. They interconnect. Indeed it will prove impossible to effect a radical separation between distance and relation.) Part of the value of the second – relation – is that it has the capacity to allow for the introduction of the ethical. In order to return to the initial problem of the doubling of space it will be essential to begin with distance. The distance between elements is a fundamental component of the constitution of their specificity. The door and the window are held apart. The floor and the ceiling are distanced. Corners emerge out of the interplay of the meeting and distancing of walls. The wall works to divide. The staircase while joining floors nonetheless marks their distance. This takes place in a way that differs from the manner in which two floors are joined and distanced by walls. The constitution of the house necessitates distance. In addition it demands the experience of that distance. The experience of dwelling is, though in an as yet to be specified way, premised upon the experience of distance. (Distance need not, of course, be limited to the architectural. Both Buber and Heidegger have, in their own ways, tried to demonstrate that distance is a decisive element in the constitution of the being of being human.)[2]

What then is the experience of distance? Is it no more than the experience of a relation, albeit one that generates specific identities? The problem of experience cannot be posed as thought it took place prior to spacing and distance. Experience is always going to involve a division between the experiencing subject and the object of experience. This distinction is not a heuristic primitive since it is still possible to ask the question of the conditions of possibility of experience itself. Now, however, as opposed to the doubling of space that takes place within the attempt to reflect upon it – ie space existing as an object of thought – what is at play here is slightly different. The difference will reside in the nature of the distinction that can be drawn between experience and interpretation. This distinction can never be absolute since both take place in relation to tradition. And yet neither is it completely defined by tradition and thus relative. There is a further dimension here, namely that any understanding of experience is going to involve the activity of interpretation. The difference is going to involve the activity of interpretation. The difference is rather that interpretation as an act – as a philosophical task – will, and of necessity, involve different ontological and temporal considerations than those at work within experience; even in an 'interpretation' of experience. The unfolding of these considerations will be traced. An initial marker can however be found in the presence within experience of the 'lived'. Experience is that which takes place within the bodily and cognitive encounter of the world of experience. The question then of the experience of distance will refer, though always only ever in part, to what can be described as the reality of lived experience.

Demanding that experience be allowed the further description of 'lived' is not to link experience to an unproblematic and thereby simply posited empirical existence. (The empirical understood as involving a purported unmediated giveness to consciousness.) It is exactly in these terms that the empirical is thus already an 'interpretive' term. Hence there is no straightforward suggestion of an opposition between interpretation understood as discursive and therefore of experience as lived (ie as non-discursive). It is rather that experience and interpretation involve different relations both to history (or in philosophical terms to tradition) and to the present.[3]

Now distance seems to bring with it a choice. It is not as simple as the alternative between closure and openness. The choice, here, is more difficult to define. It concerns the nature of the relation. Consequently it resides in the possibility of a distinction between a relation in which distance comes to be effaced and one in which while it is maintained – one where distance endures – distance is experienced in the absence of totality and more significantly in the absence of teleology. (This absence must be clarified since it is not just non-presence: that would be the logic of the either/or.) In other words distance comes to be experienced as always involving the ineliminable presence of an otherness that can never be overcome in the struggle for synthesis. The real problem here will always concern the possibility of precisely this type of experience. The distance in which distance comes to be effaced is one articulated within and thus expressed – also experienced – in terms of teleology. Experience becomes predictive experience. What emerges therefore as a fundamental component of these considerations is the predictive. The temporality of prediction involves a split – a spacing – between a now in which the prediction is advanced and a future; one having a specific nature. In the first instance it is open awaiting the realisation of the prediction. It then closes, enclosing what had been held apart, when the prediction comes to be realised. The awaiting that 'attends' prediction defines and directs both the possibility of experience and the specific object that comes to be experienced. The spacing of prediction therefore is one that involves both an opening and a closure. Space – distance – is effaced in the realisation. As a consequence spacing, understood as a site of potential plurality, is denied by the progressive realisation demanded by teleology. It would, of course, be far too hasty to conflate prediction and teleology. It is best to leave the specificity of prediction – the predictive – open and cite instances.

In outline it can be suggested that the philosophical strategy associated with the Hegelian element within German idealism is another instance of a predictive philosophical strategy.[4] Here the predictive involves an Absolute that encloses; enclosing while defining the nature of the differences within it. The movement towards the experience of the I=I of Absolute self-consciousness encloses the history of experience. The actuality of philosophy, in Hegelian terms, perhaps even the actuality of experience itself, occurs within the closure that marks the realisation of the absolute as the absolute. The distance established within teleological prediction or within the attempted realisation of the absolute, understood as taking place with the experience of the absolute qua absolute, is overcome in the synthesising realisation of the predictive. In other words predictive experience will, in the process of its coming to be realised, close the initial distance and thereby exclude any need to take up the question of the relation. (The ethical potential is thus denied.) The problematic element is the housing of non-predictive experience. The problem is compounded for within concrete space teleology emerges in terms of function. The predictive and function are interarticulated. It is the distance between wall and window, between the experiencing subject and the object of experience, that comes to be effaced when the house is experienced in terms of function. The conditions of possibility for this type of experience are to be found in the tradition in which unity and totality are taken as prior and as having priority. Distance is overcome in a synthesis. The held-apart, the distanced, are henceforth rearticulated within a totality. The counter move is not to take the elements of distance in their radical individuality (once again this would repeat the nihilistic gesture of attempting to counter totality with the assertion of unmediated singularity or individuality) but rather to dwell on the possibility of thinking unity or totality beyond the determination of synthesis and therefore beyond a projected or posited essence and thus in terms of the possibility of unity/totality being the belonging together of the different; a fundamental and constitutive part of which will be distance. Distance will thereby emerge as an anoriginal presence. The anoriginal is the mark of an original dis-unity. Instead of taking distance and spacing as an opening up of that which had hitherto been a unity, they will be taken as primary; as anoriginal. The issue at play here rather than being stated in advance will come to be worked out.[5]

It is only once the move of reworking identity and difference is made in terms of the anoriginal that the ethical/political problem of relation can be investigated. The reason for this being the case is that the relation, as a relation between the different, can itself only emerge with the distancing of the possibility of synthesis and the effacement of distance. A process that rearticulates and repeats its own presence, yielding the anoriginal presence of distance which generates the relation as a relation. Relation will provide a way of approaching the belonging together of the divergent. Recognising the possibility that relation rather than being imposed after the event can be argued for as always anoriginally present. It is always possible that a relation between the different can come to be reworked in terms of sameness. In fact a great deal of ethical and political argument will depend upon this being the case. The important point is however that the move to sameness takes place in relation to anoriginal difference. Sameness will occur out of difference. Sameness, unity and totality will involve a pragmatic dimension; moves in a game. Therefore difference and identity, their specificity and the 'difference' between them will have to be rethought beyond the confines of tradition. Rethinking and tradition will themselves be distanced from each other. Finally the mark of the anoriginal will always figure within the secondary sameness checking any claims of absolute synthesis or totality. Thinking difference will depend upon the anoriginal.

Having come this far it is now the question of how to understand the distinction between the predictive and the non-predictive that is of fundamental importance. Not just because of possible answers but because of the very formulation of the question. The distinction between the predictive and the non-predictive is not, despite surface appearances, (and in spite of the implicit irony) either a simple binary opposition, or a distinction articulated in terms set by the logic of the either/or. If it were, if, that is, the distinction involved a straightforward oscillation between the positive and the negative, then the distance opened by the distinction would itself have vanished. The already suggested distinction between experience and interpretation is central here. In order, therefore, to analyse further the nature of the relation between the predictive and the non-predictive it will be essential to investigate some of the ways in which experience and interpretation can be differentiated. What is at stake is their distance.

It has already been suggested that the distinction between interpretation and experience lies in their differing relations to tradition and the present. Tradition is not a univocal term since there are differing and marginal traditions, and yet tradition intends to be univocal. There is, nonetheless, a dominant tradition. It is precisely in terms of this dominance (taking the interplay of margins and intentionality into consideration) that tradition can be understood as a determination in advance. The foreclosing of the future within such an understanding of tradition is necessary if there is to be an adequate conception of change and experimentation since they will come to be defined by tradition and yet in the process will come to redefine tradition itself. The determination in advance is the articulation of a repetition governed and dominated by the Same. Understanding tradition in this way gives rise to a conception of change/experimentation in which what comes to be presented – what takes place as a founding moment – is an original repetition. The Same does mean absolute identity; that to which it refers is a repetition of conditions of existence: and thus of the possibility of thought.

The distinction between a repetition of and within the Same, and, an original repetition, brings into consideration the problem of the history and in particular and history of thinking; ie the history of philosophy. As has been indicated what is intended by the Same here is not the repetition of the same, identical mode of thought. But rather the Same as itself is a unifying process that determines what can be thought. It does not follow that this determination is necessarily successful. It is a determination on the level of intentional logic,[6] ie one that takes place in relation to the dominant tradition's self-conception. (It is this 'self-conception' that provides access to what has already been designated as the present since the present can be understood as the moment implicated in the formulation of the philosophical task.

The 'moment' [not the present moment but rather the 'moment of the present'] will be inscribed within the task, and insofar as it is applicable, generate the concepts of past and future proper to that task.) The original repetition, while situated within the same chronological time as the present of tradition, displaces itself. It pluralises the time that is the present, establishes a distance – a space – such that the displacement of, for example, the original repetition, cannot be reduced to the present of tradition, while, nonetheless occupying a place within the same chronological present. It is thus there will be an inevitable connection between chronology and the present of tradition. The connection will not admit of any type of reduction. It will however allow the original repetition to be dated. Spacing will be constitutive and thus involve anoriginal presence. It is the anoriginal nature of spacing that will relocate the ethical. Its locus will become an already existent relation. The mode of being proper to this 'existence' is problematic. It is not actual existence. It will involve a presence which while present is not actualised as such. This is primordial presence. (Delimiting the specificity and the ontology of primordial presence remains to be done.)

The relationship between interpretation and tradition needs to be re-expressed in terms of the relationship between a dominant mode of interpretation and the philosophical task of interpretation. Setting up the distinction in this way allows for the inclusion and consideration of the presence of repetition and the effacing of distance. The particular self-conception of the philosophical task of interpretation that seeks conformity with the modes of thinking handed down as tradition will attempt to overcome the distinction between mode and object of interpretation. Within these terms the task of interpretation will have been completed to the extent that a homology between mode and object has been established. Homology will mark the attempt to exclude distance. Difference can always be thought within homology however it is a difference that is sustained by the Same. Difference will always take place 'after'. It will have to announce the two-fold priority of unity and identity. Here on the other hand identity will always precede difference. Difference and spacing are therefore continually at work within thinking. The thinking of tradition can be viewed as parasitic upon an original presence despite the fact that it works to exclude it. The thinking of tradition therefore, as well as the possibility of identity, will be premised upon an an original spacing that comes to be excluded and effaced within the attempt to realise the tasks that tradition sets for itself and which are thus fundamental to its own identity or self-conception.

While interpretation generates complex problems, the most complex, in this instance, concerns experience. Consequently what must now be investigated is how the present and tradition figure within experience. There will always be an analogical relationship between interpretation and experience. What is at play here however is not the analogue – ie not the similarity – but the way in which they differ. As an approach to experience it is essential to draw an important distinction between two types of experience. The first concerns those experiences that can be made objects of reflection. The second are the experiences that fail to be noticed; ie to figure within consciousness, in other words experiences of which there can be no actual memory. (Memory is not simply a negative characteristic since it is obvious that memory will play a fundamental role in the first type of experience.) While there are importantly different reasons why there may be no memory of a given experience – the differences will range from indifference to repression – emphasis here will be given to the first type. It is perhaps already clear that the move from experience to reflection could be thought to be another expression – though perhaps a reworked one– of the distinction, and therefore of the relation, between experience and interpretation.[7]

It is essential to recognise that there must be a unity in experience. This would occur in a similar way to there being a unity in perception. The 'all' that is experienced must be experienced in its totality. While this is the case to remain at this level is to fall into the trap of offering no more than a phenomenological description. What must be investigated are the conditions of possibility for the unity of experience. One argument would be that time provides the answer. The experience or perception of the 'all' takes place at the same time; an argument that is for example pursued by Husserl.[8] Its unity therefore is temporal. The temporality of the experiencing subject would be identical with the object of experience. This would, in addition, define the relations between the elements of the percept, or object of experience, in temporal terms. The relations between X, Y and Z, assuming that X, Y and Z form the given object of experience or perception, would exist because they were in that particular set of spatial relations at the same point in *time*. To the extent that this particular argument is followed perception and experience will not just involve a temporal simultaneity, their existence will be defined by it. This is, of course, far from sufficient for the question of how this unity emerges as a unity cannot be answered by recourse to time on its own for time (in the sense that time has been used in the above) will never address the question of the 'what' of experience or perception. The 'what' of the object is not commensurate with the existence of the object qua temporal entity. The 'what' is precisely what the object is. The nature of the 'what' cannot be separated from the more general problem of the conditions of existence. The reason why this is the case it that objects of experience are always experienced in terms of this 'what'. Either the 'what' is unproblematic or it remains as a 'what' that is as yet to be determined. This state of the as-yet-to-be-determined can, in the main, be resolved by attention to detail, sharper focus, greater clarity, etc. Nonetheless there will be a stage when the as-yet-to-be-determined will have a qualitatively different nature. It is this stage that will be of specific interest since it delimits what can be called avant-garde or limit experiences. Such experiences will call upon thinking and thus to that extent will demand philosophy.

The status of the object of experience or perception is not explicable in terms of its objectivity, its pure being as object. Indeed it is possible to go further and suggest that except in those cases in which the object is indistinct or out of focus (or other similar states of affairs) what comes to be experienced or perceived is never pure objectivity. The 'what' of the object intrudes into the experience or perception to the extent that meaning occurs. The absence of meaning – the incomprehensibility of the perception of the experience – can only be explained by the object having retained its objectivity and not having attained its 'whatness'. The consequence of this is that the existence of the object as no more than object entails that its specificity has yet to be determined, it fails to signify beyond objectivity and hence it is yet to mean. The further problem that emerges here concerns shared experiences or perceptions. It is on one level clear that the 'same' object of experience or percept has been experienced or perceived but this will only be strictly true in terms of the objectivity of the object. When what is at issue is the exact nature of the experience or perception then that which comes to be addressed is its meaning: its 'whatness'. It is at this point that the presence of disagreement and conflict occurs. The possibility of such an 'occurrence' is grounded in the fact that it does not follow that the experience or perception of the 'same' object will entail an agreement in regards to its 'whatness'. It is here that a link between experience and meaning can be established. Experience does not occur in terms, as it were, of its own pure objectivity. Experience will exist in relation both to the object and to that which makes possible the experience of the object as a meaningful object, namely tradition. Moreover, it is the interconnection between experience and meaning that will allow for an explanation of conflicts and disagreements.

The link between experience and meaning takes place in relation to tradition and the present. As has been suggested what is intended by the present is neither the instant, the *nunc stans*, nor is it the pure temporal moment within chronological time. The present is the 'time' of the self-conception of the philosophical task. It is therefore the self-conception of the age. An age that is itself described within the formulation of the task. The reciprocity here is inescapable. What it marks is the recognition that any age will always define itself in its own terms. (The self-description only reinforces the radical separation of the time of the present; ie ephocal time and chronological time). However this description will not be one that it gives to itself but rather it is a description that is announced in the actual formulation of the philosophical task. It will occur therefore both within the conception of the task and also within the ontological and temporal preconditions at work within that task. These preconditions need not be explicit. Indeed their implicit presence often serves to check the realisation of the self-sustained task. It will always be essential to add that the present will not be a unified site, there will nonetheless always be a dominant self-conception. The repetition of this dominance is tradition.

The relationship between this repetition and experience involves a conception of meaning or understanding as a determination in advance. It is possible to go further and suggest that the pre-existence of the categories of the understanding, being those through which any 'new' experience or perception is understood, will entail that within meaning and understanding, tradition acting in terms of rules – and hence enacting rules – will have a regulative function. Such rules will determine what can be understood and what can mean: have meaning. (This determination taking place as tradition working through and as the understanding.) The legislative function is the presence of dominance. There is an important corollary here. One that concerns the concept of the avant-garde since it involves what is generally understood as 'resistance' to tradition.

The interplay of meaning and tradition could give rise to a conception of the resistance to dominance as the assertion of non-meaning. The constraint of the primacy of meaning yeilding such a response. The basis of such an argument would be the presence of the possibility of meaning residing in the determination in advance. Meanings, for which, the future was always determined, and to that extent never really futural would be countered by the promulgation, at the instant, of purported non-meaning. Comprehension confronted by the perpetual impossibility of comprehension. However it is precisely because of the relationship between the understanding and meaning that the contrary will be the case. Since non-meaning falls within the purview of the understanding it does not mark its limit. The limit will not be an absolute but rather exist as a site of tension at which in spite of its being present the understanding can no longer be said to dominate. The closure of homology and tradition opens. Even though they are present the understanding and tradition would have become displaced; replaced by their representation as displacement. The inescapable presence of the understanding – ie the historicality of the possibility of meaning and comprehension – entails that what passes as 'resistance' will always have to be defined in relation to tradition and more importantly to the self-conception of tradition; its present. The result of this is simply that resistance on its own will no longer be an adequate description of the avant-garde project. Resistance becomes nihilism; pure negation devoid of even dialectical mediation. It therefore cannot be thought to mark the moment in which the understanding and tradition no longer either determine or delimit the possibility of meaning, thought and experience.

This potential, the possibility of the avant-garde will be connected – while not being reducible to – the imagination and hence to the aesthetic. The exclusivity of the imagination is not an option because of the capacity for an experience of the as-yet-to-be-determined generating reflection. Reflection, in this instance, will emerge at the limit of the understanding. In other words at that point at which distance is maintained; namely at the point where the percept, object of experience, etc is such that it cannot be automatically assimilated to, and hence only be explicable within, the terms decreed by the determination in advance. Experience can be made the object of reflection, here however the possibility for meaning, understanding, depends upon reflection. Reflection in this latter sense will always differ, in the way it operates, from the understanding since its practice marks not only the understanding's limit as was suggested, but, is at the same time the limit of tradition. One consequence of this is that it draws an important connection between understanding and tradition within experience. A further possible division within experience is established by the presence of the limit. On the one hand there is the experience of/at the limit. On the other there is the capacity for a re-experience which would amount to a renewed holding-apart of experience and object of experience, thereby overcoming the automatic assimilation and thus, finally of allowing spacing. The renewed holding-apart would be a form of original repetition. The doubling of spacing would no longer be a paradox – or logical contradiction – but rather the actuality, the reality, of thinking at the limit. While this opens up themes that will have to be explored in greater detail elsewhere it will allow for greater precision in examining the distinction between interpretation and experience.

When a non-limit experience has been made an object of reflection, then what takes place is a retracing of how the meaning or comprehensibility of that experience is established. What comes to be noted is its conformity to the understanding and thus to tradition. Within the attempt to reveal the precise determination of the 'what' of experience the 'retracing' will both reopen and close the distance between the original experience and object of experience and their subsequent presence within reflection. The experience will be of a conformity or a homology. These characteristics are not intrinsic to the object. They delimit the relationship between the object – its 'whatness' – and that in terms of which this 'whatness' is determined, namely, the understanding and tradition. This is the nature of predictive experience. It is not as though the 'whatness' could be experienced in another way if it is to have either meaning or comprehension within the experience. Once again this is not intended to preclude the possibility that, either in terms of re-experience or reflection, the 'whatness' could come to have a different and perhaps even conflictual determination. It is simply that insofar as the interrelationship between understanding, tradition and meaning is concerned the 'whatness' – in relation to non-limit experiences – is determined in advance. Within such experiences distance can only be said to figure in its being effaced. It is with the emergence of the question of re-experience that the homological nature of experience can be opened up. Distance and spacing become reinscribed. Plurality would seem to intrude. Experience gives way to interpretation. Re-experience is the potential at work with tradition that the understanding need not dominate. While the possibility of re-experience need not involve an original repetition the fact that it can means that harboured within the present is a past which will not be re-presented but will be presented anew.

One of the defining elements of the non-limit experience is homology and thus the absence of plurality in relation to the 'whatness' of the object. Once the moves towards re-experience and reflection are made then this unity became pluralised. The potential for plurality will always lie in the reworking of the 'whatness' of the object. It is, of course, exactly this reworking of the 'whatness' that cannot take place as experience. The possibility of this reworking is not to be located in the object of experience per se but in the possibility of thinking beyond the determinations of the understanding and tradition in relation to the object. Here the analogy with interpretation comes into play. Interpretation can always involve homology, however the difference is that while homology may be an aim it is not the precondition for interpretation. The precondition lies elsewhere. The problem at this stage is not with the activity of interpretation but the way in which plurality figures – in a positive and negative sense – within that act. This will be another way of distinguishing between interpretation and experience.

Interpretation will involve distance. Spacing does not become an integral part of the activity of interpretation, it is a constitutive element. The temporality of interpretation concerns both the specific act of interpretation as well as the capacity for either different interpretations or for reinterpretation. The potential is inscribed within the object and as such may figure within the interpretation itself. The interpretation that demands homology – a unity between subject and object – must fail to address or try to exclude that element that cannot be reincorporated; ie to use Walter Benjamin's terms, the potential 'afterlife' of the object. The specificity of the 'afterlife' cannot be determined in advance; to the extent that it is the future becomes present; to the extent that it does not the future potential resides in the present. It is therefore futural in the sense that it is always yet to be determined. The problematic aspect of this argument concerns the claim that this potential is inscribed within the object and that hence it may come to figure within the process of interpretation. This needs to be understood as involving the following considerations.

The desire for homology can be viewed as a desire for that unity or totality within which the truth of the object comes to be established via the act of interpretation. Truth, in this sense, marks the closure of distance. It is here that an otherness prior to both unity and totality – an otherness that founds the initial desire – comes into play. The primacy of becoming over stasis will form an integral part of the mode of being proper to this otherness. The recognition of the anoriginal will entail that the distance between mode and object of interpretation can never be fully overcome. Truth is no longer an option. The result will be that the force or viability of an interpretation will have to be judged in a different way. Judgement returns as a philosophical problem. A fundamental part of this will be the consequences of holding a given interpretation; consequences stemming from its presuppositions and implications.

The next consideration will flow from the recognition that the tension accompanying a conception of the object as anoriginally heterogenous means that attention will need to be paid to style. Style and project will be both distanced and related. There will therefore be neither an absolute difference nor complete commensurability. Homology as the dictat of tradition will founder on the primordial presence of spacing. Attention to spacing opens up the critical dimension within the object, one, it must be added, that the object's intentional logical may always seek to deny.

The final consideration is that the plurality inherent within interpretation can only emerge within the practice of interpretation. This emergence, once again, needs to be understood in both a positive and negative sense. The lack of a direct comparison with experience resides in the temporality proper to each.

Experience will always involve a cognitive assimilation of the object. If this does not occur then experience gives way to reflection. There will nonetheless be those limit experiences in which what comes to be experienced is the presence of an ineliminable distance between subject and object. This presence can only even be grasped after the event. It is in this way that temporal deferral becomes an essential element of limit experiences. Having reached this stage it is now possible to return, albeit briefly, to the problem of relation.

Between any two 'points' not only will there be distance there will also be a relation. Distance and relation are to that extent interarticulated. One does not precede the other. The mode of being proper to this relation is complex. A relation will always involve distancing and spacing. It is however only if the held-apart is taken as held-apart that relation emerges as central. If the constitutive elements are given priority then individuality would be thought to take place prior to relation. This precedence is based not on the original elements of relation, but on effacing the initial relation that constitutes the elements in their individuality. The initial constitutive relation is therefore primordially present since its being present does not of necessity depend upon its having been actualised. The primordially present relation works to reinforce the description of a relation that involves anoriginal heterogenity. The relation both holds apart and brings the held-apart together. The significant element is that this process does not work to assimilate the constitutive distance between same and other. The absence of assimilation is the absence of homogeneity. The relation sustains a difference outside of synthesis. It is only once relation is held as a primodial presence marking anoriginal heterogeneity that the question of how the relation is to be understood, such that the belonging together of the different is able both to take place and be maintained, can come to be posed. The question of the relation pertains equally to the ethical as well as aesthetic realm. In this instance it is the aesthetic that is of primary interest.

Relation is important within aesthetics because the centrality of relation will yield an approach to the object that does not take the relation between subject and object as a totality but as the interplay of identity and difference; of same and other. This generates a different object. The question of how relations are to be understood is, for example, a fundamental question within architectural thinking once the domination of functionalism and determinism no longer takes place. The centrality of relation will mean that the task of interpretation will no longer be conceived in terms of the need to establish a homological relation between subject and object. One consequence of this is that what is thereby allowed to come to the fore are those elements within the object that would not sanction either totality within the object – the object would no longer be approached as though it were a synthetic unity – or a totality based on the overcoming or effacing of relation, the held-apart, existing between subject and object. Anoriginal heterogeneity therefore will play a central role within interpretation. Interpretation will henceforth work otherwise.

The distance between philosophy and architecture and their relation, the spacing within the building with its own plural inbuilt relations, are themselves to be approached, from within philosophy, in terms of the held-apart; the primordially present held-apart. It is only in this way that distinction qua distinction can come to figure within interpretation, re-experience and reflection.

Notes

1 The impetus for writing this paper came in part from trying to think through some of the ways in which philosophy and architecture may be thought to connect and how experience and the understanding would figure within it. And in part in response to rereading John Sallis' important and fascinating book *Spacings – of Reason and Imagination*, University of Chicago Press 1987.

2 The way this occurs in Buber and Heidegger is complex and will be treated in greater detail at a later stage. In sum it concerns Buber's paper 'Distance and Relation' in *The Knowledge of Man*, Humanities Press International 1988; and elements of Heidegger's commentary on Sophocles' *Antigone* in *An Introduction to Metaphysics*, Yale University Press, 1985.

3 This term is, in part, clarified in the remainder of the essay. In sum both the present and tradition provide a way of thinking philosophically about history.

4 These far too cursory lines presuppose a certain reading of Hegel. They privilege the *Phenomenology of Spirit* and, it can be argued, concern Hegel's project in the form that it comes to be announced in that work.

5 I have tried to develop the concept of the anoriginal in *Translation and the Nature of Philosophy* Routledge 1989, and 'Interpreting Mirrors, Painting Reflections' in *Oxford Literary Review* Summer 1989

6 By intentional logic what is meant is the self-identification of that particular task or project that a given object of interpretation sets out to enact.

7 These comments on the relationship between memory and experience are skeletal and stand in need of a great deal of expansion and elaboration. Part of such an undertaking would involve taking up the distinction drawn, though in different ways, by Buber and Walter Benjamin between 'Erfahrung' and 'Erlebnis'.

8 I have in mind here Husserl's analysis of experience in the first part of *Experience and Judgement*.

SCHINKEL, WERDERSCHEN MARKET BERLIN

JEAN-FRANÇOIS LYOTARD
MATTER AND TIME

One of the questions posed is that of the use of the concept of matter in contemporary philosophy. What does the question mean? What is 'use of a concept'? Is a concept a tool? And then use to what purpose?

I see in the question the predominance of a technologistic thinking of thinking, i.e. a thinking of

thinking as work. A mechanical energy, potential and/or kinetic, is applied to an object so as to transform it (movement in space; qualitative modification: alloiôs): 'productive' use.

Now such an object is called in dynamics a material point or system.

With matter comes force, and the different sorts of energy, and work.

Are these metaphors? Or else is it thus that what we still call thought operates? An energy applied to a material point so as to transform it? With in that case the 'concept' playing the role of transformer?

There are several families of transformers because there are several forms taken by energy: mechanical, calorific, electrical, chemical, rays, nuclear. Should we add thinking or spiritual, as Bergson used to put it?

The 'material points' to which each of these forms of energy is applied are all different. Cartesian mechanics studies 'bodies which are perceptible to human observation and transformations analogical to human experience.

The transformation of elements, such as the transformation of uranium 238 into neptunium, by bombarding the nuclei with neutrons, are not only not on our scale, but require an idea of matter of which the philosopher, ignorant and timid as he is, notes at least this – that it seems no longer to give any credence to the substance model.

I   Cartesian mechanics, and metaphysics, need no more than a naked substance. 'The nature of matter or of the body taken in general does not consist in its being a hard, or heavy, or coloured thing, or which touches our senses in some other way, but only in that it is a substance extended in length, breadth and depth.' (*Principles of philosophy*, II, 4). Such is the body, 'substance of material things'. Extension is infinitely divisible (§20), and thus is not constituted of simple elements (atoms), contains no void (§16-18), is homogeneous and continuous; it is indefinite (§21).

A body in the narrow sense is a part of extension. Movement is the changing of place of this body, from one bodily neighbourhood to another. The movement is only relative to an observer judged to be immobile. So that there is no substantial difference between rest and movement. Movement does not demand any particular form, it is a property of the mobile, and rest is another property of it. Mechanics is a part of geometry, study and production of figures in movement. The only relevant transformers are the axioms of classic geometry. Cartesian matter is a concept – extension – which is perfectly transparent to geometrico-algebraic thought. Everything that comes to us from it via the senses is removed from it as appearance. As my

body is a part of extension, it cannot inform me about extension in general and its mathematical logic. Physiology, to the contrary, attempts to explain appearances (hardness, weight, colour, etc) by the mechanism of figures and movements alone. The machine has to be rediscovered under the sensibility which is no more than a theatrical effect of it.

We would say today that there is no matter in Cartesian thought. The foreclosure of the 'material other' inspires the decision to deny the 'knowledges' of the body proper. The union of soul and body remains an intractable enigma. The soul unites only with itself, via its own transformers, innate ideas, the categories.

The soul has as its disposal the only language. The body is a confused speaker: it says 'soft', 'warm', 'blue', 'heavy', instead of talking straight lines, curves, collisions and relations.

Matter thus denied, foreclosed, remains present in this violently modern thinking: it is the enigmatic confusion of the past, the confusion of the badly built city, of childhood, ignorant and blind, of the cross-eyed look of the little girl loved by René Descartes as a child. Of everything that comes to us from behind, 'before'. Confusion, prejudice, is matter in thought, the disorder of the past which takes place before having been wanted and conceived, which does not know what it is saying, which must be endlessly translated and corrected, currently and actively, into distinct intuitions. Childhood, the unconscious, time, because 'then' is 'now', the old, are the matter that the understanding claims to resolve in the act and actuality of the instantaneous *intuitus*.

All energy belongs to the thinking that says what it says, wants what it wants. Matter is the failure of thought, its inert mass, stupidity.

We say: what impatience, what anguish in Cartesian modernism!

II   Nuclear transformations such as those which affect certain material elements known as radioactive, or those which take place in those transmutation-crucibles we call stars, or those which we provoke by bombarding and fission of the nucleus of plutonium or uranium 235 – such transformations not only required the long history of physics research from Descartes to Heisenberg, they presuppose a complete overturning of the image of matter. And it is against this overturned image, however confused it may be for a mind as ill-informed as mine, that contemporary thought is inevitably measured, closely or at a distance.

One essential feature of this overturning of the image of matter consists in the pre-eminence of time in the analysis of the relation of body to mind. 'The questions relative to subject and object, their distinction and their union must be posed in terms of time rather than space', writes Bergson (*Matière et mémoire*, §4). The author of *L'énergie spirituelle* recalls this sentence of Leibniz's: 'One can consider every body as a mind that is instantaneous but deprived of memory' (Letter to Arnauld, November 1671).

The instant which in Descartes marked the spiritual act, which was the timeless time of the understanding, here swings over to the side of material actuality. The bare monad forgets itself from one moment to the next. True mind is memory and anamnesis, continuous time. None the less, this memory remains local, limited to a 'point of view'. God alone has or is the memory of the whole, and of its programme. He alone has at his disposal all the 'notions' of the monads, of all the properties they develop, have developed, and will develop. Absolute memory, which is at the same time timeless act. The localisation of the created monads is the spatial version of their temporality. They have a 'point of view immanent to space because they are immanent to time, because they do not have enough memory, because they do not gather themselves sufficiently together.

Considered spatially, every monad is a material point in interaction (direct interaction in Bergson, in Leibniz mediated by divine wisdom, which ensures the harmony of all the interactions) with all the other material points. This is why Bergson can call this material point an 'image' (in *Matière et mémoire*), and why Leibniz endows it with a 'perception'. The whole world is reflected in each material point, but what is the furthest from it, which thus takes the longest time to be made distinct (as one counts distances in temporal terms in mountain walks or interstellar expeditions), can only be inscribed on the 'mirror' if the material point has the capacity to assemble and conserve a lot of information at once, as we would say. Otherwise, the recording can certainly take place but remains unknown. So we must imagine that from matter to mind there is but a difference of degree, which depends on the capacity to gather and conserve. Mind is matter which remembers its interactions, its immanence. But there is a continuum from the instantaneous mind of matter to the very gathered matter of minds.

If there is such a continuity between the states of matter, this is because all material unities, even the 'barest', as is said in the *Monadology*, can only consist in their form, as Aristotle had understood it. For matter considered as 'mass' is infinitely divisible, and the unity it can produce is only phenomenal. This is the case with each human body, which doesn't stop changing in its mass, and has real and exact unity only through its difference, its 'point of view', itself determined by its 'form', i.e. its ability to gather up the actions exerted upon it (what we're calling interactions). If there are 'atoms of substance', these are therefore 'metaphysical points'; 'they have something vital and a sort of perception, and mathematical points are their point of view, to express the universe', in the words of the *Système nouveau de la nature*.

This quasi-perception – which makes me think so strongly of the 'pre-reflexive cogito' that Merleau-Ponty tried to isolate, or of the 'pure perception', perfect co-extension of perceived and perceiver hypothesised by Bergson at the beginning *Matière et mémoire* (I'll come back to this) – is none other than the 'expression in a single indivisible being of divisible phenomena or of several beings', writes Leibniz to Arnauld (about 1688-90). No need, he adds, 'to attach thought or reflection to this representation': the perception can remain unperceived. And it must be shown that there are these 'material expressions which are without thought' not only in animals, but in living creatures such as vegetables, and even in 'bodily substances', writes Leibniz.

So I imagine this formal atom as the point at which all the images the monad has of the universe come to be projected. None of them has the whole of the universe in its mirror (*Monadology*, §56), otherwise it would be indiscernible from another monad. Now a *being* is a being. In matter, it is not the 'mass' which obeys the principle of the identity of indiscernibles – on the contrary, it is a crowd – but rather the form, which is the projection on to a mathematical point of a texture of relations. And if the images change on the mirror of each formal atom, then all the other mirrors must reflect, each according to its point of view, the complementary changes of the first. This harmony is ensured by divine wisdom, alone in representing everything, whilst the differentiation of the 'points of view', the multiplication of the monads, which causes the diversity of the world and the complexity of bodies, is a result of the principle that the all-powerful must deploy all its possibilities.

Our laicised science calls that 'all-power' energy, and it refers the responsibility for the convergence between the points of matter, their compossibility, not to a wisdom, but the chance and to selection, which 'fix' (for immensely differing 'lifetimes') material organisations, 'formal atoms', always precarious.

III I return for a moment to the 'pure perception' imagined by Bergson in *Matière et mémoire*, to bring out how Leibnizian in principle is his problematic of the relation between matter and mind. Of course the working hypothesis is entirely different – pragmatic, if you like: the living body is an agent of the transformation of things, all perception induces an action. But what is not pragmatist is that this term 'perception' is applied by Bergson to every material point: 'The more the reaction must be immediate, the more the perception must resemble a simple contact, and the complete process of perception and reaction must be scarcely distinct from a mechanical impulse followed by a necessary movement' (*Matière et mémoire*, p 28).

The further one climbs the ladder of organised beings, the more one observes that the immediate reaction is delayed, 'prevented', and that this inhibition explains the indeterminacy, unpredictability and growing freedom of the actions these beings can perform. Bergson sees the reason for this inhibition in the extension and complexity of the nervous relays interposed between the afferent or sensitive fibres and the efferent or motor fibres. The 'mirror' gets more complicated, and the influx on its way out can be filtered down many paths.

It will only go down one of them – and this will be that of the real action performed. But many other actions were possible and will remain inscribed in a virtual state. This is how perception stops being 'pure', i.e. instantaneous, and how representational consciousness can be born of this reflection (in the optical sense), of this 'echo', of the influx on the set of other possible – but currently ignored – paths which form memory. (And even then we are only talking about immediate memory or habit. Recollection [*souvenir*] will be the memory of that memory.) This is how what is given one by one, blow by blow, or, as Bergson puts it, 'shock' *(ébranlement)* by shock, in the amnesiac material point, is 'retracted', condensed as though into a single high-frequency vibration, in perception aided by memory. The relevant difference between mind and matter is one of rhythm. In an 'instant' of conscious perception, which is in fact an indivisible block of duration made of vibration, 'memory condenses an enormous multiplicity of shocks, which appear simultaneously to us although they are successive' (*Matière et mémoire*, p 73). In order to get back to matter from a consciousness, it would suffice to 'divide ideally this undivided thickness of time, and distinguish in it the desired multiplicity of movements' (ibid).

Let us take as an example one of the those 'secondary qualities' abandoned by the mechanistic explanation, the colour red. Science which takes this as real matter sees in red light a vibration of the electro-magnetic field at a frequency, according to Bergson, of 400 trillion vibrations per second. The human eye needs two thousandths of a second to make a temporal dissociation between two pieces of information. If it had to dissociate the vibrations condensed in the perception of red, it would take 25,000 years. But if it synchronised itself to that rhythm, it would no longer perceive red at all, and would, says Bergson, register only 'pure shocks', since it would be co-extensive with them. It would be, instant by instant, each of those shocks itself. It would be a 'pure' or 'bare' material point.

IV The continuity between mind and matter thus appears as a particular case of the transformation of frequencies into other frequencies, and this is what the transformation of energy consists in. Contemporary science, I believe, shows us that energy, in all its forms, is distributed in waves, and that, to quote Jean Perrin, 'all matter is in the end a particular and very condensed form of energy'. The reality to be accorded to such and such a form of energy, and therefore of matter, clearly depends on the transformers we have at our disposal. Even the transformer that our central nervous system is, highly sophisticated in the order of living creatures, can only transcribe and inscribe according to its own rhythm the excitations which come to it from the milieu in which it lives.

If we have at our disposal interfaces capable of memorising, in a fashion accessible to us, vibrations naturally beyond our ken, i.e. that determine us as no more than 'material points' (as is the case with many forms of radiation), then we are extending our power of differentiation and our memories, we are delaying reactions which are as yet not under control, we are increasing our material liberty. This complex of transformers, still seen from the pragmatist point of view, well deserves the name it bears, that of techno-science.

The new technologies, built on electronics and data processing, must be considered – still from the same angle – as material extensions of our capacity to memorise, more in Leibniz's sense than Bergson's, given the role played in them by symbolic language as supreme 'condenser' of all information. These technologies show in their own way that there is no break between matter and mind, at least in its reactive functions, which we call performance functions. They have a cortex, or a cortex-element, which has the property of being collective, precisely because it is physical and not biological. Which cannot but raise some questions which I shall not address here. I should like instead to end by trying to respond to our initial question: what impact can the idea of matter I've just broadly summarised have on philosophy?

It is possible to give a pragmatic turn to a philosophy of matter, as does Bergson in *Matière et mémoire,* which then – whatever Bergson may have thought about it – can easily be linked with the ambient technologism or techno-scientism. The link of the one philosophy with the other does, however demand a correction, which on reflection is no mere detail, and of which Bergson was perfectly aware. Pragmatism, as its name suggests, is one of the many versions of humanism. The human subject it pre-supposes is, to be sure, material, involved in a *mileieu,* and turned towards action. The fact remains that this action is given a finality by an interest, which is represented as a sort of optimum adjustment of subject to environment. But if one looks at the history of the sciences and techniques (and of the arts, of which I have said nothing, even though the question of matter, of material especially, is decisive for them), one notices that this was not, and is not – especially today – in fact their finality.

The complexification of the transformers, theoretical and practical, has always had as its effect the destabilisation of the fit between the human subject and its environment. And it always modifies this fit in the same direction – it delays reaction, it increases possible responses, increases material liberty and, in this sense, can only disappoint the demand for security which is inscribed in the human being as in every living organism. In other words, it does not seem that the desire – let's call it that – to complexify memory can come under the demand for equilibrium in the relation of man with his milieu. Pragmatically, this desire operates in the opposite direction, at least at first, and we know that scientific or technical (or artistic) discoveries or inventions are rarely motivated by a demand for security and equilibrium.

That demand wants rest, security and identity; the desire has no use for them, no success satisfies nor stops it. In order to reduce this objection, Bergson introduces the notion of an *élan vital,* a creative invention. This is where he leaves pragmatism behind, and exchanges a metaphysics of well-being for a teleology of life. This teleology is not new, it is romantic or pre-romantic, and has given up its all in the speculative dialectic.

But in the current state of sciences and techniques, resort to the entity 'Life' to cover what I call, for want of a better term, desire (*conatus, appetitio* for others), i.e. the complexification which disavows – de-authorises, so to speak – all objects of demand in turn; this term seems still far too derivative of human experience, too anthropomorphic. To say that a Life is responsible for the formation of systems such as the atom or the star or the cell or the human cortex or finally the collective cortex constituted by machine memories is contrary, as are all teleologies, to the materialist spirit, in the noble sense, Diderot's sense, which is the spirit of knowledge. It can only invoke chance and necessity, like Democritus and Lucretius. Matter does not go in for dialectic.

Obviously I do not intend to solve the problem. But if I invoke Democritus and Lucretius, this is because it seems to me that micro-physics and cosmology inspire in today's philosopher more a materialism than any teleology. An immaterialist materialim, if it is true that matter is energy and mind is contained vibration.

One of the implications of this current of thinking is that it ought to deal another blow to what I shall call human narcissism. Freud already listed three famous ones: man is not the centre of the cosmos (Copernicus), is not the first living creature (Darwin), is not the master of meaning (Freud himself). Through contemporary techno-science, he learns that he does not have the monopoly of mind, that is of complexification, but that complexification is not inscribed as a destiny in matter, but possible, and that it takes place, at random, but intelligibly, well before himself. He learns in particular that his own science is in its turn a complexification of matter, in which, so to speak, energy itself comes to be reflected, without humans necessarily getting any benefit from this. And that thus he must not consider himself as an origin or as a result, but as a transformer ensuring, through his techno-science, his arts, his economic development, his cultures and the new memorisation they involve, a supplement of complexity in the universe.

This view can cause joy or despair. I should have liked to have had the time to show, through *Le rêve de d'Alembert,* for example, but many other texts too, that it was in its essentials the view of Diderot. It was also that of Marcel Duchamp and Stéphane Mallarmé. Perhaps it is enough, in all sobriety, to give us a reason for thinking and writing, and a love of matter. Matter in our effort performs its anamnesis.

SYLVIANE AGACINSKI
SPACE AND THE WORK

Our place here will not be within the space of a work, even a short or minor one. Nor, perhaps, will it be within the space of worklessness (désœuvre) either, if one means by that a kind of activity which, without mastery of its own beginning or end, takes shape as a series of juxtapositions and partial articulations and, without ever closing, always combines with that which is already there.

The issues I want to raise in relation to the space of the work turn on the theme of the articulation and disarticulation of the *whole* contained in the notion of 'the work'. For instance, to analyse space *on the basis* of the theme of the work is to ask whether the work is not always and in its essence a process of articulation, whether its aim is not the absolute articulation of its features, its inscription and writing, to the point where, in effect, something which still remains to be thought with regard to the notion of space – but also, clearly, the notion of time – is effaced. Or, more generally, one might say that the work has the ambition of instituting its own time and space, denying any inscription in a space that would not be *its own,* a space that would always be *other,* never already there, and that such an ambition is present even in the case of Maurice Blanchot, when he comes to write *The Space of Literature.*[1]

These questions make it important to dissociate the classical – theological and philosophical – idea of the work from what in the case of a visual work of art might, in privileged fashion, constitute an 'experience' of space.[2]

I am forced here to leave to one side the philosophical problem of space as it is posed outside of the question of art. But a brief summary would soon reveal that the question of space, indeed space itself, does not have the same meaning, for instance, in texts like the *Critique of Pure Reason* as it does in the *Critique of Judgement.* In the first, as an a priori form of sensibility, one is dealing with a de-realised and pure and empty space, while in the latter space is either the volume of real material things or else the space of things represented.

As soon as one approaches the question of art philosophically – though we shall attempt later to distance ourselves from this approach – the theme of space is immediately bound up with that of an exterior world in which a subjectivity is expressed. The plastic arts, in Kant, for example, are arts of sensuous truth, and deal with the real space of material things (sculpture and architecture), while painting is of the realm of sensuous semblance and is concerned only with representation. Nevertheless, the plastic arts and painting, as Kant puts it, 'both use figures in space for the expression of ideas'.[3] In Hegel, painting similarly occupies a place apart, in that it is an art of the *representation* of space, and not an art of the real space of material things. It *reflects* spiritual interiority outwardly. It is a representation of a representation *(Vorstellung einer Vorstellung),* and is thus mediated by subjective thought.

In this way, then, the implications are clear: on the one hand, as in painting, spaced materiality is reduced to the level of a simple means, to a mere support of subjective representation, which implies that representation must efface the space of the support, so as not to be confused with it, but rather take its place and subjugate it within representation. Or else, as in the case of architecture, spaced matter serves as an exterior enclosure for spiritual subjectivity that itself remains unspaced (as spirit, presence, life). In this perspective, irrespective of whether the work of art is being produced, used or contemplated, it appears unnecessary for subjectivity to undergo the 'experience' or test of space.

Hegel lays much emphasis on the difference between real space and represented space. This is at the heart of the conflicts between architecture and painting and the reduction of mural space to pure neutrality. It is essential that architectural space should not be the subjectile of painting, nor may it act as its *support.* But it is not possible to speak of the representation of space without the same sentence also meaning: the representation of spatial things, of spaced things. This immediately implies that space is not a 'complete vacuum' but the apparent or real volume of bodies. In that case, space refers both to the whole and to the part, the containing volume as well as the volume contained, it marks, doubly, both outside and inside. A plastic work of art, for instance, could therefore be envisaged either from the point of view of the spatial volume in which it appears, or the space that it institutes itself, its own volume, as it were. All space therefore could be treated as a volume to be inserted inside another, and so on to infinity. At any rate, the space of the work as the unity of a space *proper to the work* seems to me totally implicit in the very idea of the work and to coincide with the idea of volume and homogeneous totality.

Now, this space of the work which forms a *volume* – including that of the book – can become *one* only if it articulates, connects and interconnects its component parts in such a way that the gap between them is abolished or overcome. Once incorporated *within the work,* these parts are wrenched from their spatial dispersion and ordered within the proper space of the work, and thus referred back to the space they themselves describe but which simultaneously also includes them.

The Unity of the work in some way overcomes spatial difference, the spacing of that with which it is constructed or written, and thus time, that is, the very movement of its elaboration. This is the reason why it seems to me that the idea of the work as a totality instituting its own space can be viewed as an effacement of space, but space conceived differently, understood as divergence, difference, spacing, or interval, i.e. that space to which one refers when one speaks of something being *spaced out,* having a relationship of difference with itself and diverging from itself. (Here, though no doubt in a very approximate fashion, one might be getting nearer to a Leibnizian conception of space, since, if there were no bodies in it, space would have no meaning for Leibniz. For Leibniz, space is neither empty nor absolute, but refers to the interval between actual bodies, to the *relations* between them.)

Be that as it may, the process of totalising articulation of the work is inscribed philosophically within a problematic of the foundation and origin of the work, either because the origin transcends the work, in the idea of a space able to overlord or dominate it from 'outside' – as for instance from a position of pure interiority – or because it is already embodied within the work like an invisible void, from which it re-emerges, in a single leap, through the creative act.

According to this other figure of the origin, which might be called phenomenological and breaks with the philosophical distinction between subject and object, the presence of the work is deployed from within itself, by opening itself to itself. Clearly, the origin of the work is not a plenitude of sense, rather a sort of gaping absence. On this reading, the work can never be in the world – like a simple object – because it *is* itself world, and this constitutes a radical way of stating the self-sufficiency of the work, and of contrasting this sufficiency with everything that is of the order of the simple 'task' or 'fragment'. One may be reminded here of the contrast drawn by Worringer between the work of art *(Kunstwerk)* and the artistic fragment *(Kunstück)*. The work as world 'gathers' the world together, saving it from fragmentation – *aufheben* can also mean to 'gather together'). For this approach, which is the one adopted, for instance, by Henri Maldiney in his *Art et existence,* the work is of the same order as existence, as *being-there,* or *being-it-there,* and is thus held in suspense in the void, the nothing or the blank which name the origin, that is to say, an origin where all and nothing are *one.*

As a process of self-engenderment of itself, the work is far from excluding, indeed, on the contrary, it presupposes the institution of a *proper* space, cleansed of all contamination with borders or margins. Maldiney writes that 'the creative artist's beginnings show us . . . the borders of art, and not the leap. There is a clear distinction to be made between explaining things by reference to this beginnings and understanding the origin.' The work is not born from its borders but from itself, in a movement first of expulsion, then of meditative communion that recreates the world. The result, of course, is a rejection of fragmentation and of real space and of all imitation. As a diverging from the demand for unity and meditative communion, *worklessness (désœuvre)* maintains a different relationship to *border,* to the *fragment,* even to imitation.

To return to classical aesthetics, one might say, to put it very crudely, that the theme of interiority, which is inseparable from that of subjectivity, always refers back to something unspaced, something that somehow eludes spatial division. Now, the difficulty, for me, is how the distinction between interior and exterior, inside and outside, can be thought prior to any delimitation or division of space. Two questions are worth picking out: firstly: is the question of interiority not derived from the question of the envelope, that is, from the opposition between something that envelops and something which is enveloped? Secondly: is this opposition between the enveloping and the enveloped not itself secondary with regard to that of the work, notably of the work par excellence which is the tomb?

My feeling, and I shall return to this shortly, is that the Hegelian interpretation of the Egyptian pyramid, and of the mummy that is sheltered inside, suggests that one can conceive of the emergence of subjectivity as being contemporary with the building of a shelter around the dead body, and thus with the body preserved and enveloped and still living by dint of having been enveloped and protected from the outside in this way. It is possible that architecture, and above all architecture as an edifice

for burial, represents something like the archetype of the work, if it is true that the classic theme of the work is at one with that of the dwelling, the shelter, or the place of habitation suffused with presence and meaning. But if, at the same time, this presence or meaning cannot be distinguished or grasped in advance of what it is that shelters it, then presence and absence become interchangeable, and in their original role may be equivalent. This equivalence, together with the proximity or close relationship between the work and the tomb, can be said to make it less 'bleak' than is sometimes assumed to think of the possibility of giving up the idea of the work, and with it the idea that thought and art ought necessarily to be always *at work (à l'œuvre),* busy with the work at hand. Abandoning the work in this way has, of course, become routine today, but there is nothing deliberate nor wilful about it. And there is nothing 'desperate' about it either.

In the same way, as he points out himself, there is nothing 'disastrous' about what Maurice Blanchot calls the 'writing of disaster' *(l'écriture du désastre).*[4] It is rather a writing which has 'broken with the star *(astre),* that is, with all forms of totality, and forever re-affirms its own divergence from the tenacious and insistent demand for unity. What it diverges from is the idea of the work as a *whole.* Indeed, the work itself, one might say, is nothing other than the aesthetically beautiful whole that is ordered according to the sense it gathers together in a totality in which origin and end meet in a perpetual circle. This fascination for unified totality and for order, for an edifice founded on a fixed external point, is at times disturbing, but disturbing in a different way. One might say that the object of this fascination is something *of the order* of the monumental.

I cannot tell whether Georges Bataille is right to claim that monuments are the real masters of the people. I cannot tell if there therefore exists in general, as Bataille puts it, 'an animosity of the people towards monuments', which culminated according to Bataille in the storming of the Bastille. (It is worth pointing out, however, that in French the word *Bastille,* which derives from 'bastide' and from *'bâtir',* links the dressmaker's art of weaving or braiding with the art of *fortification.* The word, *'bâtir',* was used as early as the 11th century, according to Bloch and Wartburg's etymological dictionary, in the sense of 'constructing fortifications by weaving wooden stakes around a castle'.)

One can accept more easily Bataille's idea that the liking for architectural building, far beyond the realm of monuments in the strict sense, is due to a liking for human or divine authority. It is clear for example that many totalitarian regimes, as well as developing strategies for the domination, intimidation and subjugation of the masses, also demonstrate an extraordinary need for architecture. This is not restricted to the architecture of the blockhaus or bunker, for the crucial point is the need to provide a display of *monumentality.* With regard to monumentality, it is worth recalling the word *monumentus* in the Latin sense of the term, which contains the idea of perpetuating a memory, of commemoration, of building an epitaph or funereal monument. Everything that constitutes a *monumentum,* everything that 'recalls something or somebody' is linked to the sign and the tomb. There is of course no question of somehow getting rid of such a 'need' for monumentality. But when a nation wishes to immortalize itself in granite monuments in the Egyptian mode and thus erect its own epitaphs while still alive, it is surely the case that what is being celebrated here, at one and the same time, is unity and death. Franco Borsi is clearly right in this respect to emphasise the funereal character of Nazi architecture in his book, *The Monumental Era: European Architecture and Design 1929-39.*[5]

There is the monumental architectural edifice, whenever its massiveness is displayed, something fascinating, which does not just come from the assertion of the link between totality and its *arché* or foundation, and thus help to exorcise the anguish of fragmentation, particularly the fragmentation of the community. There is also the intuitive sense that there is some connexion between order, authority and massiveness. Order must always be something massive, simple, without fault. No uncertainty, no hesitation in the expression and ostentation of order is allowed. There is always a kind of massiveness about edifices which assert order monumentally, and this was why Victor Hugo claimed to be able to see the hieroglyphs of papal unity in the works of Romanesque art.

It is possible that power as such, in so far as it takes command (*arché*) and becomes the founding authority, is unable to rid itself of the architectural model of that authority, of a system of thought which links the work and the power of the work to the power of the architect, in whom, for my part, I would readily see the archetype of the author. One could also say that with totalitarian power what is also realised is the desire for a putting into order and putting into work of architecturally dominated society. This putting into work could be seen as a response to the desire, in society itself, to exorcise and lay the ghost of its own division. Ought one's conclusion therefore be: 'Unhappy the society which has a need of architects'? If by that one means the desire of a community to retreat into itself, to abolish within the totalising work its difference from itself, its multiplicity, its complexity, its plurality, the answer must be: yes, and I should simply like to refer you here to Jean-Luc Nancy's book, *La Communauté désœuvrée (The Workless Community)*.

I am not suggesting, of course, that the work of art in general, or architecture itself, is somehow 'totalitarian' in its essence. If I emphasise the totalising and founded character of the work, that does not mean that all 'art' in general should be understood on that basis. There is always more or less worklessness (*désœuvre*) in what one calls the 'works of art'. I merely want to draw attention to a certain (theologico-philosophical) model of the work, one which art and politics ascribe to one another mutually. In this sense, there is nothing fortuitous in the 'magic power' that the 'word architecture' exerts over political power – as Speer notes in connexion with the power of the Nazis.

Plato used the identical concept of *techné* to refer to the art of the demiurge, the politician, and the carpenter. In the value and function of the *arché* there is something like both a commencement and a command, making possible the collusion between architecture and power, between the architect and the primal leader. The form of this collusion can change in character together with the changes affecting understanding of the work of art. But political thought may also diverge from the model of the work. Even if the polis is still thought of in terms of a 'totality' or a whole, the whole is also conceived as that which survives only by resisting unification, only by being continually affected by division, difference, plurality, diversity, separation, and this was already the case as long ago as when Aristotle launched his critique of Plato. But Jean-Luc Nancy's book, *La Communauté désœuvrée*, details rigorously the demands, conditions and characteristics of a political thinking which breaks with the work – and I can speak here of 'worklessness' (*désœuvre*) only by underlining my debt to Nancy's admirable text.

Wherever the theme of the work is in operation as a model, resistance to it is found in the form of that movement of difference which is not subordinated to the *arché,* which is thus not sutured and, at bottom, does not refer back to what stands at the beginning and is in command. Here is something which fails to *refer back to the founding moment.* This movement of differance, in Derrida's term, may be described as a play of traces without anchorage in any primary or original presence; it is what Derrida, in *Of Grammatology,* calls *writing* in the

broadest sense of the word. You may remember that differ*a*nce as a play of traces, as purely differential play, is also termed *spacing* by Derrida because of the way traces refer back to one another without ever being gathered together in the presence of a here or a now. In this way, writing as spacing functions so as to defer *presence* – and sense as presence – unceasingly, making presence into 'an effect of traces'. This is the presence that the book or its lapidary equivalent, the edifice, claims to be able to shelter and gather together. But spacing might constitute a means of speaking space, of speaking the spacedness of space, in such a way that space is not subjugated, no longer absorbed into one place, word, or idea, and therefore not reduced to anything that is unspaced (like sense, presence, or subjectivity, etc). To think the arts on the basis of the putting into play of differential elements, of articulations of elements which have value only though the interval that is neither presence nor absence, would be to emphasise the activity of *worklessness* in the acceptance of spacing, to the detriment of an idea of the work that would be either *in* space, or constitutive of *a* space, its own *proper* space. Worklessness decentres, it is without medium, inner kernel or outer shell; its places are crossing points or passages, not sites. With worklessness, therefore, comes also disorder.

The work, on the other hand, opens a *site;* it institutes a space within a space, a world within a world, a totality within the totality that is the world. The putting into work has the demiurgic quality of claiming to break with the *already-there* of space by opening *a single* space. The idea of the work corresponds to a desire to repress space, to enclose it within itself or subordinate it to representation by reducing it to a single plane articulated around a central point. For this to happen, it is necessary for the architect, or demiurgic artisan, to *appropriate* space rather than encounter it. He must therefore start from nothing and make, *from beginning to end,* what in due course will become a chamber, a room, a space *(Raum).*

This pure idea of the architect as maker is untenable to the extent it depends on some agency in which the fixed point has its origin and which guarantees it as both end and beginning. The architect, therefore, must be – and is – a subjectivity representing for himself the end of his work, anticipating and pre-empting it. As the one who 'builds in his head', he is the classic model for all makers, planners and designers driven by the idea of mastering space and time by effacing the gap between the end and the beginning of the work. And the architect also needs to appropriate himself, and find in himself his own beginning, his own end. This is why, in this regard, philosophy is architecture's crowning glory.

I am not claiming, of course, that such an architect could ever have existed. To begin with, the architect never did built 'in his head', as the standard phrase has it (from Aristotle down to Marx); the process of 'construction' pre-supposes certain supports (whether in the form of paper or a computer programme) with the help of which a drawing or sketch or spatial diagram are produced. Clearly, these materials and supports can vary, and the question of scale may change. But there is a tendency to confuse the process of creating models with the idea of thought as a *pure* anticipatory activity, a kind of seeing through the mind's eye that can compress the spatiality of space, and gather together the movement of spacing into a single comprehensive view. But neither painter nor architect have any visual or mental mastery over space. The question is one dealt with by Paul Valéry in a series of texts devoted to Leonardo. I just want to pick out the remarks relating to drawing as a sort of *test* or *ordeal.* For Leonardo, drawing was experimentation which could not be dominated or pre-empted by any notion of seeing through the mind's eye. As valéry argues, the *graphic* is not something that has its source in ideas or speech. Instead there is, as it were, a putting of thought to the test *through* the mark, the act of tracing. This has little to do with the representation of what seen things look like. But it is constitutive of a new approach to things in space. It is not *vision* that presides over drawing or painting, but the demand of the mark, the space of the mark, forcing the painter to treat space as a movement of bodies. 'Leonardo', Valéry writes, 'utilises all material modes which react to ideas and on which ideas can be tested out, and which create opportunities for unexpected relationships between ideas and objects'. In his 'Introduction to the Method of Leonardo da Vinci', Valéry says of the artist that 'from this point of view his intellectual labours are part of the slow transformation by which the notion of space – at first that of a *complete vacuum,* an isotropic volume – has little by little developed into the notion of a system inseparable from the matter it *contains,* and from time.'[6] The word 'contain' is thus no longer appropriate: space does not 'contain' matter, it is already itself matter in the process of spacing. It is true that the test of drawing seems to be inspired here by a desire for *knowledge,* but this knowledge is not something that transcends drawing itself. (I shall leave to one side the question whether or not this test that 'all material modes' inflict on thought prefigures the coming together of *knowing* and *doing,* which for Valéry was one of the major characteristics of the modern science he enjoyed so much.)

Vitruvius's *Ten Books on Architecture* offer further examples of this primal involvement of the architect with irreducible spacing, if only on the level of the drawings representing the building. When Vitruvius mentions the different 'representations' of buildings the architect has at his disposal when erecting the building, he lists: the plan (ichnography), the elevation (orthography) and perspectival elevation (scenography). He adds that the plan is only the physical outline of the building transposed to a *smaller* space. He also says that these 'representations' are what the Greeks call *idea.* The use of the word *idea* by Greek architects, unlike the use of the term in metaphysics, already makes clear the spatial character of the model the architect creates in the act of drawing. *Idea* does not refer to something purely intelligible, nor purely sensuous, but rather to a graphic spacing of which drawing itself is only one instance. Nevertheless, this graphism can still be put in the service of spatial planning, such as, for example, the rational planning or urban space.

In this instance, the town planner may well undergo the test of drawing on the blank, unmarked space of his page, but he fails to take into account the space of things already there. His idea is that architecture, or the city itself, should have their beginning with him. He wishes to create the city, instead of 'carrying on' from the already there. In short, this is another form of 'totalitarian' temptation: he wishes to make the city into his *work.* This type of archi-urbanism could be contrasted with the disorder or worklessness of medieval towns where buildings are grafted on to one another without these juxtapositions being subordinated to any controlling principle. Worklessness is also authorlessness. With Le Corbusier, however, the architect, designing on to the blank page, appropriates the pure space of his own creation, and dreams of rebuilding the entire world. The utopian space of design is an instrument of unlimited control over real space. When Alain Guiheux, in an article published in the journal, *Traverses,* 43, calls for a 'retention of creativity' and a 'withdrawal of the architect', it is, to my mind, to protest against this attempt to organise space in a uniform, homogeneous way and subordinate it to the imagination.

It follows from these different remarks that the theme of the work is on the side of a thought which seeks to master space, while what, for want of a more satisfactory expression, I have termed the *experience of space* corresponds to the abandonment

by the worker (or the *ouvrier,* the one who opens) of any perspective that strives to transcend the playing of space with itself, or matter with itself, for in that play the opener is already implicated, even undone. This experience of space is also that of worklessness, which is the loss of the essentially expressive aim of the work corresponding to the ambition of subjectivity to impose unity to what it believes to be its own outside, i.e. matter or materials in their spacing. Abandoning this position is in itself a response to thought beginning to take account of those experiences and tests of alterity that submerge the subjectivity which thought it could contain the other, both in the sense of enclosing it and restraining it by compression.

Obviously, such abandonment is never pure and simple. Similarly, worklessness always finds its way into the work. Worklessness shows, however, the disappearance of the illusion that the work might begin and end or remain closed upon itself, within itself, around the inner kernel of meaning. Worklessness diverges from totalising ambition because by opening itself, by working directly on space and the body, the task has always already begun. Workful composition is always delayed with regard to the space in which it is inscribed, the space of its own inscription. The support is what spaces itself already, in a way, programming the work, and unworking it. One remembers how Artaud would work relentlessly with pieces of wood or on paper. He wrote that 'space and time resist manual work', showing an acute awareness of his dispossession by space and voicing his own revolt against this dispossession.

Worklessness can also be taken to indicate the between-spaces, between appropriation, mastery and dispossession by space. In the manner of working, it displays the inclusion, or inscription of the worker into the fabrics on which he 'labours'. It is however less a case of carrying out purely manufacturing operations than of what one might call a series of passive manipulations, grafts, juxtapositions and discordances, of ever partial articulations always 'plugged into' the already there. There is no moment of rest.

It is worth noting, to return to what 'affects' us, too, that our age, as one calls it, with all the things that typify it as a moment in the deconstruction of the philosophical thought of the subject, is turning more and more towards a thought of *existence* affected by space from the outset, that is to say, a sort of existence which no longer has any masterful 'comprehension' of space or can overcome spatiality by converting it into something else, like, for instance, time. In his lecture 'Time and Being' Heidegger concludes that 'the attempt in *Being and Time,* section 70, to derive spatiality of existence from temporality is untenable'.[7]

I want just refer you to an important book written on the subject of this untenable attempt by Didier Franck, entitled *Heidegger et le problème de l'espace.*[8] It becomes clear from Franck's book that the independence of space from being as time played a decisive part in the interruption of *Being and Time.* What is central for Franck is the idea that, if sensing oneself is a property of all embodied existence, we are always already outside ourselves, as Heidegger also wrote in his *Nietzsche.* But the phenomenon of embodiment as such is not taken into consideration in *Being and Time.* And, in fact, it is clear that a being of flesh and blood, an existence that has a body and senses itself in a variety of different ways, cannot treat space as a simple outside (or even as a simple bodily inside). If the flesh does have a relation of exteriority from itself, if the flesh, as body, is always divergent from itself and spaced in relation to itself, then the body can no longer be that which is unfolded as an outside or folds back on itself. From the outset, existence has to do with movements of spacing, divergence and delay.

Though this may not be the best place for it, one ought here to consider everything that, as flesh, is folded or folds back on itself, which opens and closes, and even penetrates itself in a play that is at the limit of inside and outside. One can cite the famous example of the child sucking its thumb with passion (though active and passive cannot be dissociated here), which I tend to think is not a substitute for anything exterior, not only because it is a source of satisfaction for the small child from the foetal stage onwards, but because it perhaps simply satisfies a kind of eagerness of the flesh for itself. Bodily spacing, if one may use the term, clearly does not exclude the possibility that for what one calls the body there still remains an inside and an outside. But the simple identity of the flesh with itself, its unity as a body, seems rather to be infinitely delayed, as though it were only realised in passing, in death. But you may be wondering what the relationship is between this and the work. Let me return to my main theme.

For philosophy to forget the flesh, which is a strange distraction, and to think of the soul in terms of pure interiority, what was needed was for a particular spacing of existence (space and temporality) to be ousted by the more straightforward opposition between a material, three-dimensional outside and a pure spiritual, unspaced inside, or if you will, between an outer shell and an inner kernel.

The outer shell and the inner kernel are the terms employed by Hegel in his *Aesthetics* to describe how, in India, solid phallic columns, which were compact and massive constructions, were hollowed out and turned into sorts of pagodas. These narrow, high pagodas, born from the separating of the shell from the kernel, are certainly not *houses* in our sense. They are more closely related to Egyptian columns and obelisks. But the process of hollowing out was a decisive stage compared with the solid monuments of before. It served to usher in what, for other works, became the form of the dwelling place.

The solid cubic tower described by Herodotus as standing at the centre of the temple of Baal was very different. This was not hollowed out inside, but solid, capped with up to eight towers piled one on top of the other. At the actual summit, there were no statues, and men were not allowed to spend the night there. Hegel, evidently, doubts whether the god, as the priests claimed, came to visit the temple and rest on the camp bed left at the top. 'However,' Hegel continues, 'we cannot put this gigantic structure on a par with temples in the Greek or modern sense. For the first seven cubes are entirely solid ... so that the whole structure rises really independent by itself.'[9] Hegel lays similar emphasis on the colossal and the massive in his description of the Egyptian temples whose purpose was neither to shelter a god nor serve as a meeting place for worshippers. This entire independent and symbolic architecture – but symbolising nothing, since the pyramid constitutes the real symbol (in the section on 'Symbolic Art') – consisted here in building for the sake of it, without any concern for sheltering men or gods.

Quite different from these uninhabitable edifices are the ones that mark the transition from independent architecture to classical architecture 'proper'. This begins with excavation, thus allowing the building of a shelter. Architecture as dwelling place – and this is quite an original point in Hegel – does not start with the hut, but with the hole, by burrowing underground, by caves. In India, as in Egypt, according to Hegel, underground workings came before buildings on the surface, and when these were built they were like imitations of the first: 'to make a nest in the ground,' writes Hegel, 'or to burrow, is more natural than to dig up the ground, look for material and then pile it up together and give shape to it'.[10] The remark is an interesting one, for it could be taken to place underground building on the border line between the work and worklessness: digging a hole is both a doing and an undoing.

The first dwelling place is the pyramid, the place of habitation designed for the dead. Hegel's description is well known. The realm of the invisible, as the realm of the dead, arises with the strange architecture linking underground art with edifices in the open air. There are therefore three types of working: holes, solid buildings, and hollowed out buildings. Architecture proper, the sort that builds a dwelling place, is a sub-division of hollowed out buildings, but it first occurs by combining the underground hole and the surface edifice, i.e. in the pyramid. Let me summarise some work I have done elsewhere and say that the moment of the pyramid figures, in Hegel's writing, three births: that of the symbolic work of art (in 'Symbolic Art'), that of the sign (for which, in the *Encyclopedia*, it serves as example and illustration), and lastly that of the dwelling place. It realises the vocation of architecture proper, which is to envelop and enclose. It is the first enclosure in architecture. But what is the 'meaning' of this initial edification? Its role was to construct or edify the realm of the invisible as the realm of the dead. The invisible is preserved by the visible work of the inorganic envelope and constituted as such, as sense, presence, the intelligible face of the sign, and primarily as an individuality enveloped in bandages and stone. The preserving, or keeping, of the body functions, for Hegel, necessarily as a means of conserving individuality – something indivisible – as spirit or as *spiritual individuality*. Consequently, the embalming of the body attests, paradoxically, to the individuality of existence as distinct from the bodily envelope.

The work as hollow envelope attests to, but also guarantees and affirms, perhaps also produces the idea of the invisible permanence of the thing enveloped, and it guarantees it primarily as a permanence or preserving of the dead body. The paradox, which is only apparent, comes from the fact that the body splits into two distinct entities: the first is the enveloped bodily *individuality,* prefiguring spiritual individuality, while the second is the external bodily envelope, doubled by the bandages and the building itself. The funereal dwelling place, by sheltering it from the outside, makes possible the survival, the life of interiority, and contrasts this life inside with death as inorganic exteriority. On the other side of life or spirit, the corporeality of the body becomes the *representation* of spiritual individuality. Hegel writes that 'it is individuality that . . . is preserved, and the corpse is considered as representing it in a direct and natural way.' It is as if the monument to the dead is like a monument to the body also, hollowing it out in order to secrete within it a presence that is both persistent and invisible. The moment of the Egyptian pyramid is interpreted philosophically as heralding the identification by the Greeks of the body with the tomb and the sign. One could add, too: with the work. The funereal building is what marks the birth of a non-bodily, undegradable individuality hidden at the centre of the work and represented by it. (And one might wonder whether this does not, in the process, make the body into something comparable to a work). It is important to stress here that *individibility* means something indivisible, non-material and unspaced.

The work is constructed therefore as a voluminous unfolding that encloses an absolute that cannot be unfolded, that is, folded back on itself, and unspaced, as well as arresting and founding spacing. That which cannot be unfolded is what is usually known as sense or full presence, on the basis of which or in view of which it is the nature of what is unfolded to be unfolded. Presence as sense thus governs the spacing of the fold in all works, especially the book or edifice, which are two variations on the theme of *the dwelling*. This is a structure of shelter, it is an articulated construction, centred on something which cannot be articulated, a pure point, eluding the play of relations between bodies. This point can equally well be a void, or a presence or absence, life or death: all that is needed is for it not to be a part of the whole.

It seems to me that if philosophy so often uses architecture as its model, it is not only because a system is a construction founded on something fixed, but because both share this idea of the dwelling, as Heidegger shows us. For Heidegger, thought, residing in close proximity to poetry, is the gathering and shelter of being. Heidegger describes speech as the 'house of being'. In a short passage from the essay, 'Art and Space *(Die Kunst und der Raum)'*, Heidegger speaks of spacing in the sense of a tracing, a clearing and an opening, but what is at stake here is the opening of a space by the work, a releasing of 'the open *(das Offen)'* 'for a settling and residing of man'. Heidegger contin- ues: 'Spacing brings forth the locality *(Ortschaft)'* which makes ready a residing', indeed, 'in spacing', he writes, 'a taking place *(ein Geschehen)* both speaks and is concealed.'[12]

Let me ask your indulgence for not dealing with this at greater length. But what one can say perhaps is that, so long as thought speaks of itself as working with the aim of sheltering, gathering, preserving, so long as it sees itself as a dwelling, in a way it also retains as its horizon the simplicity of an origin which it sees itself as having carefully to preserve. Over and beyond the 'destruction' of philosophy, the theme of the dwelling endures in the thought of the work and in the work itself.

Notes

1 Maurice Blanchot has subjected the theme of the work to the most profound and radical questioning. What we are dealing with here is a thought of the work that diverges from all metaphysical aesthetic perspectives. In Blanchot's writings what is spoken is the break between 'the work' and any idea of totality, as well as the break of the bond between the work and the authority of the author. To put oneself to the work, to begin writing, for Blanchot, is to undertake that which is 'interminable', 'without end and without goal', and cannot have to do with the work as a finished totality, nor even with truth, nor even with preserving as a mode of remembrance. Writing takes place in the very element of forgetting and of solitude, which is a term to be taken, for me, as an entrance into the risk of absolute *exposure,* and is also called 'intimacy with the outside', a disturb- ing, almost frightening expression: 'Where I am alone,' writes Blanchot in *L'Espace littéraire,* 'the light of day is only the loss of a dwelling place. It is intimacy with the outside which has no place and affords no rest. Coming here makes the one who comes belong to dispersion, to the fissure where the exterior is stifling intrusion, is nakedness, and is the chill of where one is utterly exposed. Here the only space is the dizziness of spacing', (Maurice Blanchot, *The Space of Literature,* trans Ann Smock, University of Nebraska Press, London, 1982, p 31, trans adapted). Solitude, intimacy *with the outside,* these words speak of a kind of ecstasy of the writer. But the difference with Bataille is enormous, and ecstasy in Blanchot is cold, as though it were without pleasure, emotion or laughter. There is another more profound difference in that, for Bataille, nakedness or solitude is not achieved via writing as such or by 'the work'. The *writer* is not the one who experiences them. For the author of *Inner Experience,* writing is equivocation. Any word spoken is an attempt to pass beyond the non-knowledge of 'experience'. Maurice Blan- chot, however, thinks of original experience as art: art becomes an essential presence, both origin and beginning. Blanchot never ceases to link the question of the work to that of the origin or the original. The work is primarily the origin of art: 'For what is glorified by the work is the work itself, and what it gathers together is art.' The work begins nothing, but is pure beginning – 'The work speaks beginning' – writes Blanchot. The work is not another world, it is *the other of any world, that which is always other than the world.* To say 'beginning' is already to precede all beginning. The work is 'the first light that precedes the light of day'. It *initiates* and *enthrones.* It is the origin which always precedes us. Without a *before.* Also, the theme of the beginning cannot be dissociated from that which distinguishes the work from customary objects and from nature. Only the work reveals 'the presence of matter' which, without it, would remain hidden. (The sculptor should not be confused with the roadmender.) And, beyond the materials it glorifies, the work opens up to the original, and is turned, not towards the elements and elemental materiality, but its essence which is 'elemental darkness', 'the elemental background', the 'depth of the shadow of the element' which the arts bring forth. In this sense, it is impossible to speak of the space of literature, the space of art, or the space of the work without falling back into the theme of the origin of the work, or of the work as origin. For me, worklessness speaks of a *resumption,* not a 'beginning'.

2 I am using experience here in the sense of a test or ordeal, the fact of having to 'suffer' in the sense of sustaining, being traversed, touched, affected by that of which there is 'experience'. I would also say, in relation to Georges Bataille, that that which is being experienced, which can *only* be experienced, is born of non- knowledge and remains part of it. With experience, there is always some loss, not necessarily the experience *of* loss, but experience *as* loss, disengagement: as disarray, disturbance, ecstasy, spacing. If, in experience, the other is what *comes over me,* I as a subject am no longer the one over whom the other comes, and the other is no longer simply other either.

By the expression 'ordeal of space', I mainly want to indicate that which by initially engaging existence or thought 'in' space puts it already, as it were, at a distance from itself.

3 Immanuel Kant, *The Critique of Judgement,* trans James Creed Meredith, Oxford University Press, Oxford, 1952, I, 186, § 51.

4 Maurice Blanchot, *L'Escriture du désastre,* Gallimard, Paris, 1980. The book is translated in English as *The Writing of the Disaster,* University of Nebraska Press, London, 1986.

5 See Franco Borsi, *The Monumental Era, European Architecture and design 1929-39,* Lund Humphries, London, 1987.

6 See James R. Lawler, ed, *Paul Valéry, An Anthology,* Routledge and Kegan Paul, London, 1977, pp 33-93.

7 See Martin Heidegger *On Time and Being,* trans Joan Stambaugh, Harper and Row, New York, 1972, p 23.

8 Didier Franck, *Heidegger et le problème de l'espace,* Editions de Minuit, Paris, 1986.

9 GWF Hegel, *Aesthetics: lectures on fine art,* trans TM Knox, Oxford University Press, Oxford, 1975, p 634.

10 GWF Hegel, p 649.

11 Martin Heidegger, 'Die Kunst und der Raum' in: *Aus der Erfahrung des Denkens, Gesamtausgabe,* Vol 13, Frankfurt, 1983, pp 206-7.

BERNARD TSCHUMI, ZKM KARLSRUHE, INTERIOR

GEOFFREY BENNINGTON
THE RATIONALITY OF POSTMODERN RELATIVITY

The relativity and quantum revolution in language remains to be carried out. (Le Différend, §188)

I   The so-called 'debate' around 'postmodernism', 'postmodernity' and 'the postmodern' is probably most distinguished for its confusion.[1] Clearly something is going on, but there is a perhaps unusual degree of disagreement as to what it is, and even as to whether it is 'really' going on, or somehow 'manufactured' by those who find their advantage in saying that it is. Perhaps the disagreement is all that is going on. And if disagreement (or dissensus) be taken as a sign of the postmodern, then it would indeed seem reasonable not so much to look for a 'true state of affairs' behind that disagreement as to take the disagreement as the true state of affairs. In this sense, disagreement about the meaning or existence of the postmodern would itself be the postmodern, and we should have enforced at least the consensus that there is a dissensus. And if a corollary of the conception of the postmodern as disagreement is that the disagreement (which becomes a *différend* in Lyotard's sense) cannot be dominated and resolved by one of the parties to the disagreement (and Derrida, for one, has linked postmodernism to the end of a project of domination),[2] then it follows that it would be naive to attempt an 'overview' of the so-called 'debate'. (A supplementary complication would arise from the suspicion that the major items in the 'debate' are nevertheless attempts at overviews.) The situation is complicated further still by a recent tendency, in my own field at least, to conflate postmodernism with 'so-called poststructuralism'. Some people try to put some order into this by saying that post-structuralism is merely part of a more pervasive postmodernism, but the general aim of such conflation is to lump a lot of things together the better to get rid of them without having to think very hard. A determined rationalist might well see in this very situation the sort of unbridled relativism ('anything goes') s/he finds intolerable. I shall be suggesting that it is still possible to discuss these questions rationally but not rationalistically.

A slightly trivial and certainly naive illustration of some of the difficulties of this situation is provided by Charles Jencks' recent work, *What is postmodernism?*[3] In the course of his remarks, Jencks suggests that the reaction of committed Modernists to post-modernism (a reaction he calls 'The Protestant Inquisition') is as 'paranoic, reactionary and repressive as their Beaux-Arts persecutors were before them' (p 14). On the one hand, Jencks rather welcomes this: 'I do believe that these characterisations have not done what they were supposed to do – stem the tide of Post-Modernism – but rather have helped to blow it up into a media event' (Ibid), and goes on: 'My nightmare is that suddenly the reactionaries will become nice and civil'. (Before moralistically condemning Jencks for what seems to be a complacent welcoming of 'media hype', we might pause to wonder what sort of 'event' today (and indeed what sort of event in general) would not be a 'media event', and to wonder also if this might also be a component of a 'postmodern condition'.) In any case, having apparently welcomed this violence of reaction and the consequent 'media event', Jencks goes on to deplore it too, because it has hidden what he calls 'the root causes of the movement'.

Jencks then proceeds to offer the reader the 'true story' of the movement called postmodernism. Despite the claims made on the cover-note about 'typical Post-Modern devices of exposition' (irony, parody and so on), this story is in fact academic and classical enough. Jencks in fact defines Post-Modernism in the most traditionally dialectical way imaginable, as 'the continuation of Modernism and its transcendence' (p 7): cancellation and preservation in a nice Hegelian *Aufhebung*. In view of this, it perhaps comes as no surprise to find Jencks at the end of his text endorsing and appropriating Peter Fuller's call for 'the equivalent of a new spirituality based on an "imaginative, yet secular, response to nature herself"', seeking '"a shared symbolic order of the kind that a religion provides", but without the religion' (p 48). Jencks explicitly sets this against the 'relativism' he suggests must inevitably result from Lyotard's arguments: but the result is that the 'disagreement' I was suggesting might be constitutive of the postmodern is here rapidly defused and absorbed into the pious projection of a horizon of consensus and even redemption, beyond current rows and media events. Nothing could be less postmodern than this type of schema of argument, and nothing could more invite deconstruction than the unquestioned value of 'nature herself', which is of a piece with the simple view of history I have described: let me quote from *The Truth in Painting* to illustrate this difficulty: which the work of Charles Jencks might be taken as an example – Lyotard links Jencks' notion of the postmodern to an eclecticism attuned to the demands of capital),[5] and a *prescription* as to the appropriate (affirmative) way to think about that situation. The problems that arise from the third proposition I have isolated are more difficult and thereby more interesting. Jencks finds the idea of the postmodern somehow coming 'before' the modern 'amazing' and 'crazy' (irrational, then) (Ibid. 39-42) (although 'original'), and suggests that it leads Lyotard to 'confuse' postmodernism with 'the latest avant-gardism': he goes on to admit that 'it's embarrassing that Post-Modernism's first philosopher should be so fundamentally wrong', and to suggest rather condescendingly that because Lyotard is a philosopher and sociologist of knowledge, he is simply not sufficiently attuned to cultural differences to make sense of what is going on.

One of the reasons for Jenck's bemusement is that he takes the eminently rational view that the prefix 'post-' in 'postmodernism' must imply that the object it labels simply comes after modernism (although he would see this as a necessary but not sufficient qualification). This reasonable view is widespread, and the cause of a lot of trouble. Fredric Jameson, for example, in the longest of his contributions to the 'debate'[6] begins by saying of postmodernism that 'the case for its existence depends on the hypothesis of some radical break or *coupure*, generally traced back to the end of the 1950s or early 1960s'. This type of view, which is not entirely absent in Lyotard's own earlier writing on the subject (see for example the beginning of the introduction to *The Postmodern Condition*, though the statement is complicated by a number of features of the text, and in particular modalised by the status assigned to what Lyotard describes as a 'working hypothesis') habitually makes a link between postmodernism and so-called 'post-industrial society', and tends to centre on the question of the reality of the referent of the term 'postmodernism'. Reading Jameson, I confess that I am unsure as to his conclusion on this point: on the one hand he seems quite confidently able to identify certain features supposedly typical of postmodernism, such as superficiality, the 'waning of affect', loss of critical negativity, and so on – but on the other he seems concerned to cast doubt on the 'radical break' supposed to be necessary to the establishment of that reality, to argue that post-modernism is a dialectical development of the culture of capitalism (a third stage following realism and modernism), just as post-industrial society would in his view be a third stage of the capitalist mode of production, rather than a radically new departure. I think it would not be difficult to show that this tension (which I imagine that Jameson, good Hegelian that he is, would have no difficulty in determining as itself a dialectical contradiction awaiting sublation) affects the very writing of Jameson's text: I am grateful to Rachel Bowlby for drawing my attention on the one hand to the abundance in Jameson's text of expressions of 'a whole new...' something or other (as if he were trying to sell the latest product himself), of 'our now postmodern bodies', and so on; and on the other to a persistent, awkward but determined use of terms such as 'authenticity' and 'realism'. As always in Jameson's work, there is a resolute and stirring promise of a breakthrough to a dialectical understanding yet to be achieved (though this always seems to involve regaining or recapturing something), in which we shall have produced (in this future perfect) 'a some as yet unimaginable new mode of representing' the postmodern, in spite of the postmodern's acknowledged challenge to representation, and in which 'we may again begin to grasp our positioning as individual and collective subjects'. What Jameson terms 'the political form of postmodernism, if there ever is any', 'will have as its vocation the invention and projection of a global cognitive mapping, on a social as well as a spatial scale' (p 92).

So although Jameson appears to argue for the 'reality' of the post-modern, the discourse he uses to defend that reality is one which consistently ignores the questions that same 'reality' would put to that discourse's basic operators, which consistently aim, in however mediated a form, towards unification, totalisation and universalisation. Lyotard is, happily, philosopher enough to be suspicious of the sort of view, be it that of Jameson or Jencks, that would reduce what he is trying to think (provisionally and, I think he would agree, imprudently) under the name of the 'postmodern' to such terms. If Lyotard is right to insist on the temporal complexities of what he calls the *event* of presentation or even of presence, then we can be quite certain that standard sociologising and historicising accounts of what he is doing must be reductive at the very least. Our problem is and will be that what I would call journalism (with no pejorative intent), in its constitutive preoccupation to identify 'news' now, will almost necessarily reinforce that sort of reduction.

I should now like briefly to document Lyotard's arguments around these questions, not to administer a triumphant corrective, but to complicate, complexify, the issue if possible. First from A*u juste (Just Gaming)*. Here Lyotard appends a footnote to a discussion of the question of the addressee of works of art, which question he thinks he can use as a principle of classification. In the body of the text, he works with a broad two-term distinction between 'classical' and 'modern'; and in the footnote

wants to complicate the latter term:

> The modern addressee would be the 'people', and idea whose referent oscillates between the Romantics' Volk and the *fin-de-siècle* bourgeoisie. Romanticism would be modern, as would the project, even if it turns out to be impossible, of elaborating a taste, even a 'bad' one, that permits an evaluation of works. Postmodern (or pagan) would be the condition of the literatures and arts that have no assigned addressee and no regulating ideal, yet in which value is measured by the standard of experimentation. Or, to put it dramatically, which is measured by the distortion that is inflicted in the materials, the forms and the structures of sensibility and thought. Postmodern is not to be taken in a periodizing sense. (p 16)

This is still a difficult remark, because if the insistence on postmodernism's not being a concept of a 'period' is clear (and in the text itself Lyotard states categorically that 'the date is of no importance at all'), then its being placed against such a precisely historically defined notion of the modern is difficult. This complication is not immediately reduced by comments from the essay 'Answering the Question: What is Postmodernism?'. First, Lyotard claims that the postmodern is 'undoubtedly part of the modern' (p 79), and, in a sense, *prior* to the modern (this is what Jencks finds 'crazy'): 'A work can become modern only if it is first postmodern. Postmodernism thus understood is not modernism at its end but in the nascent state, and this state is constant' (Ibid). Although Jencks is sufficiently amazed to stop reading at this point, Lyotard suggests that this understanding is too 'mechanistic', and goes on to describe the postmodern as a particular modality of the modern: broadly speaking, an affirmative rather than a nostalgic modality. The nostalgic modality stresses a loss of reality and the powerlessness of the subject to comprehend the world: the affirmative modality stresses a power to conceive beyond the constraints of given reality or understanding, or the given rules or theory of artistic activity. This affirmative, postmodern modality (which Lyotard is not dating as necessarily contemporary, insofar as Montaigne is thought to be postmodern in this sense) puts forward works which demand judgement, in the absence of any available criteria to ground such a judgement. The other. 'modern' modality puts forward works recognisable to a common 'taste' which would permit judgement to be made.

These descriptions obviously trouble any simple historicising conception of the postmodern (ie *all* conceptions of the postmodern), and I shall stress that trouble by quoting what is the most important paragraph of Lyotard's essay:

> The postmodern would be that which in the modern alleges the unpresentable in presentation itself; which refuses itself the consolation of good forms, the consensus of a taste which would allow nostalgia for the impossible to be felt in common; which inquires into new presentations, not in order to enjoy them, but the better to convey that there is the unpresentable. A postmodern artist and writer is in the situation of a philosopher: the text he writes, the work he accomplishes are not in principle governed by already-established rules, and they cannot be judged by means of a determining judgement, by application to the test or work of known categories. These rules or categories are what the work or the text is looking for. The artist and writer thus work without rules, and in order to establish the rules of what will have been done. Whence the fact that work and text have the properties of the event, whence too they come too late for their author or, what comes down to the same thing, their mise en oeuvre always begins too soon. Postmodern would have to be understood according to the paradox of the future *(post)* perfect *(modo)*. (p 81: tr mod).[7]

In this description, the postmodern would correspond neither to Jencks' 'post-Modernism' (which Lyotard, as I have mentioned, would think of as a sort of eclecticism pandering to aesthetic confusion and in the service of Capital) nor to his 'Late-Modernism', but to an attempt to work with a particular question of temporality or historicity, and more specifically with a valorisation of the event as a configuration which breaks simple linear temporality by opening the 'inside' of anything like 'modernity' to an 'outside' not (yet) namable as such. (A similar type of argument can be found earlier, about literary modernity, in Paul de Man's essay 'Literary History and Literary Modernity.')8

Jameson, unlike Jencks, does acknowledge, in the Foreword to *The Postmodern Condition*, that Lyotard precisely does not 'posit a post-modernist stage radically different from the period of high modernism and involving a fundamental historical and cultural break with this last' (xvi: thus apparently contradicting the statement about break or *coupure* quoted above, but perhaps simply already preparing the argument that Lyotard is not in fact talking about the postmodern at all), and recognises elsewhere that postmodernism involves a 'crisis of historicity'. But such a 'crisis', is located, as always, only in opposition to some lost authentic and good 'properly historical' possibility which is the absent plenitude which underlies all Jameson's thinking and lends his work its relentless pathos and rather tedious nostalgia. Similarly, Terry Eagleton, in an article which is in general hasty and keen to be as harsh on Lyotard as possible, does give the argument some 'qualified credence' at this point (the vital point: most of Eagleton's attacks on Lyotard are either unargued, or aimed at positions Lyotard does not in fact hold), for correctly locating in Modernism 'a revaluation of time itself'9 and Eagleton links this to the same Walter Benjamin he had earlier castigated Lyotard for not taking seriously enough. But both Jameson and Eagleton rapidly draw back into more familiar notions of history in their anxiety to account for the postmodern in terms of their presupposition that whatever is going on now must be bad and alienated, and replaced as soon as possible in a perspective of redemption.

Jencks, Jameson and Eagleton are thus all keen to absorb events into continuities, genealogies and teleologies (Jameson's assertion that genealogy neatly escapes the problems of teleological history is never argued or put to the test). There is really little to choose between them in this respect. If they are able to think of an 'event', this must be thought of as a break and new start. Such a view is irremediably 'Modern' in inspiration,10 and cannot begin to understand the temporal complexity Lyotard is attempting to address: it may well be that the very term 'postmodern' invites such a view so strongly that it self-destructs, that it cannot fail to be another 'modern' term – but it seems clear that attempts to periodise and classify so as to judge and expel or extol can only take place on the basis of a repression of the question of the event which Lyotard is attempting to elaborate.

Questioning in this way the essentially rationalist presuppositions which underlie the responses to Lyotard of Jencks, Jameson and Eagleton does not at all commit one to relativism and still less to irrationalism. Lyotard's purpose is not to attack rationality as such, but a particular rationalistic determination of reason. In the Kantian terms with which much of Lyotard's recent work is concerned, this involves a protest against the claims of the understanding to dominate the entire field of reason. In the realm of aesthetics, such a determination would involve a priority of the determinant over the reflexive judgement, in proceeding according to already-determined rules: for Lyotard, the situation is not that the rules already exist, with the task of artist or architect (but also of politician and scientist, for he would wish

to extend this situation to the reas of knowledge and politics too) being to produce 'cases' fitting these rules, but to 'experiment', to produce cases for which the rule must subsequently be discovered by the reflexive judgement. Whether or not the rationale or rationality of contemporary science really does conform to this schema (as *The Postmodern Condition* claims – and Lyotard's analogy between 'postmodern science' and the concern with justice which is the real guiding-thread of his book is certainly difficult, precisely because of its analogism, and would need patient analysis) is perhaps less important than the fact that nothing in this set-up would justify the charge of irrationalism, in so far as this activity of experimentation is, if not guided, then at least regulated by Ideas of Reason (such as Justice, to be sure, but also Architecture or Painting) resistant to determination by the understanding. If this entirely provisional insistence on the specificity of the Ideas of Reason11 against the encroachments of the concept is enough to constitute relativism, then Lyotard evidently is a relativist: but if relativism be taken to imply that in the absence of conceptual determination everything is equivalent, and anything goes, then he clearly is not – if there is a meta-prescription implied in Lyotard's recent thinking, it would involve the obligation to judge precisely in the absence of determining criteria. Clearly this can be an uncomfortable ethical demand in the wake of our obsession with questions of epistemology and the critical panic which can ensue when epistemologies collapse. Talk of thinking (but also building, painting and politicking) in terms of 'tasks', 'honour' and 'dignity' can seem to involve an unappealing pathos. But it could quite easily be shown that pathos (in the rhetorical sense of aiming to produce an affect in the audience in the absence of rigorous argumentation) is more the quality of the works of Jencks, Jameson and Eagleton: this is the sign of the 'slackening' Lyotard deplores, rather than of the experimentation he advocates. By attempting, in their various ways, to exorcise the threat of 'relativism' they see in Lyotard, Jencks, Jameson and Eagleton all appeal to a superficial rationalism which rapidly does collapse into the pathetic. This does not indicate so much a triumph of relativism as the inadequacy of the opposition between rationalism and relativism (and still less irrationalism) to describe what is at stake in the 'postmodern'.

II   The same sort of point can be made about Derrida and deconstruction. Derrida suggests in his discussion of Tschumi that terms in post – are used 'as if yet again one wished to put order into a linear succession, to periodise, distinguish between the before and the after, limit the risks of reversibility or repetition, of transformation or permutation: progressivist ideology' (4 tr mod: this configuration would also mean, as Derrida has argued more recently,12 that the 'new historicism', for instance, immediately denounces itself as old historicism in its very claim to be 'new' (the oldest claim there is)13 – I suspect that the prefix 'post-' in terms such as 'postmodernism' and 'poststructuralism' can be worked with interestingly – non-journalistically – only if linked to Derrida's exploration of the postal system in *La Carte postale*.14 Derrida's appeal to the word 'maintenant' in his analysis of Tschumi's project is an attempt to escape this type of temporal organisation, and the tension of that 'maintenant' is directly comparable to what Lyotard means by the event. The term 'deconstruction' does not carry the immediately unfortunate periodising connotations of the term 'post-modernism', although it is in some ways an unfortunate and misleading label (as Derrida himself has often said) for the work he and those inspired by him have done, Even accepting the label 'deconstruction', it would, for example, be quite inaccurate to suppose that this simply names something like a method or a technique or a theory or even a philosophy invented by Derrida in Paris at some ideally dateable moment in the 1960s. There are important and specifiable reasons why it is wrong to think of deconstruction as something Derrida or anyone else does or has done to a text or an argument or even a painting. Let me quote briefly from Derrida's short text, 'Letter to a Japanese Friend', which discusses, with a view to its translation into Japanese, the status of the term 'deconstruction':

> In spite of appearances, deconstruction is neither an analysis nor a critique ... It is not an analysis, in particular because the dismantling of a structure is not a regression towards the simple element, towards an indecomposable origin ... No more is it a critique, whether in a general or a Kantian sense ... I'll say the same thing for method. Deconstruction is not a method and cannot be transformed into a method.[15]

Our historicist and subjectivist or objectivist impulses are so ingrained that it is difficult to think this, but we have to try to understand that deconstruction is neither something done at a given date by an active and willful or even heroic subject to a more or less resistant or complicit object, nor quite something that that object is shown to do to itself anyway, whether we like it or not. Here's Derrida again, in the same text:

> It is not enough to say that deconstruction cannot be reduced to some methodological instrumentality, to a set of rules and transposable procedures. It is not enough to say that each 'event' of deconstruction remains singular, or in any case as close as possible to something like an idiom or a signature. We should also make clear that deconstruction is not even an act or an operation ... Deconstruction takes place, it is an event which does not wait on the deliberation, consciousness or organisation of the subject, nor even of modernity. (p 391 [51])

In *The Truth in Painting*, for example, Derrida does not more or less perversely deconstruct Kant's *Critique of Judgement*, but nor does Kant's *Critique of Judgement* deconstruct itself. The point is rather to locate in Kant's text elements which the overall argument has difficulty in containing satisfactorily and which have unsettling effects on that argument in its entirely: what Kant calls the parergon cannot adequately be described as either inside or outside the work of art, although without parerga the work of art would have no inside and outside. *(Mutatis mutandis, this questioning of the frame – in the most general sense of the word – is also what interests Lyotard in the work of Daniel Buren, which is why Buren's 'installations' are difficult to locate as either inside or outside the institution of art: and one can be sure that if we were to try to frame Buren by deciding to call him a deconstructionist, he would respond by sticking his striped pieces of paper all over that frame too.)*

If deconstruction is not, strictly speaking, a theory (given what Derrida calls the 'singularity' of its events: I suppose this is what gives some obscure motivation to Merquior's rather crass characterisation of it as a 'dismal unscience'), then it cannot be taken to prescribe a practice. It is hard to imagine a painter scouring *The Truth in Painting* for instructions as to how to proceed. The two central essays, on Adami and Titus-Carmel, which can indeed be taken to express some admiration for the work discussed, hardly amount to a manifesto of what art should be up to now. But if deconstruction has effects on certain philosophical determinations of art, and if art has always been more or less complicit with its philosophical determination, never separable from busy discursive activities of all sorts, then of course deconstruction might give rise to artistic events of various types, to be invented. But insofar as deconstruction does not simply question the philosophical determination of the work of art from within, say, aesthetics, but questions the coherence of the systematic philosophical organisation in which the domain of

the 'aesthetic' is located, then just as Derrida is no longer strictly speaking writing philosophy, then deconstructive art would no longer strictly speaking be art, and just as deconstructive literary criticism is no longer strictly speaking literary criticism, so deconstructive art criticism would no longer be strictly speaking art criticism, even if its object were work which appears to fall happily within the traditional determination of art. These consequences follow quite rigorously from the argument I quoted above from *The Truth in Painting*, where they are linked to the form of the question 'What is Art?' Whence the comments in the essay on Adami on the 'silliness' of discourse on painting in so far as it is compelled by a drive to philosophical or poetical 'mastery', and the effort made in that text to respond to Adami's work differently, answering the *trait* of Adami's line with a proliferation of words beginning in *tr*, producing a text which escapes our familiar sense of assessment, academic value and translation. The claim would be that something is happening in Adami's work: the academic response to that event is to bind it tight in the strictures of commentary and explication and historical location (including the structures of the label 'deconstruction'), Derrida tries to let something happen in his text which is certainly not purely independent of Adami's event, but which bears a relationship to that event which is not simply servile and therefore masterful, not trying to sublate the sensuousness of paint into the truth of the concept. Despite appearances, this is not essentially different from what Lyotard is attempting to do when he writes about attempting to respect or bear witness to the event of presence given in painting, the 'that it happens' of the event which is what he is attempting to write in the 'post-' of the postmodern: such an event is 'prior' (and in this sense perhaps art indeed 'a thing of the past') to the temporal organisation of history as a narrative which Jencks has to presuppose.

According to the generalised sense of 'text' with which Derrida works, this type of approach also blurs the frame between work and commentary. Adami reads Derrida as much as Derrida reads Adami – no established criteria are going to decide which of these two 'texts' deserves priority in any sense. And Titus-Carmel's work is already as 'philosophical' as Derrida's discussion. There is no claim here that this situation is radically new or unprecedented: the most traditional philosophical views of art as mimesis, and its most academic practice, have always necessarily left uneasily open a sense of art as a dangerous event in which something happens to disturb the integrity of 'nature herself' (and not just 'respond' to her), somewhere resisting the grasp of concept and commentary, and through the insufficiency of attempted explanations of this event in terms of talent, inspiration or genius something of this deconstructive edge or 'point', as Derrida says, has always been at work. To this extent, art has always already been in excess of its concepts, already deconstructive, and deconstruction the motor or movement or element of art, whether in the relatively and historically variably unstable domain of painting or in the equally unstable domain of criticism, just as much as in philosophy. If there were ever to be a deconstructive movement in art, it would be a movement already dissolving its determination and resisting the restitution of its events to anything so stable as a namable movement. Derrida again: '*Of Grammatology* places in question the unity of the 'word' and all the privileges with which it is in general credited, especially in its nominal form' (p 392 [6-7] – the messy and tense area left between determination and indeterminacy, where odd things happen, is where deconstruction is at work.

III In this situation, where these several authors are clearly not all talking about the same thing, still less in agreement, it might however be possible to begin some tentative and entirely preliminary elaboration of the question of the event as it might possibly relate to architecture: I shall briefly consider the work of Venturi, Eisenman and Tshumi.

I take my cue here in the first instance from Venturi's *Complexity and Contradiction in Architecture*,[16] and specifically from Chapter 9 of that book, 'The Inside and the Outside'. The question of the event appears explicitly here: arguing against the 'flowing space' of Modernism and the tendency to impose a continuity between inside and outside, Venturi argues that 'Since the inside is different from the outside, the wall – the point of change – becomes an architectural event' (p 86). And in so far as most architecture is concerned at some point to build walls separating insides from outsides, then it would appear simply enough that architecture is all about events.

In arguing for his complex and contradictory architecture, Venturi draws most of his cultural authority from sources in literary criticism, and notably in the tradition stemming from Eliot – and indeed Venturi opens his preface with quotations from Eliot about criticism and tradition. It seems to me that these references are inadequate to what Venturi is trying to think. It would not I think be difficult to trace the genealogy of his notions of complexity, contradiction, the 'difficult whole' and so on through this tradition. Mannerist and Baroque buildings are to Venturi what the English Metaphysical poets are to Eliot. In this tradition of literary thought, 'complexity' is valorised in so far as it is thought in terms of ambiguity, irony, balance: the 'difficulty' of the whole may well be partially an academic obscurity, and would exclude the potential populism of Venturi's 'is not Main Street almost all right?' (p 104) and of *Learning from Las Vegas.*

To someone approaching Architectural criticism from literary studies, these fundamental references in Venturi's work are a little surprising: the rather stuffy urbanity of Eliot's critical writing seems often to control rather than respect the more disruptive energies that might be detected in literary Modernism, and which would nowadays be approached through the work of Kristeva or Derrida rather than Eliot. In Derridean terms, this would lead to a wariness of the value of 'contradiction', because of its Hegelian ancestry – the determination of difference as contradiction invites the sublation of that contradiction into a totality (however 'difficult'),[17] and it would equally lead to suspicions about the notion of ambiguity: even extended to mean 'polysemia', ambiguity remains in the ambit of a notion of meaning as ideally unitary and recoverable – Derrida has detailed analyses questioning these values, especially in 'La Double Séance':

> If, then, there is no thematic unity or total meaning to be reappropriated beyond textual instances, in an imaginary, an intentionality or a lived experience, the text is no longer the expression or representation (happy or not) of some truth which would come to be diffracted or gathered in a polysemic literature. It is for this hermeneutic concept of polysemy that should be substituted that of dissemination.[18]

Dissemination disrupts the totality and any search for 'meaning', and to this extent is an uncomfortable for Venturi's book as for any other (but the constitutive vagueness of discursive terms in architectural criticism – does anybody for example really know what the word 'meaning' means when applied to architecture? – makes this problem both more urgent and, perhaps, more approachable here). But Venturi's book also invites closer reading with Derrida: in 1966, *Complexity and Contradiction* has its chapter entitled 'The Inside and the Outside'; in 1967, Derrida's *De la Grammatologie* has a chapter with the same title. Derrida is of course analysing the notion of the sign, especially as formulated by Saussure, whereas Venturi is analysing buildings. But the (inevitable) tendency of architecture to be discussed in

terms of meaning should allow some cautious use of analogy between the analyses: and Derrida's appeal to initially spatial categories of inside and outside in what must, at least at first, seem like an analogical way (for what would it mean *literally* to suggest that signs have an 'inside' and an 'outside'?) suggests that the analogy does not only work in one direction.

Some care must be taken here to avoid hasty misunderstandings: at first sight, Derrida is suggesting that the opposition between inside and outside cannot be sustained, and duly follows his chapter with one affirming that the inside *is* the outside:[19] Venturi, on the other hand, is *attacking* the continuity between inside and outside he sees promoted by Modernism, with its 'emphasis on the oneness of interior and exterior space', and stressing that 'the inside is different from the outside; (p 70). But the matter is more complicated than this apparent opposition would suggest: Venturi may indeed by arguing for separation as against any 'ultimate continuity of space' (70), but the point of this is to move against the Modern dictum that 'the inside should be *expressed* on the outside' (*Ibid,* my emphasis). And this presummposition that the outside expresses (or represents or signifies) an inside is of course also the object of Derrida's investigation. The whole classical notion of the sign as divided into signifier and signified rests on just such an inside/outside opposition, and on the presupposition that the outside somehow, more or less obliquely, reveals or manifests the inside. As Derrida shows, an underlying assumption here is that the inside, the signified, exists ideally prior to and independently of the outside: the outside is the accidental ('arbitrary') means of access to the inside, and should ideally not obstruct that access, should be transparent. The plate-glass 'walls' of the Modernist cube would appear to be analogous to such a transparency of the outside. On the other hand, in so far as there is an inside, then it must necessarily have an outside to define it as an inside: the border, even made of glass, must be at least as much a place of separation as a place of communication (this combination of separation and communication defining the notion of the limit as a place of articulation).[20] Even Modernist buildings must provide at least a *thermal* difference between inside and outside, as Venturi points out.

If one pursues the analogy a little further, then the modernist pretension (as analysed by Venturi – 'the truth of the matter' is not what is at stake here) to reduce the barrier between inside and outside to the diaphaneity of a sheet of glass would be an extension of the set-up diagnosed by Derrida as 'logocentrism', taking the need to 'express' the inside on the outside to the limiting case of reducing the outside to almost nothing. Or, in terms of Derrida's analysis of writing, such architecture would correspond to the Western investment in the excellence of so-called 'phonetic' writing, as opposed to the mysteries of hieroglyph and ideogram, which, as against the democratic accessibility of phonetic script, protect an inside as a potential mystery, accessible only to the select few.[21] Paradoxes proliferate in this situation: phonetic writing, which apparently *reduces* the separation of inside and outside, might also be said to *enforce* it all the more – Derrida shows Saussure anxiously confirming writing in its exteriority to speech precisely by stressing the demands of the phonetic: if writing could only become that diaphanous means of access to interiority, then it could not be said to affect or penetrate that interiority at all, but to remain in its place outside.

A number of moves might be made in this situation, which is complexity itself. We might argue, for example, that one effect of Derrida's analysis is to demonstrate the impossibility of conceiving the inside prior to and independently of the outside. Only an outside defines an inside – in the analysis of the sign, this leads to the idea that in a sense there is no signified: a signified is no more than a signifier placed in a certain position by other signifiers. Look up a word in the dictionary to 'get at' its signified and you find more signifiers referring to ever more signifiers. What has always been thought of as the signified is no more than an effect (not quite an illusion) of the 'play of signifiers'.[22] Once this has been argued, then it is difficult to retain the notion of signifier (and this marks Derrida's difference from doctrines of the 'materiality of the signifier', which is moreover a contradiction in terms):[23] 'signifier' can only imply 'what signifies a signified', and if there is really no signified to be signified, then there is really no signifier to signify it either (whence Derrida's introduction of the notion of the trace). The inside is the outside, but this rapidly leads to the conclusion that there is no outside either, but a generalised differential space organised into 'effects' (not quite illusions) of inside and outside. A radical 'flowing space' would not simply reduce the wall to a sheet of glass, but would show that the inside is merely a fold or invagination in a generalised 'outside'. The plate-glass window maintains a separation all the more securely for promising its abolition – it might suggest a possible continuity and yet break your nose if you try to take that promise up: whereas nobody would walk into an honest wall.

Venturi, also suspicious of the expression of inside on outside, fights against the 'Saussurean' solution of reducing the outside the better to keep it outside (in our loose analogy, the 'transparent' walls of the Modern office-block keep the outside out all the more securely by displaying the power and mystery of the inside as power and mystery). Venturi's suggestion is that if the attempt to reduce the separation of inside and outside is an illusion, then better accept that separation and make something of it – Venturi likes the difference to be great and mysterious, and it is no accident that temples at Karnak and Edfu appear to illustrate the text at this point, or that he should refer to the 'partial mystery inherent in a sense of privacy' (71) in this chapter.

It would be nice, but I think an over-simplification, to conclude that Venturi, faced with the failure of a certain Modernism's apparent denial of the inside/outside opposition, takes fright and moves regresively back to an insistence on their separation, whereas Derrida moves progressively on and demands that the opposition be deconstructed altogether. I would not deny the presence of 'regressive' moments in Venturi's text and 'progressive' ones in Derrida's. Such moments would encourage the placing of Venturi as the 'conservative' 'historicist' 'post-modernist' he undoubtedly partially is, and Derrida as the radical Modernist taking modernity to its ultimate conclusions. But it is just as easy to imagine a counter-argument whereby Venturi is the progressivist, arguing for a flexible and livable negotiation of inside and outside, whereas Derrida's arguments lead him to the arcane mystery of an apparently hermetic script. The ease with which such characterisations can be constructed suggests that there is something wrong with them.

We can complicate this picture (and note that to do so we must jettison any simple notion of contradiction) so far as Venturi is concerned, by noting that his rejection of the Modernist argument for a continuity of inside and outside does not simply retreat into an affirmation of their radical separation. His use of the Egyptian temples does not in fact concentrate on any mystery eventually to be found at their centre, but on the graduated series of enclosures of enclosures. Such a set-up does not always imply a central mystery – Roland Barthes, for example, made persistent use of the formally identical model of the onion as an image of the text which was precisely made up of layers within layers but contained nothing at its centre: reading becoming the process of negotiating the layers rather than the triumphant arrival at any central 'core' of meaning.[24] Moreover, by advocating quite aggressively a different treatment of inside and outside surfaces

of the wall, Venturi is splitting the line of limit or border in a way that might easily look to Derrida rather than Eliot for its language. And against his own declared location and valorisation of 'contradiction' between inside and outside, Venturi also makes more subtle moves, leading to an idea of 'residual spaces' which cannot simply be accommodated into a rigidification of an inside/outside polarity:

> Residual space in between dominant spaces with varying degrees of openness can occur at the scale of the city and is a characteristic of the fora and other complexes of late Roman urban planning. Residual spaces are not unknown in our cities. I am thinking of the open spaces under our highways and the buffer spaces around them. Instead of acknowledging and exploiting these characteristic kinds of space we make them into parking lots or feeble patches of grass – no-man's lands between the scale of the region and the locality. (p 80, my emphasis)

In this description, 'residual space' could not simply be described as either inside or outside: rather it would seem to be a pocket of outside within the inside, the 'no-man's land' of frontier and margin at the centre of the city's inside. (In Lyotard's terms, the zone of the pagus, from which Lyotard derives his notion of the 'pagan'[26]). In spite of Venturi's insistence on 'the inside's being different from the outside', and his best or worst intentions in that direction, his own description of 'residual space' productively disrupts the very dichotomy he is trying to reinforce.[26] This disruption can be further illustrated in a quotation from Aldo van Eyck provided by Venturi, apparently wanting it to support his own arguments:

> Architecture should be conceived of as a configuration of intermediary places clearly defined. This does not imply continual transition or endless postponement with respect to place and occasion. On the contrary, it implies a break away from the contemporary concept (call it sickness) of spatial continuity and the tendency to erase every articulation between spaces, ie between outside and inside, between one space and another (between one reality and another). Instead the transition must be articulated by means of defined in-between places which induce simultaneous awareness of what is significant on either side. An in-between space in this sense provides the common ground where conflicting polarities can again become twin phenomena (p 82).

Despite the manifestly dialectical character of this description, it would not be difficult to take this notion of the 'in-between' (see Derrida's play on 'entre' and 'antre' in 'La Double séance')[27] and see it, not as the ground of a dialectical mediation between contradictory or 'conflicting polarities', but as the generalisable 'medium' or milieu of the same (not the identical, as both Heidegger and Derrida insist)[28] in which differentiation takes place. In this type of reading, the in-between space would be something like the spatiality of space, the spacing of spaces, which cannot itself be simply defined as inside or outside, nor indeed as simply 'in' space at all. And, as the quotation from van Eyck suggests, architecture would then consist in the 'configuring' (differentiating) of space into spaces which are always intermediary. This reading would of course exercise a certain amount of violence on van Eyck's text, as it would lead to the idea that, in a sense, this does imply something of a 'continual transition or endless postponement' with respect to both place and occasion. We are very close to Derrida here, and specifically to his derivation of différance, differing and deferring.[29] This also takes up on the temporal aspect of what van Eyck says: for if we are to make any sense of architecture as to do with the event, then we must be talking about time as well as space. And to have a closer look at these possibilities, we shall have to leave Venturi and move to two architects who explicitly invoke the work of Derrida, namely Eisenman and Tschumi.

IV Paradoxically enough, the explicit invocation of Derrida in texts by and around Eisenman makes the discussion rather more difficult than in the case of Venturi. It may be that in some sense Eisenman is proposing more or less rigorously 'deconstructive' architecture: this clearly does not imply that the discursive links of such an architecture with the work of Derrida are successfully negotiated. For example, in one of the essays in the *Fin d'Ou T HouS* project, Jeffrey Kipnis picks up on the notion of in-betweenness I have just been discussing, and says the following: 'The betweenness reading, which Derrida calls "différance", is the always in flux space that constitutes the relations that are reading itself; scene of intrinsic subjectivity, it is the playground named Mind'.[30] Now whatever exactly 'intrinsic subjectivity' means here (or 'mind' for that matter), it is an odd way to talk about Derrida. Kipnis has earlier in his text introduced the notions of reading and subjectivity which inform the sentence I have just quoted: he says for example that 'Writing, in Derrida's formulation, is any and every organisation of form that stimulates an organised experience of reading' (p 15), and that 'writing' in the generalised sense given to that word by Derrida, consists in 'subjectivity vested [...] forms caught up endlessly in referring to other forms ...' (*Ibid*). I really do not know where Kipnis has found the authority for these appeals to reading and to subjects, for there is no such appeal in Derrida. The inspiration is apparently much more Barthesian, for whom the proclaimed 'death of the author' (which would correspond closely enough to Eisenman's heralded absence as architect from his own programmed architecture) is all too rapidly paid for by the birth of the reader:[31] Derrida's 'writing' is in fact the death of the reader as much as the death of the author. In *Of Grammatology,* for instance, Derrida says that writing is other than the subject, in whatever sense one chooses to take those words.[32] And if 'experience' is invoked by Derrida around the argument that writing in his generalised sense is (among other things) the 'formation of form', this is an 'experience' which takes transcendental phenomenology to its limits before crossing through the notion of experience as derived and secondary to that of the trace. In passing, Derrida comments on the necessity of passing through these transcendental arguments, as otherwise the 'ultra-transcendental' text (which he is proposing) can all too easily look like the 'pre-critical' text, which I fear Kipnis has provided.[33] (The same error that Derrida's philosophy is somehow a form of subjectivism is also perpetrated in the presentation of the recent interview in the review Domus.[34])

Eisenman's own presentations are also quite obscure and uneven. In the Romeo and Juliet material,[35] for example, the attempt to disrupt the value of presence by opposing it to avoid and by re-defining absence, is potentially confusing: and that re-definition of absence as 'either the trace of a previous presence' (in which case it 'contains memory'), or else as 'the trace of a possible presence' (in which cas it 'contains immanence) could be shown to fall short of the Derridean account of the trace on which it is clearly attempting to draw: this account is essentially that of a phenomenology such as is traversed by Derrida in *Of Grammatology* and *Speech and Phenomena.* By thinking in terms of memory and past or future presences, Eisenman is still within the metaphysical and essentially linear account of time which Derrida has so patiently undermined. It is also noticeable that Eisenman is still thinking in a fundamentally dialectical way, both in this account of absence and the temporality of the site, and in the three 'structural relationships' he takes from the story of Romeo and Juliet (the dialectic of division, union, and then union-and-division of the lovers in the tomb). Derrida's own discussion of Romeo and Juliet (which there is no reason to assume that Eisenman would or should have known)[36] disrupts this simplicity with a non-dialectical complexity, in which 'division' inhabits union as a non-accidental 'accident', and division inhabits identity in, for example, the simultaneous unity and division of Romeo and his name. It may well be, of course, that Eisenman's project in some sense *shows* this, even if his discourse does not quite *describe* it. But as the logic of Eisenman's work is that it is difficult if not impossible to perform a neat separation of building and discourse, this unevenness cannot be ignored.

Whatever the value of Eisenman's descriptions, and whatever the doubts that might be levelled at his particular appeal to the notion of self-similarity, which could lead to closure as much as to opening if too quickly interpreted in terms of the *mise-en-abyme,* (and Eisenman's idea of the architectural object becoming 'internalised', 'self-definitive', 'true to its own logic', progressing 'an intrinsic value system' suggests that he is no stranger to that over-hasty interpretation)[37] it is clear that his is an attempt to think time in the space of architecture, beyond the obvious and simple sense of the time of a building's building or existence. If it is true that this is an attempt at an architecture of the event, then it clearly cannot simply mean that the building of a building is an event, nor that it provides a space in which events may take place.

It is precisely this concern which Derrida explicitly finds at work in Tschumi's Villette project (see §3 for the point just made). I asked before if anyone really knew what it meant to talk of meaning in architecture: even in no-one really does, the fact would remain, according to Derrida, that in general the meaning of architecture is that it should have meaning (Derrida presents this as the basic postulation underlying four invariables traversing the history of the concept of architecture (§8). The meaning of architecture cannot itself be architectural, and to this extent architecture is governed from principles outside itself (§9). Derrida's complex argument is designed to suggest that Tschumi's project disrupts this configuration. It is clear that this is again a question of the deconstruction of an inside/outside polarity, if not quite in the sense I was trying to sketch out a propos of Venturi. It is emphatically not a question, in Derrida's reading of Tschumi, of simply refusing the outside, the 'extrinsic' meanings imposed on architecture, in favour of some notional internal purity or propriety of architecture, as we might still suspect to be the case with Eisenman. Just as Venturi's apparent desire to mark a strong separation of inside and outside led to a complication of the structure of the limit separating inside and outside, so Tschumi's project both includes the outside (it does not refuse external demands of utility and so on), and opens the inside to its others (photography, cinema and so on). Tschumi's architecture would thus by definition not be *proper* architecture, and it would be unreasonable, as in the case of Eisenman, simply to separate the building 'itself' from texts, drawings and so on, which accompany it as more and less than 'projects'. In this case, it is Tschumi's fortune to be able to include a text by Derrida Kipnis in his intertext.

In Derrida's reading, Tschumi's effort is to 'maintain the disjointed as such', to 'give dissociation its due, but to put it to work as such in the space of a gathering' (the gathering that is the fundamental motif of Heidegger's 'Building, Dwelling, Thinking'). The logic here is precisely that which governs Derrida's general thinking on inside and outside (and thereby his thought in general, in so far as separating inside and outside is the act of separation itself, the analysis, critique, conceptualising which defines philosophy): the 'points' on Tschumi's grid gather their own separation, hold together and apart both togetherness and apartness, 'associate and dissociate both association and dissociation', in a tension which refuses the dialectical solutions proposed by Eisenman, and which could not give rise to the suspicion of closure invited by Eisenman's appeal to 'self-similarity'. (§§ 13-5: I would want to argue that such an 'economy of dissociation' is identical to that briefly proposed under the sign of 'dissensus' by Lyotard at the end of *The Postmodern Condition*, against Habermas – Derrida here talks of 'a socius of dissociation (§14).) This tension cannot be thought in simply spatial terms, nor in terms of a temporality itself thought of as *external* to space (it is not simply a question of providing a space in which temporal events might occur). But the spacing of Tschumi's grid (which is not just its space, as we suggested above in relation to Venturi and Van Eyck) is an attempt to work at the root of space and time – each of Tschumi's differentiated cubes is caught in the play of all the others: none is simply a self-present and self-sufficient unity. Effects of inside and outside are certainly produced here, but they are neither the simple separations recommended by Venturi, nor simply the flowing space he is concerned to attach. Tschumi's points interrupt the flow as much as they allow for it, and are themselves as divisible as they are punctual. The 'maintenant' stressed by Derrida, the now and the maintaining, is a maintenance not of presence but of spacing and interruption, of what he calls 'the relation with the other as such' (§16).

The relation with the other as such (the 'as such' is important,

marking that what is at stake here is respect for the alterity of the other, not an attempt to reduce that alterity to familiarity), which defines some of Derrida's most 'technical' thinking,[38] and which marks that thinking as fundamentally ethical, is still all to do with insides and outsides, walls and events. Our 'deconstruction' of the wall in Venturi is not an attempt to deny the force or urgency of his insistence that the outside is different from the inside, but to modulate its mildly exasperated common sense into something like Tschumi's 'folies', where the difference of outside and inside is, as it were, already inside anyway. The 'promise' or invitation to the Other located by Derrida in Tschumi's project is not at all simply an invitation (addressed to 'the public') to come into the warm, nor to become a community (again). The ethico-political importance of this would quickly be made clear in a comparison of the Villette project and *Learning from Las Vegas*, where the socius in dissociation is apparently to be abandoned to the virtues of the strip. Dissociation, which is an absolute condition of the political, rather than the unfortunate failure of community it is often taken to be, need not accept its traditional (even dialectical) negative marking: as the active and necessarily unpredictable negotiation of walls between insides and outsides rather than their intolerant institution or illusory abolition, dissociation proceeds as an aleatory series of events. What will happen at La Villette remains: to be seen.

Notes

1 This is the full text of an essay parts of which have been used elsewhere: as a lecture to the Architectural Association School of Architecture in February 1987; as a paper at the Architectural Association's conference on 'The Relative and the Rational', in May 1987; and as a paper at the Tate Gallery International Symposium on deconstruction, May 1988. The later part of the essay appeared in a slightly earlier and edited version, under the title 'Complexity without Contradiction in Architecture', in *AA Files*, 15 (1988), 15-18.

2 Jacques Derrida, Interview with Eva Meyer, 'Architecture ove il desiderio può abitare', in *Domus*, 681 (1986), 17-24.

3 Charles Jencks, *What is Post-Modernism?*, Academy Editions, London: St Martin's Press, New York, 1986. References will be given in the text.

4 Jacques Derrida, *La Vérité en peinture*, Flammarion, Paris, 1978, p 25, tr *The Truth in Painting*, University of Chicago Press, 1988, p 21.

5 Jean-François Lyotard, 'Réponse a la question: qu'est-ce le post-moderne?', in *Le Postmoderne expliqué aux enfants*, Galilée, Paris, 1986, pp 13-34 (p 22) tr Régis Durand as 'Answering the Question: What is Postmodernism?', in *The Postmodern Condition*, University of Minnesota, Minneapolis: Manchester University Press, 1984, pp 71-82 (p 76).

6 Fredric Jameson, 'Postmodernism or the Cultural Logic of Capitalism', *New Left Review*, 1984, p 146.

7 For some further explication of this paradox, see my paper 'Towards a Criticism of the Future', forthcoming in *Writing the future*, ed D C Wood, Routledge, London, 1989.

8 Paul de Man, 'Literary History and Literary Modernity', in *Blindness and Insight: Essays in the Rhetoric of Contemporary Criticism*, second edition, Methuen, London, 1983, pp 142-165.

9 Terry Eagleton, 'Capitalism, Modernism and Postmodernism', in *Against the Grain: Essays 1975-1985*, Verso, London, 1986, pp 131-47 (p 139).

10 Cf Lyotard, 'Note sur les sens de "post-"', in *Le postmoderne expliqué aux enfants*, pp 119-26 (120-1): this is a rewritten version of the 'Defining the Postmodern', in Lisa Appignanesi, ed, *Postmodernism*, (ICA Documents 4 and 5) (1986), 6-7 (reprinted

London: Free Association Books, 1989: pp 7-10.

11 I say 'provisional' because, since *Au juste* at least, Lyotard points out a problem in attempting to think 'multiplicity', 'divergence', 'dissensus', etc, according to the Kantian description of the Idea. Cf my *Lyotard: Writing the Event*, Manchester University Press, 1988, p 160.

12 In an unpublished paper delivered at the 1987 University of California (Irvine) conference, The States of Theory.

13 See again De Man, op cit, pp 144 and 161.

14 See my 'Postal Politics and the Institution of the Nation', in Homi K Bhabha, ed, *Nation and Narration*, Methuen, forthcoming.

15 'Lettre à un ami japonais', in *Psyché. Inventions de l'autre*, Galilée, 1987, pp 387-393 (p 390); tr in Wood and Bernasconi, eds, *Derrida and Differance*, Parousia Press, Warwick, 1985, pp 1-8 (pp 4-5): page-references will be given in the text (I have modified the translations a little here and there).

16 Robert Venturi, *Complexity and Contradiction in Architecture*, Museum of Modern Art, New York, 1977. Page references will be included in the text.

17 This implies that contradiction, despite appearances, in fact works towards homogenisation, whereas a thought of difference, despite its apparent modesty, respects heterogeneity.

18 Jacques Derrida, *La Dissémination*, Seuil, Paris, 1972, p 294.

19 Jacques Derrida, *De la grammatologie*, Minuit, Paris, 1967. In fact, in a notorious gesture, Derrida crosses through the copula in this chapter-title, to stress a movement of excess with respect to traditional ontology, and to block potential confusion with the Hegelian 'speculative proposition'.

20 See for example *De la grammatologie*, Chapter 3, Section III, but this logic of the limit pervades all of Derrida's thinking.

21 See especially the analyses in 'Scribble (pouvoir/écrire)', preface to William Warburton, *Essai sur le hiéroglyphes*, Aubier, Paris, 1974.

22 On this sense of the word 'effect', which cannot be reduced to the couple cause/effect any more than to the couple truth/illusion, see especially Derrida's *Positions*, Minuit, Paris, 1972, p 90.

23 Simply because the identity of the signifier is secured despite its potentially very disparate material repetitions, and must therefore essentially involve ideality. It is odd that Derrida has been so widely

misread on this point, given the clarity of his statements: see for example *De la grammatologie*, pp 20, 45, 138-9.

24 See, for example, Barthes' own reflection on his use of this type of image, in *Roland Barthes*, Seuil, Paris, 1975), pp 54-5. Compare with the empty centre of Jewish tabernacle or temple, at least in the description given by Hegel's *Spirit of Christianity* (see Derrida's commentary in *Glas*, Galilée, Paris, 1974, 60a tr John P Leavey, Nr, and Richard Rand, University of Nebraska Press, 1986, 49a-50a.

25 See Jean-François Lyotard, *Instruction païennes*, Galilée, 1977, pp 42-3; *Au Jusu*, Bourgois, Paris, 1979, pp 74-5, *Le Différend*, §218.

26 This is also true of Venturi's remarks about 'open poché'.

27 *La Dissémination*, pp 240-1.

28 See especially Derrida's essay 'La Pharmacie de Platon', and Heidegger's *Identity and Difference* and 'Building, Dwelling, Thinking'. This difficult theme of the non-identical same-in-*différance* is vital to an understanding of Derrida's thinking.

29 See especially Derrida's essay 'La Différance' (in *Marges – de la philosophie*, Minuit, Paris, 1972, pp 1-29).

30 Jeffrey Kipnis, 'Architecture Unbound: Consequences of the Recent Work of Peter Eisenman', in Peter Eisenman, *Fin d'ou t hous*, AA Folio V (1985), pp 12-23 (p 16). I should like to thank Jeffrey Kipnis for his very gracious acceptance of these criticisms since the appearance of the first version of this paper.

31 Roland Barthes, 'La Mort de l'auteur', in *Le Bruissement de la langue*, Seuil, Paris, 1984, pp 61-7 (p 67). The final sentence of Barthes' article makes it clear that he is simply proposing a reversal of the traditional model which forgets the reader in favour of the author. (This point has recently been made very forcibly by Peggy Kamuf in her recent *Signature Pieces*, Cornell University Press, 1988.) The stress on the addressee in general has been persuasively argued by Vincent Descombes to be characteristic of structuralism, and to limit its claims to break with a 'philosophy of the subject':

see *Le Même et l'autre: quarante-cinq ans de philosophie française*, Minuit, Paris, 1979, especially pp 114 and 123-4.

32 19. 'Le constituant et le disloquant à la fois, l'écriture est autre que le sujet, en quelque sens qu'on l'entende', *De la grammatologie*, p 100.

33 Cf *De la grammatologie*, p 90. It should be made clear that there are degrees of the pre-critical, or possibly a stage of the pre-pre-critical. For example, Kipnis's text is of a quality not to be confused with that of recent descriptions of deconstruction as a 'style' or a 'world-view'.

34 *Domus* interview presentation.

35 Peter Eisenman, *Moving Arrows, Eros and Other Errors*, 1986, AA Box 3.

36 Jacques Derrida, 'L'Aphorisme à contretemps', in *Psyché: Inventions de l'autre*, Galilée, Paris, 1987, pp 519-33. This text was written as a programme note for a French production, and will appear in English translation in a forthcoming volume of essays on Shakespear, edited by Nich Royle.

37 Derrida, 'Point de folie...', §9: 'In reinstituing architecture in what should have been singularly proper to it, it is above all not a matter of reconstituing a simplicity of architecture, a simply architectural architecture, by a purist or integrist obsession. It is no longer a matter of saving the proper in the virginal immanence of its economy and of returning it to its inalienable presence, finally non-representative, non-mimetic and referring only to itself. This autonomy of architecture, which would claim in this way to reconcile a formalism and a semanticism in their extremes, would do no more than accomplish the metaphysics it was claiming to deconstruct.' Much of the Eisenman material I have seen would appear vulnerable to these remarks.

38 See for example the elucidation of the 'trace' in *De la grammatologie*, pp 68-9.

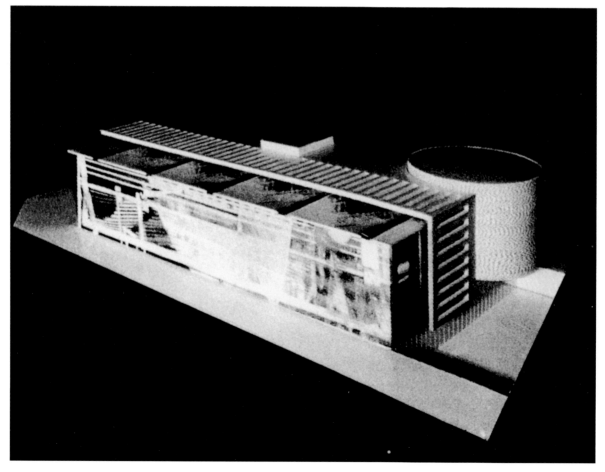

BERNARD TSCHUMI, ZKM KARLSRUHE, MODEL

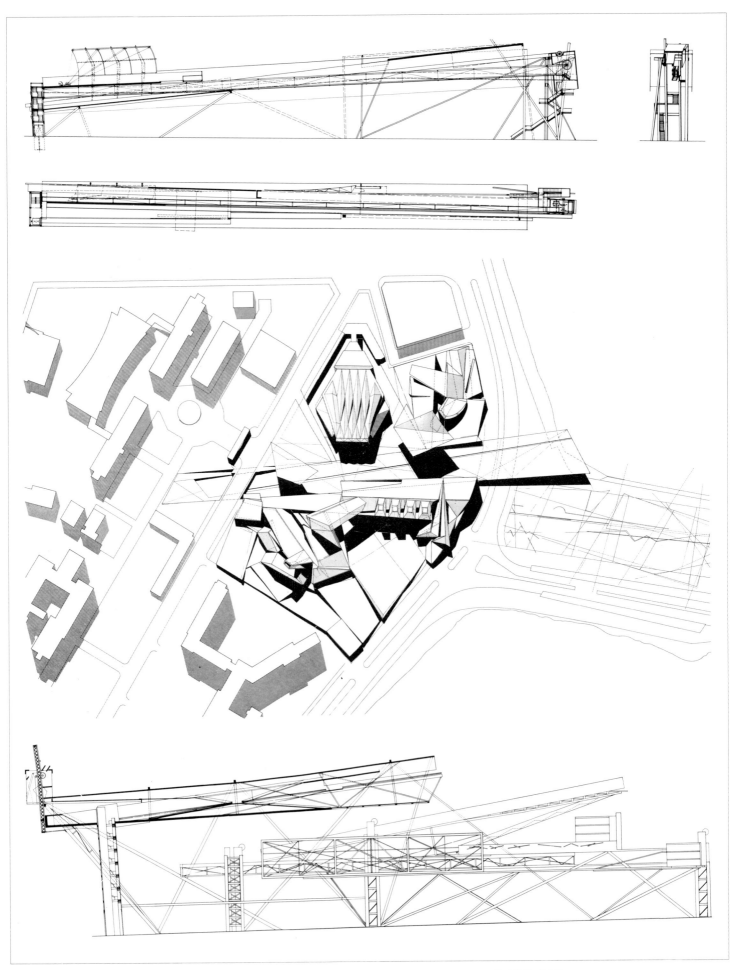

STUDIO ASYMPTOTE *ABOVE*: TIME MACHINE; *CENTRE*: ALEXANDRA LIBRARY; *BELOW*: STEEL CLOUD

JOHN RAJCHMAN
WHAT'S NEW IN ARCHITECTURE

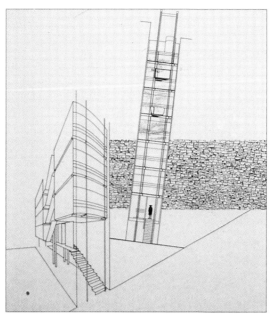

ISABELLE DEVIN & CATHERINE RANNOU, PARENTESE

Space and Time: Architecture is about space, the construction of habitable space. But how and what we build depends on when we build; the construction of habitable space has a history. The question of what is new in architecture is the question of the sort of history it has had, and may yet have. Reflection on this question has involved some contemporary philosophers in two traditional topics:

space and time. One might extract a general theme. I will call it the theme of 'other time, other space'; and I will indicate how the question of what is new in architecture may be formulated in terms of it.

In an interview concerning architecture, Foucault says modern philosophers have paid too much attention to time, not enough to space.[1] Foucault proposes to rethink space (or habitable space) in terms of his histories of the 'constitution of the subject', or, to employ a familiar, and more architecturally loaded term, his histories of the ways we *construct* ourselves. A history of space was a part of his attempt to extend the concept of 'technology' to include what he called 'technologies of the self'. I think it is somewhat arbitrary to try to dissociate the effective practice of freedom of people, the practice of social relations, and the spatial distributions in which they find themselves.[2] Urban planners, administrators of political territories, and prison wardens are all concerned with such 'spatial distributions'; just as the distribution of domestic spaces forms an integral part of the social and political history of the family.

A central idea in this analysis of habitable space was that the spaces we construct for ourselves to inhabit help to construct we ourselves, our ways of being, our *ethos*. How we are housed helps to determine who we are and may be, and one can thus examine through what means, conceptual and physical, and in

response to what problems, we have come, so to speak, to inscribe ourselves in architectural stone. Foucault's study of such spaces of our own self-construction was 'genealogical'; it was thus after all related to time. Foucault held there *events* in the sorts of spatial distributions in which we find ourselves, in the spaces we construct for ourselves to inhabit. We construct ourselves in part in response to events; and such self-constructions are in turn exposed to other events yet to come. In this sense one may speak, in Foucault's historical work, of the spatial problem of 'inhabiting a time'.

The events with which Foucault was concerned in his histories were of a particular sort – the events of new kinds of thinking, saying, being, doing, or seeing. That 'there are events in thought' was for Foucault a 'principle of singularity'.[3] An event in thought may be said to be singular just when the novelty it introduces cannot be predicted or explained in terms of context and logic alone. Ian Hacking refers to such singular events when he says that the logic neither of induction nor deduction alone can account for the emergence of the styles of scientific reasoning that determine possible domains of true or false discourse – styles like statistical or experimental reasoning.[4] We can never *infer* an event in thought from the context or reasoning from which it arises; it is always the singular arrival of something new which retrospectively transforms its very context, social and

33

intellectual. But what Foucault thus says of a statement (énoncé – that it is always 'an event which neither the language (langue) nor the meaning can ever quite exhaust'[5] – may equally be said of building or housing: the spaces we inhabit are always events that cannot ever quite be exhausted by the meanings with which we invest them.

In Foucault's early paper on architecture, 'Of Other Spaces',[6] we might find a name for such events in the spaces we inhabit. Foucault refers to spaces not of utopia but of 'heterotopia' – those spaces which appear singularly unclassifiable in our classifications and the meanings we derive from them – like Borges' Chinese encyclopedia. And, in Foucault's study of space, how we are housed is tied up with the great question of which kinds of classifications are available at a time and a place for us to characterise ourselves. The housing of the mad or the criminal in the asylum or the prison involved the question of how some things came to be classed as madness or crime, while other similar ones were not. Foucault's conjecture was that such architectural classifications arose in response to particular problems, and, more precisely, to new problems, when the response did not just follow from the context and could not be given through a logical working out of existing discourse. There arise problems that call for the invention of a singular response; they are the 'eventalising' problems in our architectural self-classifications.

Foucault called such moments 'problematisations'. A problematisation is never the simple consequence of the context or the logic of the historical process in which it arises; it is an event that interrupts the self-evidence of its context, historical and conceptual, and obliges it to modify itself. The 'other space' of a classificatory heterotopia becomes historical for Foucault when it assumes the force of the 'other time' of an event, when it problematises the history in which it figures, requiring a singular invention of thought.

Foucault's 'genealogical' investigations into the invention of those spaces that have served to construct us was thus concerned with problematising heterotopic events in the histories in which we find ourselves. He tried to start with a kind of break with the self-evidence of our current ways of going about things (and, in particular, of the sorts of spaces we construct for ourselves to inhabit). This break with our own self-constructions would offer us the possibility of a 'space' in which to re-examine the history of just how we came to take those particular kinds of self-construction for granted, and to expose us to the invention of new ones. The aim of Foucault's 'geneaology', in contrast to a certain totalising necessitarian strain in social history, was thus to 'eventalise' our history, to help articulate something new in what is happening to us.[7]

Foucault tried to show how that 'simple idea in architecture', as Bentham called his Panopticon, was a great invention in the history of the spatial distributions in which we find ourselves, and therefore in our social relations and the exercise of our freedom. But to retrospectively analyse the 'archive' in which this distribution and these relations came to figure was not to show how implacable it had become. It was on the contrary to break with its air of obviousness, the sense that there was no other way to proceed, and so to let us diagnose the possibility or arrival of other spaces, other ways of constructing ourselves. It was to free the history of our own self-constructions for our invention.

Inventions

An invention, Derrida declares in a 1983 essay, must possess 'the singular structure of an event'.[8] The essay is about how to rethink invention by rethinking event: Patent law, born of industrial technology, has learned to make invention conceptu-

ally manageable and thus 'calculable'; and such manageability has been prepared by a philosophical 'displacement' in the idea of invention that becomes stable 'in the 17th century, perhaps between Descartes and Leibniz'. To 'reinvent invention' is to extract its concept from this modern philosophical and legal context by restoring and radicalising the sense of surprise in what it initiates or innovates: the 'implicit contract' it must violate, the 'disorder' it must introduce into the 'peaceful arrangement of things'. 'Invention' shares roots with 'event'; both derive from Venire. To invent is to 'come upon' something for the first time. It thus involves an element of novelty or surprise, which would be of a singular sort when what the invention comes upon could not previously be counted as even possible in the history or context in which it arises. It is then an 'invention of the other'; it initiates what could not have been foreseen, and cannot yet be named.

The lecture containing such reflections on the event in invention is one Derrida selects out of chronological order to head off, and to entitle, a thick volume of recent writings; and in a forward he explains why. He says the lecture was a 'pivotal' one in the movement of what he terms his théorie distraite: the 'dissociated, separated, distracted'[9] elements of an assemblage in which would be variously traced something of his 'formation' in the 80s. The emergence or the arrival of a disparate multiplicity – that is roughly what Derrida understands as an event. And, by its very conception, deconstruction must have this sort of 'history'; it must proceed by constant disparate invention. 'Deconstruction is inventive or it is nothing ... its process engages an affirmation. The latter is tied up with the to-come of the event, of the advent, and of the invention.'[10] And among the disparate elements of this 'mobile multiplicity' in the thought of a rather particular first person in deconstruction, there figure the writings Derrida devoted to 'architecture', or wrote in 'corespondence' with his 'friends' in architecture, Bernard Tschumi and Peter Eisenman – friendship being defined as a shared responsibility for the affirmation of the event that is presupposed by deconstructive questioning ('If the question corresponds, if it corresponds always to some demand coming from the other, then it lets itself already be preceded by a strange affirmation.')[11]

In this manner Derrida would have again 'come upon' architecture for the first time. He would have been guided by his sense of responsibility (or co-responsibility') for those events one does not yet know how to name. And he would discharge this responsibility by introducing into architecture the concept of event ingredient in the idea of invention that is to be reinvented. Thus he asks whether 'an architecture of the event' would be possible, as though he were asking what an 'invention of the other' possessing the 'singular structure of an event' would mean for architecture, and for the architectural allegory of thought, and therefore of invention in thought. More particularly one may distinguish three points in the 'invention' Derrida brings to architecture; they might be said to constitute three points in his response to the question what is new in architecture.
1. There exist 'events' in our history: those singular occurrences that open up 'new' or 'altogether other' possibilities in the history in which we find ourselves. As Derrida uses the term, an 'event' does not refer to a narrative occurrence (as in what the Annales historians castigated as histoire événementielle). It refers not so much to what takes place in a narrative or a histoire as to those unanticipated turning-points which interrupt it, and the world its protagonists inhabit. An event is the unforseeen chance or possibility in a history of another history. Derrida would recognise such events in the history of sciences and forms of reasoning, or in the question common to a number of different historians of science: 'How does one divide up, and how does one name, those conceptual ensembles that make possible and

receivable such an invention, when the later must in turn modify the structure of this very context?'[12] But there are also political examples; Derrida calls 1968 'that event one still does not know how to name other than by its date.'[13]

To speak of an 'architecture of the event' is thus to ascribe to architecture (or to introduce into the conception of an architecture) a peculiar sort of historicity, or relation to history. In terms of the architectural allegory, it may be contrasted with the 'monumental',[14] if by 'monument' one understands something built once and for all, with a single origin or end, with a 'proper body', of which the Greek metaphysics of formed-matter would be a first philosophical articulation. An architecture of the event would be an architecture of this other relation to history: it would 'eventalise' or open up, what in our history, or our tradition, presents itself as 'monumental', as what is assumed to be essential and unchangeable, or incapable or a 'rewriting', as what is 'fixed in concrete'. It would, as it were, interrupt or dislocate, what the *demiurgos* or architect of History would be thought to have constructed once and for all in conformity with a given plan, programme or model. It would, says Derrida, *s'explique avec l'événement,* a way of spacing that gives its place to the event.

2. Our response to such 'events' in our histories requires a questioning of the 'value of habitation'. The value of habitation is the value of *Heimatlichkeit,* of being brought together in a proper appropriate place or of being able to find ourselves at home in such a place. It is a value strongly represented by Hegel, who said 'philosophy is just this: being at home with oneself'.[15] Derrida refers thus to the 'uninhabitable', what is *unheimlich,* at once strange and familiar in our being together in what we take to be our proper time and place. The uninhabitable is then what exposes or opens up our received ways of inhabiting to events.

Derrida has roughly this general story: for a long and powerful tradition of thought which we still 'inhabit', to construct a habitation, a way of living, has meant to construct a space in conformity with a plan, an ideal, a model, essence or nature, that would be independent of it, of which the well-ordered household, or *oikos,* would stand as a great paternalistic allegory. The task of inhabiting the uninhabitable is to conceive of another relation of our being-together in a space and a time than this one. Derrida's 29th aphorism says:

> To say that architecture must be withdrawn from the ends one assigns to it, and, in the first place, from the value of habitation, is not to prescribe uninhabitable constructions, but to interest oneself in the genealogy of an ageless contract between architecture and habitation. Is it possible to f*aire oeuvre* (to make something, to make a work) without arranging a mode of inhabiting?[16]

To make a work that does not arrange a mode of inhabiting is to provide or maintain in a work a space for the chance of another history. The problem of 'inhabiting the uninhabitable' is the problem of how to construct ourselves and live in a world, when we accept that at bottom there is no essence, no plan, no programme of our being-together in the spaces we inhabit; that, in those spaces there always exists the possibility of an event that would dislocate what we assume to be natural, essential or 'monumental' about it.

3. In response to the 'surprise' in our received ways of inhabiting things, we must let ourselves be put up for 'invention'. We cannot say we must invent o*urselves,* for it is just ourselves who are 'surprised' by the event; and Derrida refers to a '"we" that finds *itself* nowhere, that doesn't invent *itself.*'[17]

> ...[the event] does not happen to a constituted w*e,* to a human subjectivity whose essence would be arrested and which would *then* see itself affected by the history of this thing named architecture. We only appear to ourselves

from the point of an experience of spacing already marked by architecture. What happens through architecture constructs and instructs this *we.* The *we finds itself* engaged by architecture before being the subject of it: master and possessor.[18]

One might say that in constructing and instructing us, architecture involves itself in a central question which Derrida puts in his pivotal essay on invention by saying '*we are to be invented*'. This may be, in Derrida's idiom, the question of our *freedom.*[19]

Points of Folly, Lines of Actuality

'An architecture of the event', says Derrida, would be an architecture of a peculiar kind of 'impossibility'. In English as in French, we speak of an event as something which 'takes place'. And, at one point Derrida offers this definition: an event is that 'which gives itself place without ever coming back to it *(se donne lieu sans en revenir)'*. The phrase makes an idiomatic allusion to *ne n'en reviens pas,* 'I can't get over it'; an event is the arrival of something we can't get over, which does not leave us the same.

But the phrase also invokes an element of 'impossibility'. 'Such' Derrida declares, 'would be the task, the wager, the care for the impossible: to give dissociation its rights but to set it to work *as such* in a space of re-assembly';[20] and in his essay on invention, Derrida discusses this sort of impossibility. 'How can invention *come back* to the same *(revenir* au même)?' he asks rhetorically in advancing his idea of the 'invention of the other'. 'It suffices for this,' he responds,

> that the invention be possible and that it invent the possible. Then from its origin . . . it envelopes within it a repetition, it deploys only the d*ynamics* of what already *found itself there,* the set of possible comprehendables which is manifested as ontological or theological truth, programme of a cultural or techno-scientific (civil or military) policy, etc. In inventing the possible from the possible one returns the new (that is: the altogether-other which can also be extremely old) to a set of present possibilities, to the present of the possible, which insures the conditions of its status.[21]

An invention of the other, of 'the new' which is the other, is thus never possible. It is n*ot* possible in just the sense that Derrida speaks of what is *not* habitable, and the question of this 'not' is the topic of his paper *Comment ne pas parler.*[22] That paper is about a tradition of such paradoxical or paralogical pronouncements as 'to think the unthought', 'to say the unsayable', 'to see the unseeable', or 'to represent the unrepresentable'. And one may add that 'to inhabit the uninhabitable' belongs to it, starting with the discussion of the *chora* in Plato's *Timeus.* It is a tradition tied up with the 'mysticism' of the negative theology Derrida discusses, but would also include the early Wittgenstein as well as the later Heidegger; Derrida finds it as well in Freud's discussion of 'negation'. In the tradition of this 'not' Derrida discerns a notion of necessity connected to the chance of possibility of an event. We cannot avoid betraying that of which we cannot speak (represent, inhabit, etc.); we cannot *but* avoid it; such is the necessity of what is not possible for us.

In the philosophy of Gilles Deleuze we find a distinction that is useful in grasping this idea of the impossible. Deleuze offers a somewhat different account of the sequence in the 17th century involving Leibniz. He has Leibniz hesitating between two distinct concepts, the concepts of 'the possible' and the concept of 'the virtual'. (The best of all possible worlds might thus be said to be the one with the greatest *virtuality*). In his somewhat untraditional use of the terms, 'possibility' for Deleuze is the concept of something which might exist but does not; it contrasts with 'reality', as when one speaks of 'realising' possibilities. It follows that 'from the point of view of the concept, there is no difference between the possible and the real';[23] and the reason for this is that the idea of possibility is always taken from that of reality. It is this notion of possibility that is supposed by schemes of theological evolution. It is also supposed by the probabilistic view of evidence, or by induction.[24]

By contrast, for Deleuze, that 'virtual' is a reality of which we do not yet possess the concept; and it is not 'realised' but 'actualised'. Actualisation is a process of differentiation, but this differentiation cannot, by definition, be given or anticipated by our concepts; it cannot be said to be more or less probable; its description cannot yet be assigned a truth-value. A 'virtual multiplicity' is a disparate set of things of which we cannot yet have the concept; and its 'actualisation' therefore involves the invention of something which, by the lights of our concepts, is impossible. 'These lines of differentiation are therefore truly creative; they actualise by inventing.'[25] An event for Deleuze is not a history of a drama with beginning and end; it is the creative or inventive actualisation of a virtual multiplicity.

The 'virtual' thus involves something which is not yet see-able, thinkable or sayable in what we see think or say. But this negation, says Deleuze, is not a logical one; the virtual is not the obstacle or reversal of the possible: 'one has only to replace the actual terms in the movement that produces them to bring them back to the virtuality actualised in them in order to see that differentiation is never a negation, but a creation, and that difference is never negative but essentially positive and creative'[26] The impossibility of what is virtual in our time and place is thus not a logical one like the proverbial round square, but an historical one – the impossibility of what is not yet or not longer possible for us to think, what is not yet or not longer possible for us 'to inhabit'.

It is thus 'historical' in much the sense of Foucault's principle of singularity, that there are events in thought, and of that kind of genealogical critique that 'will seek to treat the instances of discourse that articulate what we think, say, and do as so many historical events ... that will not deduce from the form of what we know what is impossible for us to do and to know, but ... will separate out, from the contingency that has made us what we are, the possibility of no longer being, doing, or thinking what we are, do or think ... the undefined work of freedom.'[27]

That is why, commenting on Foucault's phrase 'a history of the present', Deleuze calls him a philosopher of the 'actual'. *Actuel* can mean 'of the present moment, existing, current'; *les actualités* are the news or current events. But the actuality of the 'present' of which Foucault would write the history is something else, something 'untimely'.

For Foucault, writes Deleuze, 'the actual is not what we are but rather what we become, what we are in the course of becoming, that is, the Other, our becoming-other. In every *dispositif*, it is necessary to distinguish what we are (what we are already no longer) from what we are in the course of becoming: the part of history, and the part of actuality.'[28]

In analysing the historical 'singularity' of what we have been constructed to be (as subjects of discipline or of a normalised sexuality) Foucault would be 'diagnosing' this present in which we are becoming something else. He would be tracing the lines of actualisation of what we are not yet.

> The analysis of the archive ... is valid for our diagnosis. Not because it would enable us to draw up a table of our distinctive features, and to sketch out in advance the face that we will have in the future. But it deprives us of our continuities; it dissipates that temporal identity in which we are pleased to look at ourselves when we wish to exercise the discontinuities of history.[29]

Foucault would be asking how to 'inhabit' those moments of 'actuality' in which we are becoming something else than what

our history has constructed us to be, those heterotopic moments of our current historical 'impossibility', the moments of invention.

In sum: we always become something other than who we are in the spaces we construct for ourselves to inhabit. It is the event of this *devenir-autre* that lets us see what is 'uninhabitable' in those constructions, and so exposes them to our invention. And yet it does so without projecting a new order, or providing a new programme of living. The necessity that compels us to interrupt our historical ways of habitation and to invent others is not a programmatic one. It is the point of disengagement from what we take for granted is required for us to be together in a proper time and place: *le point de folie*. It is from such points of folly that we may analyse the genealogy of the places assigned to our own self-constructions in those ways of inhabiting things we take as self-evident; and it is from them that we may start again the inventive task of constructing ourselves without arranging a mode of living, the task of our freedom. To diagnose what is happening to us is to trace, from the points of folly in our time and place, the lines of our actuality, of this Other we are becoming.

What is New in Architecture?

What is new in architecture; what is new in our building and our dwelling? That is a question that may be said to have obsessed our period of technological invention and possibility. It was a question central to the very concept of the avant-garde; for an avant-garde is by definition a group that carries forth a particular kind of novelty in our history.

And yet the avant-garde did not always conceive of what is new in the same manner.[30] Simplifying what is no doubt a much more complex history, one might say that the avant-garde did not conceive of novelty in terms of the 'surprise' of 'the event', and the space and time it involves. For the avant-garde wanted itself to be 'the subject' of its novelty – master and possessor, and take upon itself to educate all others to the new order of habitation, of which it was the subject. What was new could thus be shown to all in pure visible form; it was not the novelty of this impure, disparate 'multiplicity' of what cannot yet be seen, of this we who finds itself nowhere. For the avant-garde wished to resolve the tension between art and technological necessity by display-ing 'function' in visible 'form', rather than trying to expose in given forms the tension with function that is the chance of an invention-to-come. The novelty that the avant-garde carried forth was, in short, a novelty not of historical invention, but of historical progression. It was, Derrida might say, a 'novelty of the same' – the 'new' of a 'new order'.[31] It invented 'the possible from the possible', and was not (or could not know itself to be) an architecture of the 'impossible'.

The philosophical theme of 'other time, other space' offers another way of thinking about what is new in architecture. An 'architecture of the event' is an architecture not of the possible but of the actual, and so involves another idea of the new – the new is not the possible but the actual. The new is the 'altogether-other' of our invention, the surprise of what is not yet possible in the histories of the spaces in which we find ourselves. It is not the invention of a possible form to be realised, but of this disparate virtuality of which we do not yet have the concept or which we cannot yet name. Of such novelty we are not the masters and possessors; we do not inhabit the 'utopia' of what will be realised in history, but the 'heterotopia' of those 'lines of differentiation' that 'actualize by inventing'. That is why we can never find *ourselves* anywhere: our place is yet to come, our time is yet to take place. And the question of what is new in architecture thus becomes the question of how to inhabit this other time, this other place.

1 'The Eye of Power' in *Power/Knowledge* ed Gordon pp 149-50.
2 'Space, Knowledge, Power' in *Foucault Reader* ed Rabinow p 246.
3 'Preface to the *History of Sexuality*, Vol II' in *Foucault Reader*, p 335. For a brief discussion of 'event' and 'singularity' in Foucault, see Pierre Macherey 'Foucault'' éthique et subjectivité' in *Autrement*, No 102 Nov 1988 pp 92-103
4 'Styles of Scientific Reasoning' in *Post-Analytic Philosophy* eds. Rajchman and West p 155: '...styles of reasoning create the possibility for truth and falsehood. Deduction and induction merely preserve it.'
5 *The Archeology of Knowledge* p 28.
6 'Of Other Spaces' *Diacratics* 16 1 Spring 1986.
7 'Débat avec Michel Foucault' in *L'impossible prison* Seuil 1980 pp 43-46.
8 *Psyché: Invention de l'autre* p 15.
9 *Ibid* p 9.
10 *Ibid* p 35.
11 *Ibid* p 10.
12 *Ibid* p 37.
13 'The Time of a Thesis; Punctuations' in *Philosophy in France Today* ed Montefiori Cambridge 1983 p 44. It is interesting to note that the first of his own writings that Derrida dates is 'Les fins de l'homme' of 'Le 12 mai 1968', and that it ends with the question 'Mais qui, nous?'
14 See Foucault's remarks about the departure of the new history from the attempt to 'memorise the *monuments* of the past, transform them into *documents*' (The Archeology of Knowledge pp 7ff).
15 *Heimatlichkeit* in Hegel is the topic of Dominique Janicaud's book, *Hegel et le destin de la Grèce* Vrin 1975 1975. Janicaud starts with this statement by Hegel: 'Greece – in this name the heart of the civilised man of Europe, and of we Germans in particular, feels at home *(heimatlich)*.' The Greeks were the first to build for themselves a world that was their own; and this Greek *Heimatlichkeit* is the same one that leads we civilised Europeans, and especially we Germans to our Western *Heimat*. For Spirit is *not yet* at home in the Greek home; that requires the building and *Bildung* of History. Hegel's discussion of architecture is connected to this general scheme of Spirit returning to its *Heimat*. The reference to 'we Germans in particular' would help to explain why Hegel's conception of classical architecture remains entirely Greek, with no mention of the Italian Renaissance. Derrida's early discussion of the Egyptian pyramid that would house the basically *unheimlich* body of the mummy is connected to this larger questioning of the scheme of History returning to its Home.
16 *Psyché* p 514.
17 *Ibid* p 60.
18 *Ibid* p 478.
19 On the concept of freedom see Jean-Luc Nancy, *L'expérience de la liberté* Galilée 1988. My *Michel Foucault: The Freedom of Philosophy* (Columbia 1985) also takes the concept of freedom as a central one.
20 *Psyché* p 489.
21 *Ibid* p 55.
22 *Ibid* pp 535-96.
23 *Bergsonism* Zone 1988 p 97.
24 Nelson Goodman's famous second paradox of induction is designed to show that there can be no induction without 'entrenchment' of the predicates that describe the world in which one explains or predicts. It follows that events can be said to be more or less probable only for a 'version of the world', which cannot itself be said, or be said in the same manner, to be more or less probable. The Deleuzian idea of event is thus something like the event of a new version of the world in our thinking; and his idea of 'multiplicity' is like the notion of the disunity of such versions. In another context *(Representing and Intervening*, Cambridge 1983 p 219) Ian Hacking remarks: 'Leibniz said that God chose a world which maximised the variety of phenomena while choosing the simples laws. Exactly so: but the best way to maximise phenomena and have simplest laws is to have the laws inconsistent with each other, each applying to this or that but none applying to all.'
25 *Bergsonism* p 101.
26 *Ibid* p 103.
27 'What is Englightenment' in *Foucault Reader* p 14.
28 'Foucault, historien du présent' in *Michel Foucault, philosophe* Seuil 1989. (I discuss this Deleuzian formulation in 'Crisis' forthcoming in *Representations*.)
29 *The Archeology of Knowledge* pp 130-31.
30 In *Le nominalism pictural* Minuit 1984 Thierry de Duve distinguishes two models of significant pictorial novelty in the history of the avant-garde: the rejection or Parisian model and the succession of Munich model. The book is about Duchamp's *invention* of the ready-made as a particular kind of *event* in this history (Paris and Munich being the two cities of Duchamp's invention). De Duve says that where Gropius tried to combine technology with art in the figure of the functionalist *Gestalter*, Duchamp linked technology to an 'abandonment' of art – the ready-made was an industrial product endowed with the value of art through its selection and not its function. Thus Duchamp was not a utopian: the 'time' of the invention of the ready-made was not that of a new plastic order, but of an 'abandonment' of such an order. I discuss this point in my Preface to the English translation of the book, forthcoming from Minnesota University Press.
31 In *Psyché* p 475, Derrida remarks in passing that the now frequent use of 'post' in 'postmodernism' or 'poststructuralism' still remains hostage to a 'historicist compulsion', a 'progressivist ideology'. Thus the postmodern would break with the modern only in terms of the progressivist conception of a break characteristic of the modern; as such it would not have the time or the novelty of an event.

*

ФОРМА САМОЛЕТА И МЕТОДЫ ЕГО ПРОЕКТИРОВАНИЯ

DIE FORM DER LUFTFAHRZEUGS UND DIE METHODE SEINER BERECHNUNG, VON ING. K. AKASCHEFF

Всем известна форма самолета, его смелые и оригинальные линии, его законченные контуры. Вся его конфигурация на фоне неба неустанно приковывает внимание каждого, будь то простой обыватель или художник; в каждом из них форма самолета вызывает эстетическое ощущение.

Спрашивается, чем и как достигается эта оригинальность и смелость линий, каким путем идет и какими методами пользуется конструктор, чтобы получить эту эстетическую форму самолета?

Исходным пунктом при расчете самолета является требуемая грузоподъемность, т.-е. конструктор должен знать цель своей постройки: надлежит ли ему построить тяжелый бомбовоз, пассажирский самолет или легкий одноместный истребитель?

Имея это основное задание — грузоподъемность,—определяющее тип самолета, перед конструктором встает вторая задача для некоторых типов самолета, не менее первостепенная, чем первая,— вопрос о скорости самолета, хотя в конечном итоге она является функцией первого условия.

Для разрешения своей задачи конструктор определяет размеры самолета и мощность двигателя, т.-е. размах и ширину крыльев и величину хвостового оперения с общим центром давления или поддерживающей силы и центром тяжести самолета.

Решение этих вопросов построено на основной формуле аэродинамики

$$R \quad KSV^{2}$$ •

Из этой формулы следует, что при данной поверхности

$$S$$

движущегося тела сопротивление воздуха

$$R$$

увеличивается пропорционально квадрату скорости движения. Разложив сопротивление

$$R$$

по координатам x и y, имеем

$$R = R_x + R_y.$$

$$R_y$$

называется полезное сопротивление, т.-е. это есть та сила, которая поддерживает самолет в воздухе, а

$$R_x$$

—лобовое или вредное сопротивление, которое необходимо преодолеть при движении самолета по горизонтальной линии. Возьмем элементарный пример. Если взять

$$S$$

равную 1 $м^2$, то при скорости

$$V$$

равной 150 км в час, сопротивление

$$R_x$$

будет равняться 44 кг, при

V 200 км в час,

R_x 79 кг, а при

V 250 км в час,

R_x = 123 кг.

Законы вещей — законы мышления

Для преодоления этого сопротивления, на поверхность 1 $м^2$, при скоростях в 150, 200 и 250 км в час, соответственно для каждого случая потребуется мотор мощностью в 25, 60 и 15 лс. Цифры взяты на основании современных аэродинамических опытов, проверенных практикой самолетостроения при К 0,025 и з 90 .

Отсюда следует, что конструктору самолета весь свой опыт и знание приходится сосредоточить на устранении вредных сопротивлений R_x. Здесь не приходится думать о красоте формы самолета. Вся мысль конструктора сосредоточена на уменьшении вредного сопротивления R_x, так как уменьшение R_x означает уменьшение мощности мотора или, если мощность мотора останется той же, уменьшая R_x, мы увеличиваем R_y, т.-е. полезное сопротивление или грузоподъемность самолета.

Этот закон аэродинамики слишком суров и строг, чтобы позволять конструктору увлекаться изящными формами самолета, т.-е. ставить перед собой эстетическую задачу— создать элегантный, красивый самолет.

АРХИТЕКТОР!

ТАК НУЖНО ПОНИМАТЬ МАТЕРИАЛИСТИЧЕСКИЕ ОСНОВЫ ЭСТЕТИКИ КОНСТРУКТИВИЗМА

● $R = KSV^2$ — основная формула аэродинамики, где К есть коэффициент, зависящий от характеристики окружающей среды (воздуха) и формы движущегося тела; S - поверхность движущегося тела в $м^2$ V — скорость движения в м в секунду и R - общее сопротивление воздуха в кг.

65

FIRST PAGE OF ENGINEER AKASHEV'S ARTICLE 'THE FORM OF THE AEROPLANE AND THE METHODS OF DESIGNING IT' SA 1926

MOISEI GINZBURG
CATHERINE COOKE

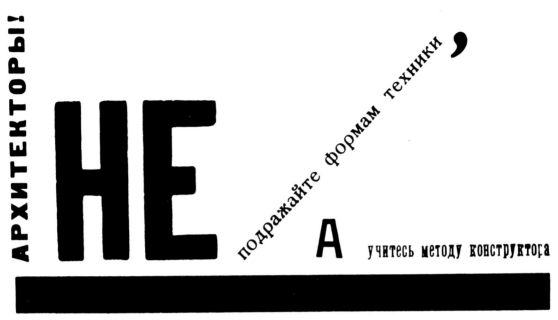

'ARCHITECTS! DO NOT IMITATE THE FORMS OF TECHNOLOGY, BUT LEARN THE METHOD OF THE ENGINEERING DESIGNER' SA 1926

'All these objects of modern life create, in the long run, a modern state of mind'.
Le Corbusier, 'Architecture or revolution', L'Esprit Nouveau, 1921[1]

In the pleiad of aesthetic theorists thrown up by the Russian avant-garde, the most interesting of those addressing architecture, in my view, was the man who became the leading theorist and practitioner of Constructivist architecture, Moisei Ginzburg.

Till his death in 1946, he was to remain a central and highly respected member of the Soviet profession, both in teaching and in practice. Much of his standing, and the richness of his thinking, derived from the unique extent to which European as well as Soviet ideas were synthesised into his theory. In a sense forced into 'cosmopolitanism' by the limited access to professional education afforded to Jews in pre-Revolutionary Russia, he studied abroad – as for example did Lissitzky. At one of Europe's most interesting moments, immediately prior to the outbreak of World War I, he thus travelled through France to Italy, to graduate in 1914 from the highly traditional school of the Accademia di Belli Arti in Milan. Graduation in 1914 meant, however, that he was there for the revelations of Sant'Elia's exhibition of the Citta Nuova in May that year, to read the remarkable Messaggio that accompanied it, where for all the iconoclasm, so much of what would later emerge as the positive aspects of architectural modernism were already expounded, and amongst it, much of Le Corbusier's programme.[2] The fundamental question underlying both programmes, as of all modern architecture, was to be the one to which Ginzburg made a uniquely

clear-headed contribution in his own writings of the twenties. It was the profound if simple question: 'What, if anything, has the architect to learn from the engineer?'

Related to this is another question: 'What can the architect learn about architecture from the machine?' In Corbusier, as in most modernist writing, the two questions are fatally confused. Ginzburg, with his focus on the designer's working method, made an important contribution to theory of modernism by reminding us they are different.

Through the inspiration of Futurism or simply to fill deficiencies in the Milan Academy's education, Ginzburg enrolled on return to Moscow for the three-year engineering degree at Riga Polytechnic, evacuated there away from Baltic hostilities. Through Revolution and Civil War he was a young architect in the Crimea, building some houses and studying local architecture.[3] Returning to Moscow in 1921, he had had time for thought, and it showed in his first two books, whose scholarly solidity was conspicuous amidst the mere journalism and manifesto writing of that unstable time.

Rhythm in Architecture, completed in January 1922, with its pictures of the Pazzi Chapel, Gothic cathedrals and Chaldean ziggurats, has the air of a belated student dissertation on proportional and rhythmic systems in world architecture. But the Nietzschean quotation which heads his text indicates the deeper waters Ginzburg is trying to probe. 'Rhythm is compulsion' wrote Nietzsche in *The Joyous Science*, 'exerting an irresistable compulsion to conform with it . . . as the spirit follows the beat and with it . . . the spirit of the gods.' In the second paragraph of his text Ginzburg brings this a little closer to materialist modernity: 'All scientific hypotheses, laws and philosophical views of the world are nothing other than attempts to find the formula and definition which can express the rhythmic pulsation of the cosmos.' On the next page he continues: 'The essence of any kind of rhythmic phenomenon consists above all in movement (the word "rhythm" in Greek means "flow".)' After all the history he concludes the book with the assertion that 'The task of contemporary architecture is to find those elements of form, and laws for combining them, in which the rhythmic pulsation of our days manifests itself.'[4]

This is the line of thought which leads directly into investigations of formal language. The theme was taken up in Ginzburg's next book, *Style and Epoch*, of 1924, in discussion of the machine as 'supreme organisedness', and of the new aesthetics of asymmetry, dynamism and ultimate economy of material and movement that it established. These concerns were more fully developed by others like the Leningrader, Iakov Chernikhov, than by Ginzburg and the Constructivists. With less reference to the mechanical model, the perceptual nature of a 'new aesthetic' capable of exerting 'psychological influence' was also analysed and taught by their rivals in Moscow, the Rationalists, lead by Nikolai Ladovsky and Vladimir Krinsky, and by Ilia Golosov. But both Chernikhov and these aesthetic Rationalists in the end belong in the same category as Corbusier, in addressing only the product of design as a generator of 'sensations', not the inner organisation of human movement within the spaces, or the 'flow' of ideas which constitute the design process itself. In Ginzburg, on the other hand, it is always implicit the 'movements' which are to be objectively studied are of two types: movement within the object (for which the dynamic organisation of the machine offers a direct model), and the movement of the architect 'through the problem', ie the process of design.

Style and Epoch was essentially Ginzburg's manifesto of architectural Constructivism. The origins of his very important theoretical ideas about the periodicity of 'constructive' periods in architectural history, and their relationship to cultural change, lie in Wolfflin, Frankl and Spengler.[5] The strongest influence behind his thinking on contemporary architecture was Corbusier, whose writings in L'Esprit Nouveau had penetrated to Moscow after the Blockade. When Corbusier insisted that 'the purpose of architecture is to move us', the terrain is of course not physical, but emotional and spiritual. The greatest emotive power, in his judgement, lay with 'primary geometrical forms', and the reason for emulating 'the engineer's aesthetic' was that these were precisely his vocabulary.[6]

As usual, Corbusier had waved a gallic hand towards something deeper, but did not probe far. 'The engineer shows the way because he proceeds on the basis of knowledge', he wrote, 'and architecture in its own domain should also begin at the beginning'.[7] Ginzburg took the message, but had to ask 'How are we to build this bridge between engineering and architecture once we understand that it is possible only through principles of creativity and not through actual forms?'[8] Corbusier offered hints for those who agreed that architecture is 'a matter of plastic emotion', but little guidance on how the architect might proceed in the task of 'organising life' which Ginzburg defined for a socialist Soviet architecture.[9]

'New methods of architectural thinking', translated in slightly shortened form here, was the lead article in the very first issue (1926, no.1) of the Constructivist's journal *Contemporary Architecture*, SA, which Ginzburg edited with Alexander Vesnin.[10] In a very real sense, it sets the agenda for the group's next five years' work, till they were abolished in 1932. As he writes here, true radicalism of form such as the engineer achieves requires absolute clarity of 'knowledge', as to both aims and architectural means. To ensure objectivity and rigour in bringing together the various bodies of knowledge that bear upon design, there must be a 'clearly organised working method'. As would be expected from the author of *Rhythm in Architecture*, Ginzburg never denies the place of aesthetic considerations. They are not to be the primary generator of form, but they are a vital means of refining it. (His own buildings, though now in tragic disrepair, indicate the quality of his aesthetic talent.) In *Style and Epoch* we find the first talk of 'a method', and he is quite explicit:

'There can be no question of any sort of artist loosing creativity just because he knows clearly what he wants, what he is aiming for, and in what consists the meaning of his work. But subconscious, impulsive creativity must be replaced by clear and distinctly organised method, which is economical of the architect's energies and transfers the freed surplus of it into inventiveness and the force of the creative impulse.'[11]

Here in 'New methods of architectural thinking' the 'aesthetic refinement stage' has a quite clear place within the architect's linear movement through the design operation. In later papers, the means of achieving aesthetic refinement were spelt out yet more fully.[12]

The method, presented here in outline form in the latter part of the article, was thus a linear sequence of 4 main stages. In his vision it formed 'a unified organic creative process in which one task leads from another with all the logic of a natural development', where 'no part is arbitrary'. In 'a movement from the main factors to the secondary ones', it must begin, according to his argument, with generation of a three-dimensional topological diagram of the building: 'a clearly established set of individual spatial parameters, their actual dimensions and the links between them.' This 'sets the direction'. It is followed by studies of suitable constructional systems, by decisions about the massing, and by refinement of the elements and details.

Ginzburg's underlying thesis was strengthened still further in SA's third issue. This gave the most prominent place to an article on 'The form of the aeroplane and methods of designing it', not signed by Ginzburg, but manifestly written by an obliging aeronautical engineer to a brief from him.[13] A typographic feature on the editorial page of this issue proclaimed 'Architect! Do not imitate the forms of technology, but learn the method of the engineering designer.'

Again Corbusier had given the clue: 'The lesson of the aeroplane is not primarily in the forms it has created . . . the lesson of [it] lies in the logic which governed the enunciation of the problem and which led to its successful realisation.'[14] But the nature of that logic had remained obscure. Here in SA, they were explicit about how they understood it. Engineer Akashev ran through the main stages of the basic aerodynamic and loading calculations. He said all the right things: the designer of aeroplanes knows what he wants, and he knows his science and technology. 'The last thing the he is thinking about initially is beauty' but he ends up, after following the 'strict and rigid' logic and the mathematics, with an object which 'evokes an aesthetic sensation in every viewer'.

Thus it is not 'romanticism or heroism of the inventor' which has at last enabled man to fly; it is what Corbusier called 'cold calculation'. But the calculation was not simply presented in SA as information: it was laid out typographically as a model of the essentially linear logic which Ginzburg described in his paper two issues previously as 'the inventor's creative method'. A typographical feature within the article itself stressed again the centrality of this material to the development of their creed:

'Architects! This is how you must understand the materialistic foundations of the aesthetic of Constructivism.'

Ginzburg agreed with Corbusier that the products of engineering exemplify the 'objet-type', his later work pursued this theme extensively, in particular in the field of housing. In this paper we see a seminal stage of the work in which he also developed in detail the different assertion, that the engineer offers the architect a 'processus-type' for the practical business of designing.

Notes

1 See also the collected edition of these articles, Le Corbusier, *Towards a New Architecture*, London, 1946, p. 256

2 The Messaggio is reproduced in full in Reyner Banham, *Theory and Design in the First Machine Age*, London, 1960, pp. 128-130

3 On Ginzburg's early life and career see S O Khan-Magomedov, *M Ia Ginzburg*, Moscow, 1972, pp. 7-10

4 *Ritm v arkhitekture* (*Rhythm in Architecture*), Moscow, 1923, pp. 9, 10, 116

5 For a discussion of these sources see Anatole Senkevitch's introduction to his translation of this book, *Style and Epoch*, MIT Press, 1982, pp. 22-25

6 'The engineer's aesthetic and architecture', *Towards a New Architecture*, p. 23

7 Ibid, p. 20

8 Stil i epokha, Moscow, 1924, p.28

9 Ibid, p. 140

10 M Ia Ginzburg, 'Novye metody arkhitekturnogo myshleniia' ('New Methods of Architectural Thinking'), *Sovremennaia arkhitektura* (*Contemporary Architecture*), Moscow, 1926, no. 1, pp. 1-4

11 Stil i epokha, p. 142

12 See C Cooke, 'The development of the Constructivist architects' design method', in: Papadakis, Cooke & Benjamin, eds, *Deconstruction: Omnibus Volume*, London, 1989, pp. 21-37

13 Engr. K Akashev, 'Forma samoleta i metody ego proektirovaniia' ('The form of the aeroplane and the methods of designing it'), *Sovremennaia arkhitektura*, 1926, no.3, pp. 65-66

14 'Airplanes', *Towards a New Architecture*, p. 102

L TO R:MOISEI GINZBURG; 'MACHINE' SA 1926

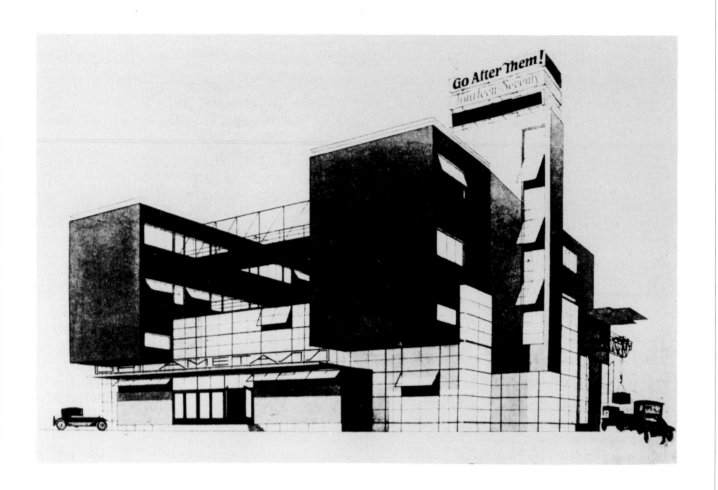

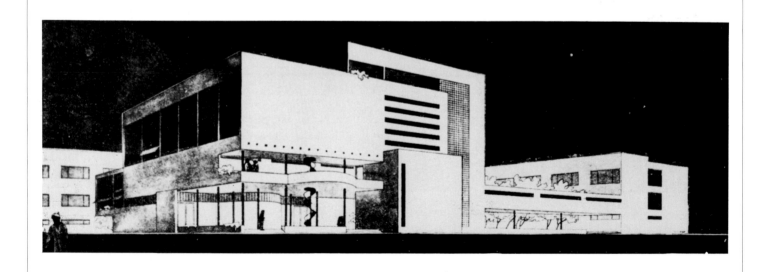

MOISEI GINZBURG *ABOVE*: COMPETITION FOR THE ORGAMETAL HEADQUARTERS, MOSCOW.1926; *BELOW*: COMPETITION FOR THE HOUSE OF GOVERNMENT, ALMA- ATA, 1927

MOISEI GINZBURG

NEW METHODS OF ARCHITECTURAL THOUGHT
Sovremennaia arkhitektura, 1926

NIKOLEV, COMMUNAL HOUSING FOR STUDENTS OF THE TEXTILE INSTITUTE, MOSCOW, 1929-30

One decade separates us from the architectural 'prosperity' of the pre-Revolutionary era, when in Petersburg, Moscow and other great centres the best Russian architects lightheartedly cultivated every possible 'style'.

Is a decade so much?

It is a small fissure in time. But the Revolution, in sweeping away the stagnant prejudices and outlived canons, has turned the fissure into an abyss. On the far side of that abyss remain the last witherings of the already decrepit system of European thinking, of that unprincipled eclecticism which always has a thousand aesthetic recipes at the ready, all of them approved by our grandfathers and great-grandfathers. Such thinking ready to ladle out truth from wherever suited – provided only it was from a source in the past.

On this side of the abyss is opening up a new path which still has to be paved, and great new expanses of space which still have to be developed and populated. The outlook and worldview of the contemporary architect is being forged in the circumstances of today, and new methods of architectural thinking are being created.

Instead of the old system in architectural designing, where the plan, construction and external treatment of the building were in a state of constant antagonism, and where the architect had to use his powers to the full as peacemaker in irreconcileable conflicts of interest, the new architectural work is characterised above all by its single indivisible aim and aspiration. It is a process in which the task is hammered out logically and which represents a consciously creative [sozidatel'nyi] process from beginning to end.

In place of the rarified [lit: abstracted] and extremely individualistic inspiration of the old-style architect, the contemporary architect is firmly convinced that the architectural task, like any other, can only be solved through a precise elucidation of the unknowns and pursuit of the correct method of solution.

The architect sees around him the fearless creativity of inventors in various fields of contemporary technology, as with gigantic steps it conquers the earth, the ocean depths and the air, winning new bridgeheads by the hour. It is not difficult to see that these astonishing successes of the human genius are explained, in general, by the fact that the right method was pursued in tackling the task. The inventor knows full well that however energetic the upsurge of his creative enthusiasm may be, it will be useless without a sober consideration of all minutiae in the circumstances surrounding his activity. He is fully armed with contemporary knowledge, he takes account of all the conditions of today, he looks forward, he conquers the future.

Certainly it would be naive to replace the complex art of architecture by an imitation of even the most sparkling forms of contemporary technology. This period of naive 'machine symbolism' is already outdated. In this field it is only the inventor's creative method that the contemporary architect must master. Any mould or model from the past must be categorically repudiated, however beautiful it may be, for the pursuits of the

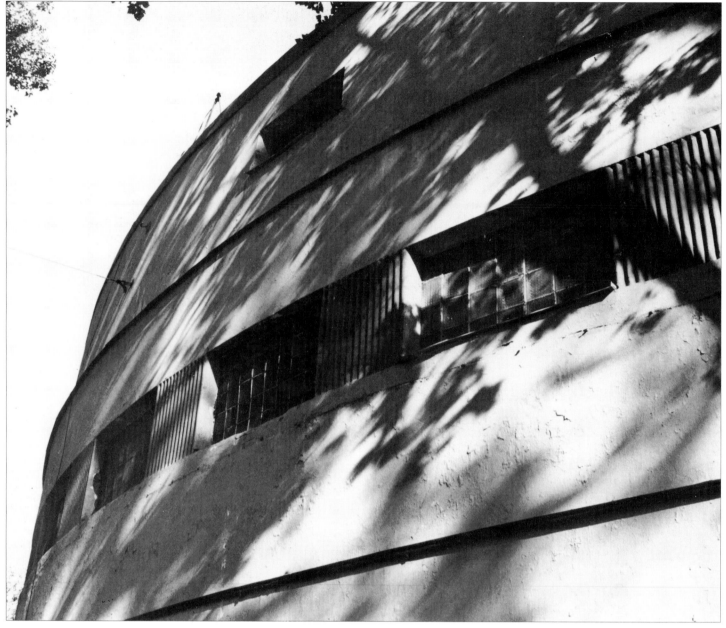

NIKOLSKY, LESNY DISTRICT PUBLIC BATHS BUILDING, LENINGRAD, 1926

architect are in their essence precisely such invention, just like all other invention. His is a work of invention which has set itself the aim of organising and constructing a concrete practical task not just in response to the dictates of today, but as something that will serve the needs of tomorrow.

Thus first and foremost we face the question of clearly exposing all the unknowns of the problem. First among these are the unknowns of a general character, dictated by our epoch as a whole. Here we are identifying those particular features of the problem which derive from the emergence of a new social consumer of architecture – the class of workers, who are organising not only their own contemporary way of life but also the complex forms of new economic life of the State. It is not a question, of course, of adapting to the individual tastes of this new consumer. Unfortunately, in posing the problem it is often reduced to precisely this, as people hastily try to attribute to the worker tastes and preferences which are essentially echoes of old pre-Revolutionary attitudes.

Least of all is it a matter of tastes here at all. What we are concerned with is elucidating the characteristics of the new consumer, as a powerful collective which is building a socialist state.

It is a question, above all, of the principle of plannedness. This must not just be a feature of the way leading state organs operate, but must become part of the work of every architect. It is a question of how the solving of individual problems becomes part of the larger productive network of the country as a whole.

The character of a contemporary architect's work is radically altered by the fact that he recognises his activity to be the establishing of architectural standards for the organisation of new dwellings and towns, rather than the fulfilment of individual commissions. He sees it as his task to be continually advancing and improving those standards, in connection with the larger characteristics of production and with the advancing technological levels both here, and internationally. In the conditions through which we are living as we develop socialism, each new solution by the architect, be it a dwelling block, a workers club, or a factory, is conceived by us as the invention of a more advanced model or type, which answers the demands of its brief and is suitable for multiple production in whatever quantities the needs of the state require. From the very start, this situation diverts the architect's energy away from the pursuit of a solution

NIKOLAEV, COMMUNAL HOUSING FOR STUDENTS OF THE TEXTILE INSTITUTE, MOSCOW, 1929

answering individual tastes, and redirects it towards further improvement of the standard type which he has devised, and a more complete and sophisticated standardisation of all its details. But in order that these type-solutions may undergo a genuinely radical renewal, in order for them to become genuinely new architectural products, they have to be thought out, of course, not for some specific individual site, not in accordance with arbitrary whim, and not within the tight framework of the tedious and arbitrarily planned town. On the contrary, they must derive from the general whole, from the new principles of rational urbanism which will satisfy tomorrow's needs as well as today's. Thus it is obvious that through a complex productive process the conditions of our state are powerfully forcing us away from viewing our task as one of individual architectural units, and focussing us on problems of the whole complex: of the village, the town, the city.

Unfortunately those specialists currently occupying top ranks of the state organs which are conducting building operations are least of all concerning themselves with this important question. Of all people they are the least disposed to look searchingly forward. They are fully satisfied, for example, by the fact that they have limited new building development in Moscow, as the USSR's largest urban centre, to a maximum height of four or five storeys.

They have nothing better in their thinking for the smaller towns and workers' settlements than the Garden City, with its little individual villas, backyards and flowerbeds. But isn't this Howardian ideal already no less than a decade behind the times, and even further behind our contemporary Soviet reality?

All the more acute is the necessity for the contemporary architect to battle with anachronisms of this kind. He must fight from two directions. On the one hand he must work out new and rational principles for planning all kinds of settlement; on the other, he must create standard architectural types which could be the precondition for creating a new and rational appearance to the town.

The social conditions of our contemporary world are such that questions of individual aesthetic developments in architecture arise only secondarily. Today's conditions focus our attention first and foremost onto the problem of rational new types in architecture, and by including the architect within the overall production chain of the country, they abolish the isolation which

45

L TO *R*: NIKOLEV, COMMUNAL HOUSING FOR STUDENTS OF THE TEXTILE INSTITUTE, MOSCOW, 1929-30, STAIRTOWER ; BARSHCH & SINIAVSKY, MOSCOW PLANETARIUM, 1928-9

previously existed between various forms of architectural and engineering activity. Certainly the complex dcevelopment of our life is such that more than at any other time, it compels the architect to specialise in a specific field, but at the same time the firm conviction has arisen amongst all contemporary architects that their different specialisms are merely subsections of a homogenous territory [ubezhdenie v odnoznachnosti ikh tvorch-eskoi deiatel'nosti]. Some are engaged in creating a new type for the dwelling, others in designing new types of community facility, and a third group, in designing new factories and workplaces. It is precisely because buildings of an industrial and engineering kind never were strongly connected with the stag-nant aesthetic traditions of the old world that they have seemed, thanks to the principles underlying their creation, to answer the needs of the moment more closely, to be better adapted to serving the needs of the new life. Not only has the boundary between engineering structures and public architecture been wiped out of our thinking, but those very engineering structures themselves have come to be seen as front-line pioneers in the shaping of a genuinely contemporary architecture.

Sober consideration [lit: calculation] of all these circum-

stances, which have been created and intensified by our present social conditions, is not just the first condition for a correct solution of our architectural tasks. It is also the source of all those purely architectural possibilities which lie concealed within the changes which have taken place in our mode of life.

But alongside these, there are a series of other 'unknowns' facing the architect, which derive quite separately from the particularities of each factor of the given peice of work, from the particular features of the task in hand, from its functional requirements, and from the productive and locational conditions obtaining in that situation.

The solving of these 'unknowns' leads to an entirely new method of architectural thinking: to the method of functional design [lit: functional creativity].

Free from the handed-down models of the past, from preju-dices and biases, the new architect analyses all sides of his task, all its special features. He dismembers it into its component elements, groups them according to functions, and organises his solution on the basis of these factors. The result is a spatial solution which can be likened to any other kind of rationally formed [razumnyi] organism, which is divided into individual

VELIKOVSKY, BARSHCH & VEGMAN, GOSTORG HEADQUARTERS, MOSCOW, 1925, DETAIL OF MAIN ELEVATION

organs that have been developed in response to the functional roles which each one fulfills.

As a result of this we are seeing in the works of contemporary architects the emergence of entirely new types of plan. These are generally asymmetrical, since it is extremely rare for functional parts of a building to be absolutely identical. They are predominantly open and free in their configurations, because this not only better bathes each part of the building in fresh air and sunlight, but makes its functional elements more clearly readable and makes it easier to perceive the dynamic life that is unfolding within the building's spaces.

That same method of functional creativity leads not only to clear calculation of the 'unknowns' of the task, but to an equally clear calculation of the elements of its solution.

The architect has then to establish his route from the first priorities to the second, from skeleton to envelope. It is only this functional architectural thinking which strictly establishes the spatial organisation as the starting point of the design and the place to which the main thrust must be directed. It demonstrates that the first function of the concrete requirements of the brief must be as a clearly established set of individual spatial parame-

ters, their actual dimensions and the links between them. For the contemporary architect this is the principal starting point. It forces him to develop his conception from the inside outwards, and not the other way round, as was done in the period of eclecticism. It sets up the direction he will follow from then on.

The second factor to be considered is the constructing of these spaces which have been developed from inside outwards, by means of specific materials and specific structural techniques. It is clear that these are unavoidably a function of the basic spatial solution.

A further step in the work of the new architect is the interrelating of volumes from the outside. The grouping of architectural masses, their rhythm and proportions will derive naturally from the first half of his activity. This part of designing now becomes a function of the material envelopes and inner volumes he has 'constructed' in the design.

And finally, the treatment of this or that wall surface, the detailed treatment of individual elements: the apertures, piers and so on. All of these are functions of some element of what has been enumerated, or of other types of consideration within the brief.

Thus the very method of functional creativity leads us to a unified organic creative process where one task leads from another with all the logic of a natural development, instead of the old-style chopping up into separate independent tasks which are usually in conflict with each other. There is no one element, no one part of the architect's thinking which would be arbitrary. Everything would find its explanation and functional justification in its suitability for purpose. The whole unifies everything, establishes equilibrium between everything, creates images of the highest expressiveness, legibility and clarity, where nothing can be arbitrarily changed.

In place of readymade models of the past which have been chewed over endlessly, the new method radically re-equips the architect. It gives a healthy direction to his thinking, inevitably leading him from the main factors to the secondary ones. It forces him to throw out what is unnecessary and to seek artistic expressiveness in that which is most important and necessary.

There is absolutely no danger in the asceticism of the new architecture which emerges from this method. It is the asceticism of youth and health. It is the robust asceticism of the builders and organisers of a new life.

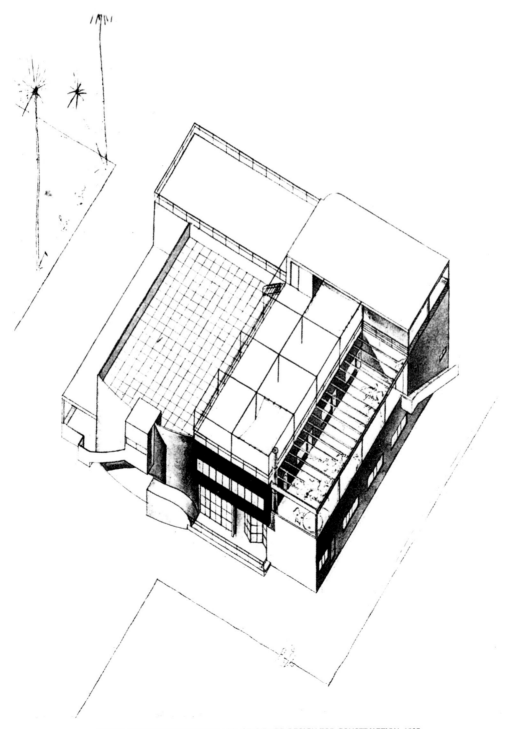

BUROV, WORKERS' CLUB COMPLLEX, STANDARD DESIGN FOR CONSTRUCTION, 1927

DANIEL LIBESKIND
FISHING FROM THE PAVEMENT
(Architecture Perfected)

Illustrated by two images of The Jewish Museum Extension
to the German Museum in Berlin on this page: *Site Plan*; on
page 64: *Plan of the Urban Scale with Invisible Axes*

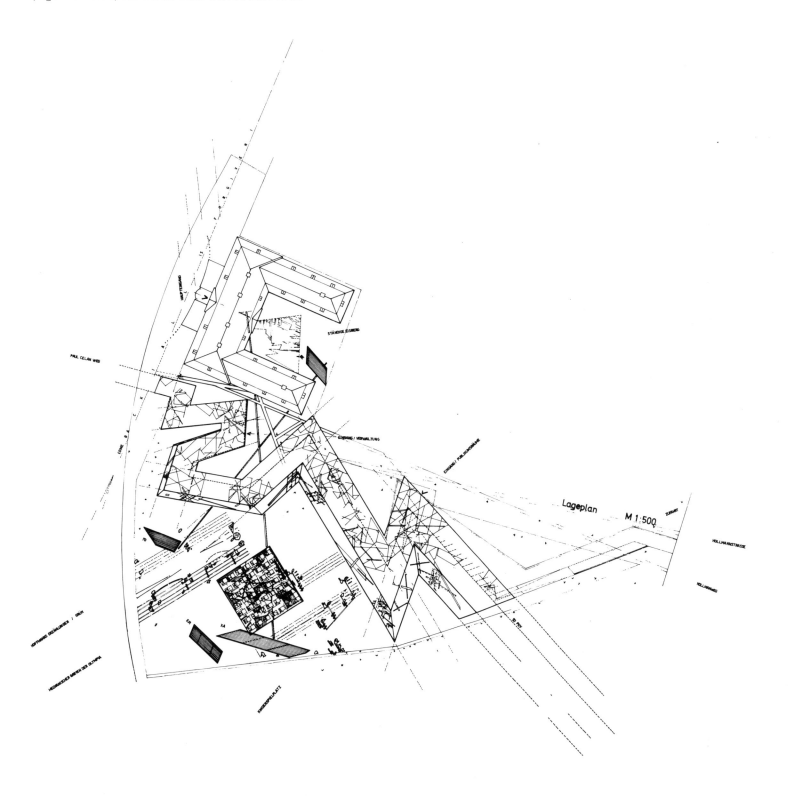

Sedition is rooted in education which only appears to equal the whistle – sound dissolving the face's angry citadel.

A fully equipped talent is attuned to the sea. Rum for sketchy farewells, static abbatoir. I am praising the city by spilling six phantoms on snows of evident docility.

– Taste excess with your cranium or advise the togaed attacker stranded on an oriental amphora that tall Saxons float in shame, ring shaped columns do not bend, Ghenghis Khan ridicules restrictions –

Are you entranced by fourteen hundred theorems, a dappled rabbit, cows bleating in the attic, ineffable apples? After all the Universal Savant is airborne on the back of a billion Sibyls who shape cameos for few cents while flying. As for repair in the loving eruption, open scissors. I think of drinking diorite: testing a pedestrian conundrum with theatrical homocide.

Edified disgorge identity by vomiting the declaration of an alias.

Weeds. Migration of promiscuous and Dutch thorns. End.

Is Kaddish comprehensible to a misanthrope? Chess logical to undertakers? Incomparable Sibelius composing in a video arcade, – tourist of enduring rest – tendon pulling nordic veal to Venice. Damnation, militant flies, Virgil, young ladies made of ice-cream.

No tantrum with respect to you – a jew with plenty of time pouring sentiment into the Kabbala. Violet-blue dripping without terror: a liability.

Dumb achiever – filtering the bride's airy song is typical of the involuntary turn. In the Tiber ridiculous Edwardian furniture,– possibility for exegesis.

To heck with Ecce Homo! – asset in eggs, dust storm. The inventory of conflict confirms the ghost, casts each soul in a minor key – sixth on the diatonic.

Last atom oddly stranded at the terminal while you

tautological darling – knock on my formaldehyde prism without angles, without lines, using a zero metaphysically corrected by a six finger guru. A cherubic picador, peaceful survivor of Armageddon s circle, calculates the position of stars while the horoscope is brimming with spontaneous tenderness.

Love violates the Old Litiaant inside the guts of Buddha who trusts the heretic s arid little hovel – opens the eternal rune to a theorizing which smacks of analphabetic s antic. Mistletoe chaise lounge which is pleasing? – a libertine's lie!

Never flee the linear figure, Pax, ancient Latin goddess, a gymnosophist from Pakistan.

The heart spills its lilacs, echoing what Titus Flavius Sabinus Vespasianus revealed about the Atlantis: steer effluvium receding, perforating the white quad with apocalyptic salt. Alliance of numbers with affliction and ectoplasmic emission.
Sweet oppression: clear photo of the international beast. Cutting with a terribly serrated knife mirrors eternity, refined harm.
Poor lightrope, selfish nectarines.

Sobbing, a condemned woman resolves to put lipstick at the scaffold. Pod instinct throwing ogive vaults across debility; awesome dots, orthogonals of salty fluid.
Erstwhile theophany: discharge from a roving beast's eye, beauty criticizing the colossus. Audacious faeries made of nuclear chromosomes form into threads, split lengthwise, associate with Don Juan s ovoid.
Enamoured with the medically depilated reflection races — are occidentals tired of animal mortar? Is a pneumatic NT. Built for sliding down Reason s annulated cadaver?
Distraught as medals thawed in Eve s tresses are the professors fussing in Erebus, humming.
– Kiss egglike, crushing the sea.
– What extinct gizzard can hush these innuendoes, guests?
– Flame, the puritan s guile!

Italian art: tacky accumulation of nubile obituaries, soft quiche lorraine displayed on the lip, scathing insult timed to ancient airs, victual. Room full of idiots ordering hours now defunct equals exterminated intellection, a vacation in Nice.
Is this not a cooling, nimble possibility — alburnum wedged between the heart and a scholar s file? — lyceum full of brilliant, disembodied Comintern members ensconced in a pleonasm?
Led under a gate the cat and his parents toast each other like domesticated cripples. For with a princenez a cat becomes an isomorph of the servants observed in cinemas, non-protestants apparently.

Harmony, a totem for money.

If I tried to imagine Time as a particular being . . . I would think of a seagull, an accountant, saucer without a cup. Stems formed into a miniature mannequin. Primordial whorls surrounding the brain with round muffs. A cad stimulating the ear of retired Dionysius. The instincts.

This race, biogenetic fake, makes real facsimiles. On the horizon a starved elephant, trees throwing up, prodigal tetrad: valence four.

Squinting poets dislocate the center; blur Ideas; daintily illuminate necessity with vacillation. The singular is spurious.

On the bald pate a tuft of grass. Impending green: neurosis flowing in veins full of asian coffee. Mohammed s metallic horses clearly debauched.

One ought to kiss the Wailing Wall without swallowing an intrusive stone or hear the Song of Solomon played on a knife.

Chained to a steep rock the gallant idolater deigns to bear his pain calmly – asks for lozenges – proud ant! If he could only hear pachalik music, Istanbul s crone, the omniscient whispering traditional curses . . .

The richtists consecrate each menhir with a writhinc movement of their wrists, reminiscent of figures in demotic writing of ancient Egypt. Curious delight: screaming with wrath rivals of the Sun Chasers make offerings of their nails to authorities, shaking a radish at the camera.

Rambunctious pinnacle, – dreadful monument on which a furious youth glows like a chromospheric flare, incinerated, god in his swollen hand. Magnificent illustration of cowards whose rings enter through the mouth in order to fire the official with aversion to dust. The bishop's phallic culm, pleasing enough though half-red, flying in particles, lashing the bearded occupant to the marrow.

Rougher activity than usual in the systole but everything on this little knee seems satisfactory to a happy prince: the Ten Thousand move the earth, mourn for each child's smile, row pride's useless ship on the sea of miracles you don t believe in.

Are you a miss Singapore date?

Jesus withered hand unable to perform the miracle; tear glitters. Bitter complaint about the wrench in combat. Creed colloseum.

Terror alone can transform a splinter of the sun into a sprig of holly: holding an old woman is a correction of the digits, premonition of new disasters.

An unknown assailant bows down to his victims – swears on the Mercator projection that Hell will hang from the roof of the Divine Mansion like a copper net of nouns.

Clear broth is an irritation to the bourgeoisie. Who knows? Before being recessed into these worthless nuggets Eve was hiding chromosomes in her cruel hand.

The voyeurs, proficient, deride the luminous because it is attached to a liquid orifice. But one who mistakes Him for a game of draughts, roll of dice, will have the zipper on his shoulder s magic line ruined.

Resist the aesthetics of urinals, seek the plastic widow: beg her for lilacs, daisies, buttercups with outrageous courtesy.

Oh, to be suntanning in Galilee, sightseeing Capernaum . . .

Deported aleph-beth, sad dog running beside a wagon pulling the beloved treble clef to its burial. Streaming cyanide purifies the air.

Unsupportable necessity yoked to sinister quantity. Irrational number washing its indivisible quotient in the black water of Beginning. Some carts aren't as flat – they curve your lip too soon.

Instil humanity by trimming your talons. The Harpies believed the Almighty; testified to the confidence game He played with you.

The ring leaders of hell squeeze the puppet. It comes to nought. Then exit at the crossroad where Copernicus asks the censor with a bulbous eye whether illconceived stars, like blue rocks, invite the blind to stomp on them. Military fashion loosens times dirty laundry. Ocular fad, the shore, is washed by aroma rather than pigment.

Let up, – offender! – hypocrite effervescent while weaving a nightmare.

Those who choose to reform the fist must be serious about crippling the fabulous glazier who informs April of the window designed to let light only at midnight.

Symbols are sharp-pointed feathers shed by eagles in flight, charismatic as Uzbeks who befriend every ripple of the mighty wave. But to awaken a race of star buds in half-sunk crystals: dim your eye's labyrinthine cavity.

Lichen on a chair floating in the Arctic. Stranaer holding indefinite conversation with lame creation. Affection steered toward syntax by horrible invectives which seek to make a throne out of your fingers.

Filthy reason! Right hand lifting the stetson, offering a demonstration or the sun's impassioned congame.

Melting of man into mirror; more honorable than a master's supplication; more turbulent than water displaced by suicides under the Brooklyn Bridge. Feeble descendants leering over noli me tancere with envy.
The etym is a cancer in wnich words are secured. Yes. But the phonetic gag makes the spoken look for other spaces. Tears forces into parallel lines are the dentils projecting under the cornice of my empty sanatorium, fluttering like butterflies in the sunshine.
Fodder for monkeys can sway immediately because charity is insured in the zoo, but chairs endear themselves only after hours of waiting or when the star is fashioning her evening wardrobe. Reticence, bullwork against yelling, lea's through the mail and other fanciful ideas.
When a paralytic tries to run the marathon the referee masticates on his tongue, laughs as he gathers the loins, – hysterical horse charging over the roses, – demands sawdust sprinkled with Assam leaves.
Curly-headed farmhands died on the cross or in the galleys howling sounds that popular tradition interprets as funeral chants. Their rotating hoes or oars were propellers for our Easter go-carts.

Oedipus is green on television but a lettuce head which germinates in the idealist s bile is pure blue.
Omens are mini-theorists on the great march across the desk. The cause they serve with such fanatical devotion is no better than Caesar s savage act of executing decemvirs at random in order to add up his detours.
Dwarfed by the sky the gods relieve their guilt by cursing what flourishes in man-made halls where nits entertain themselves by laying eggs according to the laws of linear perspective.
Rather dream up a story about a six-legged leptus or vanished Kama Sutra seeds than smell the foul air of reasonable undertakers!

Why incarnate? Sense quits with elementary humility, elopes to a grotto shaped like a skull. What gave you the idea of beheading acephalic beings? Only those who are frightened by worms possess sanity, desecrate gilded towers – endure. Yet Pisans will never disclose why fashionable safety is insecurity. Our days steadily bevel Mt. Zion into a figure resembling a tormented, destitute woman wrapping detonating charges around her forefathers before the gates were opened.

Few men feel the pain of professional dandies who, like doctors, delight in spitting into stainless steel cuspidors, prefer to live in the country with their grandmother.

Crocodiles in Mexico are unconscious of flies reciting the Kaddish while yawing but have a premonition of martyrdom because of their famous sixth sense.

Night spells polysyllabic words to the tempo of quickflowing blood rivers: supernatural, appurtenances, etc.

The Belvedere, like the Tempietto at Rimini, is a construction known for its boundless, thoroughgoing barbarism. But it is not alone in this. Karl Marx buttressed his eviscerated cause with as many pagan tributes. He demonically carried the arrogant eraser onward – and that alone made him late.

Existence, aching gland with a bandage at the exit, gently intones platitudes. What matters! The salt of the earth finally succumbs to giving stage directions to toes which have always been the tributaries for the flow of great ideas.

Rich or hot, cold or poor – a turn of the thermostat (barely an accomplishment for trained domestics) can bring about an immense revolution alone and by itself. For a magnetic field is analogous to forests where participants undergo ecstatic rights of passage fully aware of the game being played. Press forward xenolith – May's proletarian traveller!

Variation in series – solace to terms in the Talmud. Your text is correct but gullible. Muse unfit.

The Statue of Humanity which ingeniously decorates the dark alley of the mind acts like Cellini's gold Perseus: casts a shadow by fueling envy. It's easier to count all the rice grains in China, warp a machine instead of a cape, unscrew Hercules name plate without using an axe than to acknowledge the genius of the departed – their right to sell the world to the unborn.

Threatened with extinction through competition the hand engages in cultural terrorism: grasps whatever it can (Italian tutti-frutti); squeezes the fluid out of the lungs by treating the neck as a sponge.

In just the same way our hopeless precision is a delusion of alchemists in search of metallic novelty based on perjury. Universal blindness will emerge when sculptors have finished the ultimate work: carving water to represent solid matter enraged by summer heat.

Gupta's melancholic atmosphere in which, here and there, an infant could be reared, is not inferior to our suffering pierrot's.

The value of biting the ego, little fool, is perhaps greater than loitering in a major library.

You'll go far if the oft-declared necessity of chewing —inordinately mocked by facts – ceases to be respectable. Inventiveness lies in the jawbreaker and be-littles the homage you pay to these rituals of repeated incision.

Everyone knows that a bare fraction of contrition, missing gerund of abase-ment, sparrow without a roof, can fit on the nihilist's teeter-totter dignifying nausea s taste with a sprinkling of ease.

Sincere numbers are hard to fathom. They hover over the imperial turret as if accentuating the utterances of idiots; irritate the dealers of ether by quanti-fying their reaction to the angle of force.

Hay still has the same effectiveness for horses who don't look for it.

Secular martyrs, idiotic.

– just because the silly Emmanuel Kant said 'perfavor' it doesn't mean that now is the time to die, *Andiamo* . .

Easily refuted by the man with a knife in his back the Yeti continues to enter-tain the mob by cutting his name from immortal remains. Do you suffer a little from his rebellious, unfulfilled vision?

Parade of distinguished clairvoyants, small child slaughtered under a micro-scope, grouping with a side table in stone. Auschwitz or Hollywood?

A 'done' which has always 'done him in' or 'done her well'. Procession with-out the oration s dogmatic purr. Facile accomplishment of the romantic who used to number petals or damask roses and is now drunk with Spoon Ex-tract. Authoritarians are advocating chocolatas a verb for the destitute; per-oxide as the simplest form of magic.

Fashion, the backdoor of life – flies!

Knotted sunbeams – pink talent search – anthems for party members who reflect too much. A routinized westerner thinks that kamikaze vespers are not suitable for his exquisite reason; thinks himself thoroughly beyond such partisan matters as playing chorals on Ghandi s emaciated clavichord.

Skin, cowl of the soul, hides a deaf monk sucking opinions under its hood. The justice of bones is rooted in their capacity to flourish though captive in internal exile: home arrest for enemies of blood vessels surrounded by skin. They were designed with a flair by Versailles, a cunning architect who used insane, three dimensional star configurations organized around an invisible axis called science or epitaph .
What makes the sight of bones unbearable to the living is their seemingly pragmatic nature. Outside the body they look like rigid strings unfastened from a soft instrument rather than elastic playthings they really are inside any hollow box. The discovery of their resilience to time was a product of vanity – Monday morning s amateurish masterpiece!
Sacking Rome did not help the Turks in the long run nor did Lenin's immortality ensure the happiness of cosmonauts.

Humour often imprisons a person inside a water lily causes volubility. Wild animals give up eating regular meals in a cage.
'I take', 'you come': words nobly spliced according to the social contract until the maid falls ill.
Act lovingly for the sake of those who labour on Sunday even if fever finds you remonstrating against the existence of the eighth sphere in your hideaway under the lake. In this way what Aquinas called caritas swings in the oratory – becomes as immediate as spitting. For a deaf detective interrogating a bushy animal instinct is only as accurate as the foot squashing a pest.
The things we love most – ablest porters minus Mesopotamia's industry – are orphans sacrificed to armed eventuality; atrophy of folk songs. Perhaps the existence of gaps or missing links is not a worthy discovery for brain preservers, alias indelicate practitioners of evolutionary theory, authorities on the business of dessicated embryos or portable shelters.
The gambler is alarming dice. Economy will convince you that bowing down to a flag of meat dripping blood is no better than participating in Orwell s witch hunt.

Revulsion for existence fuels the turbine of universal incest — so ancient, unjust. Sorrows – fingers anticipating sticky mucus – do not tolerate being accommodated to diversions on such a small scale!

One could refute the will-to-power of the Laocoon group by comparing it with a ticking clock: both idiots need a lot of space for tiny knick-knacks, common as the desire for smooth natural marble.

Totalitarianism is a magnified idea which will eventually destroy the supremacy of white Biology. But a successful portrait of Jesus cannot be as beautiful as a painting depicting the sycamore tree unto which he swooped.

Today man can smell the fisherman smelling fish smelling water. Gnomes are short; act in cycles of short duration.

The line of incision cutting the mind is straight and long – slice manipulating dearth. Strength, teaching, art, have no power to restore sight to the blind, eliminate lisp in the follower. Nothing is ever going to mollify the petty mole riding on your chin's weakness for space.

Saying 'amen' while repeating maxims on religion Ahab is chopping his cerebrum into a pot in order to cook it. Boiled reason is excellent for a variety of diets. It is a dereliction – vegetarian blind to pity! – to refuse this morsel, cause of so many senseless, captivating disasters.

Space will not return in order to pick up castles stranded on the earth. It is generally projected by reason more feeble than gravity. Consequently flying as experienced by man is no more than an exercise of the third leg dreaming of crawling inside any woman s rib cage.

Sometimes the Great Remote can be invoked through a knowledge of meanness and stupidity. Newlyweds delighting in violent matrimonial abandon can divorce after only two days without consulting their lion or seeking Vatican s permission. But don t worry mom ... the taciturn old gentleman whose heady football I knew so well is no longer scared.

Homocide shows a complete lack of imagination characteristic of those who are too pensive or overly mesmerized by the tulip's declaration of independence. Odd teaching addressed to the Overman by the Undertaker.

Will the moon die when all the expenses incurred by Astronomy in order to create a good weather report at any cost have been repaid to it? Will the rehabilitation of poisonous snakes assuage the bitterness of Mirth? Will forearms primordially tapering into the blue continue aching?

Usually an injection of ancient venom produces thousands of antibodies against indelicate ugly feelings. The parasites are slowly consuming a shadow, while the host – horizontal alpinist – is idly bemoaning a questioner on illumination. Furrowed obstacles constitute a risk to man s limb more than to a woman s enticing discography.

The end is much more forgivable in the beginning, especially when it s a roan for a mere debutante being introduced to an all male society.

Key-in manually: F-O-R-E-V-E-R-E-V-E-R-O-F. One Thousand prayers, genuine especially late at night, cannot be equalled. Equalled be cannot, night at late especially genuine, prayers thousand, one.

Uvea a Deo! – uttering forged expletives, sailing on honey dense with cerotic acids. Oneness is experienced in Adam s frightful guess: alliance easy with a woman who debones him.

Think of a plot, wide as the dollar s unredeemable ethic, full of objects forgotten by their owner. Memory of a face speaks volumes about the blooming potato crowned with dying marigolds – rebuff to the thoughtlessness germinating in every rotten ought .

Called by etiquette arranging silverware for a dinner of distinguished classics the hairless medal confesses to having been a milliner selling women s hats which were in vogue at the time.

(An aleph on street R scrawled the preceding piece cf graffiti using cryptic notes)

Shuffling in the Louvre scratches out the paradigm of cosmic collisions on the smooth black squares of the parquet floor, – rattling pivot, – liquid pope desperately pulling a robin, – the Prussians.

Existence as a result of quantification is a colourful illustration of Alice minus Wonderland: patrimony, nihilism, the illegible. Reason sitting on a curved hip politely.

Along the canal San Francesco, – mute appearance devised by wrinkled gargoyles, – Palladio's innocent prohibition against the rock enduring in ecstasy. Ice. Enter along the concave contour of a soffit. Colourful billiard balls instead of the loggia – isolated chateau built inside the exclusive gaze – defunct vehicles. The Great Road effaced by foolish somersaults, hence by default, a dancing luminary.

A door is a permanent irritant – parmour without arteries counselling Ophelia to swoon.
The velocity of dreams equals the diameter of crystal discs which Narcissus saw reflected in his sunglasses, not water.
Tarot card in up position, datum for the lex-effect. On the equator a shattered camera begins to melt; vegetates like native myrtles. Tarantella is no longer danced though St. Vitus still collects gold pieces, jaundiced. Seamstresses sew together all the pillows in the world into one huge column supporting a mind divided into blanc definitions. Bouquet farms for the benefit of some damned emirate: The entourage dangles. Finally a prisoner tells God about the black warbler who lays five-sided cubes at midnight in the ocean and on the ceiling but never on the marble tiled terrace where the foulest youngsters are reposing.

A soul is not given. But everyone can find a pine cone in the face, sense malice in a crowd, enjoy the ultimate fulfilment of translating the vitality of a radish into the world-picture at the expense of ruinina humanity on which the future production of cradles and atonements depends.
The best masks and disguises are bestowed on those whose time is not running, are always coming home, have a passion for roaming the Siberian forest where Pushkin s deported assassin is still trying to perform the last gesture – though the former is alive – the latter long dead.

A poorly designed mechanical pendulum weighing a few pounds does not make a good pendant nor does it flatter the bare skin already singed to resemble burnt sienna.
Existence sequence: ur-sanity, fraternity, siamese twins.
The spinning top is shaped through the differential of multiple deformations which like thought-sections statically reordering the cone's inverted point propel it toward a dynamically expanding spiral dance that has no nuance or possibility of ascending compositionally in parallel segments.
Funny when information of this kind is requested by Alladin, eternally, yet unable to alert the rosy-fingered by ringing the bell very loudly.

Hector mesmerizes: unbelievable piety. The treasures of Illium troupe to his pathetic little comedy: wet biblical costumes. The percussion instruments are cactus, curling iron and a tropical rake. The tempo a wedding dress makes on the floor when the bride is hesitant.

Eau Deuteronomy – exotic side of liquid, pharmaceutical accident. Temperaments which are punitive yet perfectly moral in terms of canonic intake can withstand being tortured by drinking stroboscopes. Are they ruining anxiety?

Don't look at what is plugged! – both are liable. And Rabbi Yose had one thing in mind really: that one should cut the stubble growing on the Torah obliquely. Yet only a scholar who uses computers or calls himself Major Silence, and whose leaning toward sheer lucidity is nothing obstinate, regards the territorial damage which learning has organized on behalf of the four seasons as truly divine.

He who takes the young to what they like is the one who greets the primitive with a shriek, dips foxes into a vat full of lavender eights. But he who sleeps in the gap to what may he be likened? To one who feels the grape – a potentially shrinkable sphere – without squeezing its juice. Comment on bloody executions, gift wrap the cage.

Bororo Indians become distracted and agitated when qualified data processors, computer technicians, highranking pilots, choose their poor settlement as a place to riot for higher wages. They return a short cough when your esteem is shown or ardour for anthropology confessed. For them radar is something informal which they identify with the norm as being slightly racist, like poetry which they equate with the absence of epidemics. Actually their fault lies in kindness produced by a constant state of high temperature – an immense power to rebuff or make worse. Otherwise these Indians could not recall the apartment to which they ascend without using the stairs or experimentally perform the wicked knotting of fish in order to deform the person who is extremely long-suffering to the point of freeing him from all further striving. While those who have not seen fish-knotting are prone to defend only the local basket industry, natural knotgrass and the puzzling plastic limes they cultivate for export.

'Let your house be opened wide' reaches into the dimension of post-nuclear eloquence. It is old wisdom that a man s house should have a wide entrance on the north, south, east and west. But to become permanently replayed in the 'well, well' is to find the fifth door to the same house. And where to put the extra door?

Mad engineering ends above us. The pull of gravity would not trouble a wall provided it went completely around the stars but was no smaller than a mouth. One who speaks of money s genital, concupiscence, vocalises his losses by passing them off as clouds. He will appear strident to the wind, ca-lamitous to pure sound – will enter by sliding in all directions at once sup-pressing the foregoing.

Supplement to what horses would say to each other were they judged; namely, that a barn must be a meeting place for at least four of them, lest the stablehand open his jaw too widely – fifth door? – in order to welcome in one direction, evict in the other.

Vox populi: limited exchange of rapidly defined orders in Esperanto – attrac-tive as the idea of linking a subway to a drum through the sound which startles an ear. Both vibrations are dolorous, stupid, yet utterly comprehen-sible to one who fulminates when the debate declines to a series of aural snags, perpetually odious.

A woman s left ventricle is more vulnerable to a lapse than Hegel s strained march across his own head. You turn awry – ibis fashion – saying that the oldest life always runs out of the back, as does the oldest Lapp.

Black paraffin argot! Every yearning is condemned by its own lag to partici-pate in pogroms against itself: explicit thesis in each nursery rhyme. You wind up slicing through ice no matter how many fortunes are fed to the fire in order to kindle this exquisitely packed roll of paper.

Rivals of Time fear no hiding where nowhere is.

Television begets telepathy which in turn reforms the almost extinct craft of wrapping patients with no bias for the perpendicular into rare . parchment and idiotically displaying them on the left side of virtue. Harmonia appeals to gluttons, recumbent vandals and unsure predators for a delicate tatoo while consuming pineapples that are juicy. Heredity s entrance remains closed even if you bribe the guard with peacock's excellent meat. This prophecy suggests that spinelessness will indulge in purposeful serfdom.

The ceiling glows with romantic end all as you apply for a visa to existence, estuary to omniscience as accessible as a cliche reminiscent of heroic fanfares repeatedly sounded to alert powdered milk to ancient wrongs. The plummeting heart.

Pavement drenched in blood, the fur coat Arctic needs to become an elementary experience once again.

Authority is legitimated by fledglings whose ankles are lost in a dream where they resemble ancient family heirlooms strewn on the patio. Habitation minus variety equals an obituary, the absolutely lazy machine. Minimum existence slips on a notice.

To a sitter – pale on top of a tree – a hungry bunch of leopards dashing by resembles a buzzing colony of bees singing of summer s gaiety. Leopards are then transformed by intuition into a row of fevered mothers patiently searching for lost children. Ultimately these animals are deceived by a terrifying orator with an ascot tarnished as a medal whose face has been effaced by time and heat.

Produce your friends out of this: Heron flying over a finishing school. Remember that it took five men to make a single atom!

Today s adulation for 'I went on a holiday to Mercury' is as fraudulent as the swaggering of the anonymous voter; more powerful than the richest magnate anchoring his swollen nail – not yet ingrown but already registered – in the fog.

Frequent phenomena such as dieting peasants manning primeval Russian wheelbarrows which never touch the ground, Solomon destroying prose with ludicrous quoins, a man with several chins constitute the riddle which gushes out of the mouth, the point which never gets to it, if it did there would be no separation.

Seals do not heel. An electrical charge does not leap but personally formulates a detour round the play-square that has no right angles yet is drawn by a compass which crawls as well as the circle it draws.

64

PAUL CROWTHER
ART, ARCHITECTURE AND SELF-CONSCIOUSNESS
An Exploration of Hegel's Aesthetic

Introduction

Hegel's *magnificent* aesthetics has exercised a powerful influence on continental philosophy, but has received much scanter attention in the English-speaking world. This situation needs to be rectified, if only to break out of the *narrow* formalist approach which has dominated much Anglo-Saxon thinking about the relation between art and aesthetic experience. In this paper, therefore, I will hope to provide both an *entrée* into Hegel's aesthetic theory, and a critical development of it – with special reference to architecture's significance as an art form. In Part One, accordingly, I will outline the basic features of Hegel's overall philosophical position, and in Part Two, will trace the way in which this shapes his theory of art. Part Three will continue this tracing in more detail in relation to the specific example of architecture. Finally, in Part Four, I will offer a lengthy critical reinterpretation of Hegel's theory of art in general, and will then apply it in detail to architecture. In the course of this latter discussion, some attention will be paid to Hegel's worries about the semantic restrictedness of architecture, and how this might be invoked in criticism of certain modernist and postmodernist tendencies.

I   The key term in Hegel's philosophy is *spirit*. This does not simply mean 'mind' or 'thinking subject'; rather it involves a relation between such a subject, and something *other* than it. Through opposing or negating the other, or, (if the Other is another thinking subject) through being recognised and acknowledged by it, the subject attains consciousness of itself. There are grades of such self-consciousness. The more closely an individual can identify with his or her society and world, and the more lucidly this relation can be understood by the individual, then the 'higher' such a person's self-consciousness becomes. On these terms, in other words, spirit is self-consciousness progressively articulated and unified through concrete interaction with that which is ostensibly Other than it.

This notion of spirit must now be linked to Hegel's account of Truth. In the (so called) 'lesser' *Logic* we are told that:

> In common life truth means the agreement of an object with our conception of it. We thus presuppose an object to which our conception must conform. In the philosophical sense of the word, on the other hand, truth may be described in general abstract terms as the agreement of a thought-content with itself.1

This remark focuses on two closely related tenets of Hegel's philosophy. The first is that the truth of any judgement demands at least implicit reference to a subject who makes the judgement. This is because the objects of thought are actively shaped and determined by the process of thought itself. The second tenet is an extension of this. For Hegel holds that, in the final analysis, thought not only shapes its objects, but is, indeed, constitutive of them. The reasons for this view are, of course, profoundly complex. But one might crudely indicate the trajectory of Hegel's reasoning as follows. In experience we encounter an 'external' world of ostensibly self-sufficient and determinate things, and we think about these in terms of ostensibly self-sufficient and determinate concepts. However, things and concepts only have such a character in so far as they can be discriminated in opposition to, or a negations of, other things and concepts. This means (in the most general terms) that a*ny* finite item's ostensible claim to self-sufficiency and determinacy is in fact false, or at best 'one-sided'. This is because an item's having such qualities is *dependent* upon, or determined by, its relation to other items. *Nothing* finite, in other words, can be absolutely self-sufficient. The world is only real and self-sufficient to the degree that it can be thought through in terms of the *dialectical interdependence* of all its finite elements. This means that the only judgements with a philosophically adequate truth content are ones which are 'concrete'. Such judgements show how some familiar assertion of fact is actually 'one-sided' and incomplete and necessarily leads to its contradiction. The tracing of this relation, in turn leads to a third term which preserves elements of truth from the original assertion *and* its contradictory, but which says something new. This term itself is then shown to be one-sided, and its contradictory is generated and superseded by a third term, and so on.

Now according to Hegel, if this task of dialectical of 'speculative' thinking is carried through to its logical conclusion, the world will stand revealed as a single self-sufficient system of dialectical relations. This does not simply mean that the world can only be thought of in terms of dialectical interdependence. It means that the world just *is* a self-sufficient system of such relations. If all the facts and contradictions of the finite world are thought through philosophically, then we would find that such a world can only be explained as the embodiment of something infinite – an Absolute Spirit. The infinity of the Absolute is not, however, spatio-temporal. Rather it consists in the fact that it is self-determining, ie in contrast with the finite items which are its embodiment, it is not dependent for its existence on relations with anything other than itself. It is *the* organisational principle which is imminent to, and which shapes and sustains the finite world. Put in the most general terms, the Absolute is spirit on a cosmic scale striving for complete self-consciousness. It generates nature as its Other, and from nature generates finite spirits such as we. We in turn interact with nature, and with fellow finite spirits, and it is in, and through, these interactions through the passage of history that the Absolute Spirit gradually comprehends itself. With the formulation of Hegel's philosophy this cosmic process of thought is completed. His system is, as it were, the 'feed out' point where the Absolute attains self-knowledge. This takes the form of the world being revealed in its Truth as a self-sufficient system of items and relations, each *necessarily* related to all the others, and whose sole *raison d'etre* is to be an element in this passage to Absolute Spirit's self-comprehension. With Hegel's philosophy, in other words, we find a truth-content which is in absolute 'agreement' with itself. The contradictions of the finite world are resolved by being shown to be necessary elements in the self-comprehension of Absolute Spirit. Hegel's philosophy just *is* the Absolute contemplating and fully comprehending itself. It is Absolute Knowledge.

Given this outline of Hegel's general philosophical position, we must now briefly focus on one of its details, namely the point that it is through the activities of the finite human spirits which it generates from nature that the Absolute finally achieves self-consciousness. Now whilst this striving for Absolute knowledge is manifest in all aspects of human life, it shows through most manifestly in the historical development of those spheres where humans attempt to articulate what is fundamental about their relationship to the world. For Hegel these activities are (in reverse order of lucidity) art, religion and philosophy. Within each of these enterprises various conceptions of the individual or humanity's place in the scheme of things are manifest. These world-views are, in effect, attempts to articulate the Absolute. However, they are, (until Hegel's philosophy) inadequate, and are necessarily superseded by other modes of expression within the enterprise. With each historical transition from one dominant world view to another, the Absolute is comprehended with that bit more lucidity. Let us now investigate this in more detail in relation to the specific example of art.

II Art has many functions in human existence, but for Hegel its definitive trait is to answer a 'need of spirit' by giving expression to Beauty. But what is Beauty, and why does it answer a need of spirit? To deal with this issue it must be recalled that for Hegel spirit is self-consciousness achieved and articulated through interaction with the Other. Nature, of course, is an aspect of Otherness, and in order for self-consciousness to be fully attained through it on the road to Absolute knowledge, the human spirit must both oppose nature and achieve reconciliation with it. This process of opposition and reconciliation is the province of Beauty and Art. As Hegel puts it: 'The universal need for art . . . is man's rational need to lift the inner and outer world into his spiritual consciousness as an object in which he recognises again his own self.'[2] Indeed:

> This aim he achieves by altering external things whereon he impresses the seal of his inner being and in which he now finds again his own characteristics. Man does this in order, as a free subject, to strip the external world of its inflexible foreignness and to enjoy in the shape of things only an external realisation of himself.[3]

To some degree, any process of human labour will affect this self-recognition, but only in a crude and inexplicit way. Art, however, goes beyond this. In particular, it raises two expectations. Hegel spells these out as follows:

> . . . on the one hand, the work of art, present to sense, should give lodgement to an inner-content, while on the other hand, it should so present this content as to make us realise that this content itself, as well as its outward shape, is not merely something real in the actual and immediately present world but a product of imagination and its artistic activity.[4]

On these terms then, art involves the forming of sensuous natural material in a way that semantically energises it. That is to say, it both sets forth some idea or conception, *and* makes us aware that this meaning has been invested in the work through the rational artifice of a creative agent. This setting forth of spiritual content from nature is Beauty. In the experience of it, we encounter Truth in a sensuous form. Spirit and nature are thus reconciled.

Given this overall trajectory of Hegel's approach to art, we must now investigate more closely the relation of spirit and nature in the creation and reception of art. Consider first, the following remarks:

> In the ordinary external world essentiality does not appear . . . but in the form of a chaos of accidents, afflicted by the immediacy (ie spurious claim to self-sufficiency) of the sensuous and by the capriciousness of situations, events, characters, etc. Art liberates the true content of phenomena from the pure appearance and deception of this bad, transitory world, and gives them a higher actuality, born of the spirit.[5]

Now as we saw in Part One, our common-sense view of nature as a concatenation of self-sufficient and determinate items is in fact 'one-sided' and generates contradictions. This finite world – be it of 'external nature' or our own subjective experiences – can only be fully understood if articulated by dialectical thinking. *Then* such a world appears in its Truth, as the necessary embodiment of a self-contained Absolute Spirit striving for self-comprehension. In the above remarks Hegel is suggesting that in art, this Truth begins to be brought into focus. There are a number of reasons for this. First, in an artwork we are made emphatically aware of the necessary interrelation of parts and whole. The artwork as a *manifestly* self-contained totality prefigures the Truth of Absolute Spirit. At the same time, we know that this set of relations has not just been found or given. The creator's rational and imaginative artifice has taken some idea or content, and, by re-presenting it in a sensuous medium, has changed it for the better. He or she has deepened our understanding of it by expressing it according to rules and techniques of the medium in *publically accessible* sensuous terms. Indeed, whatever particular content in artwork may have eg as a story about such and such a character, or as a picture or sculpture of such and such a subject, the artists' presentation of this evinces a broader world view – content in the fullest sense. He or she does not create *ex-nihilo*. Rather, the way the subject is treated and the choice of medium will be informed by the artist's position within the particular framework of ideas about humanity's place in the ultimate scheme of things, which is dominant in his or her culture or epoch. For Hegel, this framework of ideas always hinges ultimately on the culture or epoch's conception of the Divine. And in our conceptions of what is Divine, we are, in effect, bringing the Truth of Absolute Spirit into focus.

What all this amounts to, is that, for Hegel, the artwork is not just one material thing amongst others. In its semantic richness it advances our self-consciousness in the direction of ultimate Truth. It is, in a sense, more real than the ordinary reality of the finite world. At this point, however, we must enter a caveat. In contrasting the essentiality of the artwork with the 'pure appearance' of the chaotic and contradictory finite world, Hegel is slightly misleading in his choice of terminology. For in his parlance 'pure appearance' is generally used as a term of *approbation* in relation to art. Used in this positive way, Hegel is able to stress that what is fundamental to art is the fact that it is sensuous material *semantically energised*. As well as being a real material object in space or time, it also opens up a *virtual* space or time, ie we see or read or hear it as an image – as referring to some imaginary event of situations. Art-s capacity to create illusion – to duplicate *creatively* and thence improve our understanding of the world, is, as we have seen, why it is of such crucial spiritual significance. However, the way in which the dimension of illusionism operates is not uniform. Indeed its diversity is the very key to the way in which Hegel understands both the different art media and the different major stylistic tendencies in art. It is also the source of most of the central problems in Hegel's aesthetic theory. I now address this dimension in more detail.

First, for Hegel the crudest form of art is what he terms *symbolic*.

> In it the abstract Idea has its shape outside itself in the natural sensuous material from which the process of shaping starts and with which, in its appearance, this process is linked. Perceived natural objects are, on the one hand primarily left as they are, yet at the same time the substantial Idea is imposed on them as their meaning so that they now acquire a vocabulary to express it and so are to be interpreted as if the Idea itself were in it.[6]

In order to understand this passage it must be borne in mind that the 'Idea' in question is that of the Truth of Absolute Spirit on the way to self-knowledge. In cultures which produce symbolic art, the Absolute (conceived of as the Divine) is known characteristically only in abstract terms. God is conceived of as say, some all powerful abstract force sustaining nature, or as a personification of powers or creatures found in nature. He is not yet understood as spirit – in the Hegelian sense of articulated and concretely unified self-consciousness. This means that art produced in such a culture is a very inadequate expression of Truth. For if the Absolute is conceived of in terms derived from nature or natural power, the art which expresses it will simply adopt a crude mode of naturalistic illusion using, say, animal shapes or hybrids of animal and human form; or else it will use brute natural material organised on mechanical rather than imaginative principles – as is the case with architecture. In either case the relation of sensuous form to spiritual content is an 'external' one. The sensuous material will not embody the Truth of spirit, but will, rather, point towards it in an arbitrary and ambiguous way. Suppose, for example, a rampaging lion is used to symbolise the wrath of God. Before being a symbol of *this*, it is simply a representation of a rampaging lion; and rampaging lions can symbolise *many* other things besides wrathful Deities. Indeed, in terms of the reference to God, the Deity has many other attributes besides that of wrath. In symbolic art, then, the relation between the symbol and the content which it symbolises is an abstract and indeterminate one. It is shot through with ambiguity. However, it does contain some element of Truth. Consider the following passage.

> ... the abstractedness of this relation brings home to consciousness even so the foreignness of the Idea to natural phenomena, ... So now the Idea exaggerates natural shapes and the phenomena of reality itself into indefiniteness and extravagance; it staggers round in them ... distorts and stretches them unnaturally, and tries to elevate their phenomenal appearance to the Idea by the diffuseness, immensity, and splendour of the formations employed.[7]

Hegel's point here is that the Truth of Absolute Spirit will strive to express itself, even though a culture has misidentified it with some abstraction from the natural world. It will lead the creators of symbolic art to grotesque exaggerations or stylisation of their content, or to use repetitive motifs, or simply to create works of a colossal size. Symbolic art raises consciousness in other words, by making the inadequacy of its content and vocabulary explicit in the extravagance of its distortions or monumentalism.

Hegel identifies symbolic art largely with the artifacts of non-Christian Eastern cultures, and pre-Christian western ones. However, it is also manifest in the Christian world in the form of architecture. Indeed Hegel sees architecture as the pre-eminent symbolic art-form. His reasons for this are complex and problematic, and I shall deal with them at length in Part Three. Before that, and bearing in mind that the Absolute is constantly striving to comprehend itself, let us consider the stylistic tendency where spirit and nature are brought into a temporarily adequate relation through art. It is in the *classical* art-form.

In the culture of classical Greece, the Divine is conceived in terms of the humanoid Olympian Gods. The Greeks understood the Absolute, in other words, as perfect form of spirit. In relation to this, Hegel remarks that:

> Of course personification and anthropomorphism have often been maligned as a degradation of the spiritual, but in so far as art's task is to bring the spiritual before our eyes in a sensuous manner, it must get involved in this anthropomorphism, since spirit appears sensuously in a satisfying way only in its body.[8]

The Greeks' conception of the Absolute as embodied humanoid spirit is one which is perfectly amenable to representation in a sensuous medium. Indeed, it is most amenable of all to representation in *sculpture* – medium which Hegel sees as the very essence of the classical art-form. In the idealised images of classical statuary the human body is presented as a perfect embodiment of spirit: ... exempt from all the deficiency of the purely sensuous and from the contingent finitude of the phenomenal world.[9] Indeed ... we must claim for sculpture that in it the inward and the spiritual come into appearance for the first time in their eternal peace and self-sufficiency.[10]

Bringing these two points together, Hegel's claim is that Greek statuary presents the Absolute in terms of idealised form occupying three-dimensions. In its idealised purity and free-standing format, in other words, Greek sculpture offers us sensuous images which correspond to the Absolute's status as self-contained spirit. The sensuous means of art, and its spiritual content find an exemplary congruence. It is for this reason that Hegel regards classical art as the highest art form – as the very *Ideal* of beauty.

However, there is a problem. For whilst the Greeks' conception of the Absolute as embodied spirit is highly amenable to sensuous expression, it is not a philosophically adequate conception. It remains 'one-sided' in that it ties the Absolute *too* closely to the finitude and particularity of the human body. This, however, highlights not only a deficiency of the Greek world-view, but also (and for the purposes of this study, more significantly) *the restrictedness of art itself* as a vehicle for expressing the Absolute. In relation to these points Hegel informs us that:

> This restrictedness lies in the fact that art in general takes as its subject-matter the spirit (ie the u*niversal,* infinite and concrete in its nature) in a *sensuously* concrete form, and classical art presents the complete unification of spiritual and sensuous existence as the *correspondence* of the two, spirit is not in fact represented in its *true nature*. For spirit is the infinite subjectivity of the Idea ...[11]

Hegel's worry here is that whilst spirit is embodied, its embodiment is complex and cannot be tied to one specific form – however appropriate that form might be. Indeed, we are dealing with an *infinite* subject. This means that for spirit to be understood in its fullest truth it must be expressed as *spirituality* – a nation which is central to the Christian religion and the cultures founded upon it. Here the Absolute is conceived of as a deeply personal relation to the Divine mediated through God's earthly incarnation – Christ. However, the 'inwardness' of this mode of self-consciousness is not one which is deeply amenable to expression in an external sensuous form. Hence, with the passing of classical art and the advent of the Christian world-view, art ceases to be the highest embodiment of our knowledge of spirit. It is superseded by religion, as, in due course, religion itself is superseded by philosophical knowledge and Hegel's system. Now whilst art is thence denuded in terms of its spiritual significance, it does not remain static. Rather it engenders a new tendency which strives to express the full depth of inwardness. This is the *romantic* art form. For Hegel, the 'romantic' means more than is conventionally understood by the term. Specifically it means art wherein qualities of illusionism – the projection of virtual space and time – are expanded, whilst the material basis of the medium is diminished in terms of its physical dimensions. Consider the example of painting:

> Whatever can find room in the human breast as feeling, idea, and purpose. Whatever it is capable of shaping into act, all this multiplex material can constitute the variegated content of painting. The whole realm of particularity from the highest ingredients of spirit right down to the most isolated natural objects finds its place here.[12]

Yet this richness of meaning is engendered from a relatively limited physical base. As Hegel puts it:

> . . . the visibility and making visible which belong to painting . . . free art from the *complete* sensuous spatiality of material things by being restricted to the dimensions of a *plane* surface.[13]

Now because the spiritual richness of romantic art serves to diminish the physical dimensions of the medium of representation, Hegel sees poetry as the most characteristic romantic art form:

> Poetry is the universal art of the spirit which has now become free in itself and which is not tied down for its realisation to external sensuous material; instead, it launches out exclusively in the inner-space and the inner-time of ideas and feelings. Yet, precisely at this highest stage, art now transcends itself, in that it forsakes the element of a reconciled embodiment of the spirit in sensuous form and passes over from the poetry of imagination to the prose of thought.[14]

In this passage Hegel makes a key transition. The Absolute's drive for self-comprehension requires for its full expression a medium which is wholly abstract yet at the same time wholly concrete. The Christian religion to some degree satisfies this, but it is only with Hegelian philosophy that the Absolute attains full self-consciousness. Thought is here left with the necessary stages of its own embodiment and becoming as its definitive object. In romantic art, this surge towards the expression of inwardness and thought is manifest in the way that the semantic richness of the romantic art media – painting, music and poetry – serves to overwhelm their physical basis. One might say that in the symbolic mode, art struggles both to articulate the Absolute in its content and to find an appropriate sensuous vocabulary to express it; in the classical mode art articulates the Absolute and finds an adequate means of expression; and finally, in the romantic mode, the on-going need to articulate the Absolute with ever more clarity leads to semantic overload wherein the sensuous means of art are compressed and diminished. It is this overload and shrinkage which marks the limits of art.

This completes my *very* broad outline of Hegel's theory of art. Before considering architecture's place within it, in more detail, several qualifications need to be made. First, whilst Hegel sees art's spiritual significance as diminished he does not necessarily imply that no more art will be produced. One would have thought that art, like the world, goes on – albeit as a perpetual variation of the romantic mode. This, however, is a controversial issue in the field of Hegel interpretation.

The second qualification concerns Hegel's chronological perspective and its relation to his understanding of the different art media. It is true that in the most general terms he does see symbolic, classical and romantic art as successive in chronological terms. It is also true that he sees each of these phases as dominated by one or other of the particular art media. There are *many* problems in the way he thus links chronology and media, but there is at least some flexibility in his position. For example, on philosophical grounds sculpture is to be seen as the dominant medium in the classical epoch. But this does not imply that there

is say, no classical poetry, painting or architecture. Of course there is – and Hegel offers impressive analyses of some of these. Similar considerations hold in relation to other epochs and media. Architecture, for example, is a symbolic art form but it has classical and romantic varieties as well. This being said, however, it must be admitted that Hegel's treatment of architecture is probably the most problematic area of his entire aesthetics. It is to this issue I now turn.

III   For Hegel, architecture is, in essence, a duality. On the one hand it must serve an 'external' need – characteristically that of enclosing space in order to provide shelter; but on the other hand, if it is to be a mode of fine art, it must also give expression to spirit – to our relation to the Absolute. Hegel remarks that:

> Its task consists in so manipulating external inorganic nature that, as an external world conformable to art, it becomes cognate to spirit. Its material is matter itself in its immediate externality as a mechanical heavy mass, and its forms remain the forms of inorganic nature, set in order according to . . . relations of symmetry.[15]

However, the relation between architecture and spirit is external and abstract. For architecture's materials and methods are much more dependent on the medium's brute physical properties and the mechanical ordering of these, than are the other art media. In particular, architecture does not, without adjuncts, create illusionistic space. It can represent no other space but that of its own physical presence. This means that reference to any specific spiritual content which it makes will be arbitrary and indirect. That is to say, we will not be able to discern it with any ease. It is this external relation to spirit which makes architecture into a symbolic art form.

This indeterminacy of the medium is matched by an indeterminacy in the spiritual content which architecture strives to address. To show some of the complexities of this issue, let us address what Hegel takes to be the three main varieties of architecture. The first of these he terms the *independent* or purely symbolic variety. Architecture of this sort is peculiar because it does not serve some external *physical* need such as providing shelter, but exists rather to express a need of spirit – specifically that of relating in individual to his or her society or religion. It serves, as it were, to focus and declare socio-cultural identity. An example of this is the Tower of Bel in Babylon (mentioned 'in Herodotus) in relation to which Hegel suggests that the symbolic content is entirely abstract. It consists in the eight storeys of the building symbolising the nightly visit of the god.

Now in most works of independent architecture, content is striven after in a comparatively less abstract way than this through the building being embellished with forms drawn from nature. Hegel sees this as an advance. As he puts it:

> . . . the symbolic content of their meanings is determined in more detail and therefore permits their forms to be more clearly distinguished from one another, as, for example, in the case of lingam pillars, obelisks, etc . . . [16]

In this tendency architecture begins to make use of sculptural elements based on animal and human form.

> . . . though whether it uses them in isolation or assembles them into great buildings, it does not employ them in a sculptural way but in an architectural one . . . [17]

This means that the sculptural elements are used on a massive or colossal scale, often in repetitive sequences, so that we simply do not view them as sculptures. We see them, rather as edifices, or as integral parts of an edifice.

Now this hybrid form of independent architecture is identified by Hegel with enormously diverse cultures – ranging from the near and middle-eastern, to the Indian and Oriental. In the architecture of all these cultures we find an extraordinary profusion of different kinds of symbols drawn from forms encountered in the natural, animal and human world. This very profusion and diversity is, for Hegel, extremely telling. In his words:

> . . . the meanings taken as content here, as in symbolic art generally, are as it were vague and general ideas, elemental, variously confused and sundered abstractions of the life of nature, intermingled with thoughts of the actual life of spirit, without being ideally collected together as factors in a *single* consciousness.[18]

Hegel's major point here is that whilst non-Christian cultures have conceptions of what is Divine (and thence of the Absolute) their conceptions are confused and abstract. They do not – as the Greeks do in their sculptural *idealisations* of the human body – grasp the Absolute as embodied and unified spirit. Lacking this insight, they search through natural form to find appropriate symbols for making what is ultimate intelligible to them, but individualised natural or human forms, or hybrids of them can at best express only limited aspects of the Absolute, and then only in an ambiguous way. This leads symbolic architects to compensate for the inarticulateness of content by creations of fantastic complexity frequently on a colossal scale. Architecture, indeed, (as we have seen) begins to adopt sculptural elements for its own ends, and it is in this pointing towards sculpture that we find the transition to the next major variety of architecture – the *classical*.

Classical architecture as Hegel understands it, is somewhat paradoxical. This paradox gravitates around the question of what counts as the essence of architecture. In the most literal sense, architectural productions:

> . . . are subservient to an end and a meaning not imminent in itself. It becomes an inorganic surrounding structure, a whole built and ordered according to the laws of gravity.[19]

However, the essence of architecture as a fine art is to answer a need of the spirit ie to advance our self-consciousness in relation to the Absolute. Now, for Hegel, the key feature of classical architecture is that (most notably in the form of the Greek Temple) it satisfies the condition for being a fine art by superlatively exemplifying architecture's more literal essence. Consider the following crucial passage:

> The beauty of classical architecture consists precisely in [its] . . . appropriateness to purpose which is freed from immediate confusion with the organic, the spiritual and the symbolic; although it subserves a purpose, it comprises a perfect totality in itself which makes its one purpose shine clearly through all its forms, and in the music of its proportions reshapes the purely useful into beauty.[20]

In these complex remarks, Hegel is making three points. The first is that classical architecture nominally moves away from the realm of fine art in so far as instead of trying to answer the needs of the spirit by using abstract indeterminate symbols, it reverts to non-artistic functionalism. It is, thence, primarily a discourse of proportion and ratio rather than one of organic imagery on a colossal scale. However, Hegel's second point is that this retreat into materials and techniques put at the service of some function nominally external to art, of itself answers the need of the spirit, by, as it were, the back door. For (in the Greek Temple at least) the function of the building is to provide a housing or frame for a *statue* of the god. This means that architecture's external and indeterminate relation to spirit is here made explicit by the fact that the building and a pre-given spiritual content (the statue) are physically distinct items. On these terms classical architecture gives expression to spirit, by thematising its own spiritual limitations *qua* architecture. It exemplifies both the gap between brute natural material and spiritual content which characterises

all symbolic art, and also the fact that architecture must make way for an art form which is more spiritually concrete – namely sculpture. Now Hegel is too astute to leave matters here, if only for the immediate problem of explaining the beauty of classical architecture other than temples. This brings us to his third and most complex point in the passage above. It is the one asserting that architecture 'in the music of its proportions reshapes the purely useful into beauty'. This concession to a more familiar architectural aesthetic, itself conflates a number of rather different questions. First, Hegel has in mind an austere aesthetic of mathematical relations. In this respect, it is telling that in relation to architecture and music he later suggests that: '. . . the two arts rest on a harmony of relations which can be reduced to numbers and for this reason can be easily grasped in their fundamental characters'.[21] However, Hegel also concedes that: 'What these relations are cannot be reduced to settlement by numerical proportions with perfect precision'.[22] This concession is crucial; for we must ask *why* architecture and music cannot be reduced to the mere following of mathematical rules. (I shall deal with this important issue at length in Part Four.)

The other approach which Hegel conflates with his 'music of its proportions' thesis, is a kind of functionalist aesthetic. The classical building 'comprises a totality in itself which makes its one purpose shine clearly through all its forms'. Again, however, this is surely problematic. For whilst a perfect congruence between sensuous form and practical function may be a sufficient condition for a building's being an exemplary building, this does not (without detailed further argument) allow us to say – be it in Hegel's or any other terms – that it is therefore a *beautiful* building. The issue of beauty's relation to the following of rules is of course, involved here, and as noted earlier, I shall return to it at length in Part Four.

Interestingly, it is this functionalist approach which Hegel makes central to the variety of architecture which succeeds the classical – namely the *romantic*. By romantic Hegel means specifically the Romanesque, medieval Gothic and some aspects of Moorish architecture. His major characterisation of this tendency is as follows:

> It has and displays a definite purpose; but in its grandeur and sublime peace it is lifted above anything purely utilitarian into an infinity in itself. This elevation above the finite, and this simple solidity, is its *one* characteristic aspect. In its other it is precisely where particularisation, diversity, and variety gain the fullest scope, but without letting the whole fall apart into mere trifles and accidental details. On the contrary, here the majesty of art brings back into simple unity everything thus divided up and partitioned.[23]

Hegel's claim here is that the impact of romantic architecture is grounded on the harmony between an immense profusion of particular details and the functional form of the building. This suggests a concrete or contained infinity ie a finite world with an infinite and immanent logic which binds it into a unified system. The work of romantic architecture, in other words, symbolises the Absolute as a self-contained but infinite whole. In its unified sensuous diversity it points towards this ultimate as it were, overload of spiritual meaning, but can, *qua* symbolic art form only indicate it indeterminately: that is to say, given the appropriate orientation we can see the romantic building as a symbol of Absolute Spirit, but this meaning cannot be read out of it with unambiguous clarity.

Let me now summarise Hegel's position on architecture. For him it is a fine art to the degree that it involves the shaping of sensuous material so as to give it spiritual content. Its central limitation, however, is its lack of illusionism. It is not a thoroughly spiritualised medium because the shaping of its material is *fundamentally* determined by mechanical and mathematical principles. This 'external' art form has three main varieties-cum-stages; the independent (in its pure and hybrid modes), the classical, and the romantic. The chronological emergence of each of these from its immediate predecessor is determined by the Absolute's striving for ever more lucid self-articulation. That is to say, the pure and hybrid independent architecture of eastern cultures had to be negated by the classical mode, so as to make the purely external and opposed relation of architecture to spirit explicit. This, in turn, had to be negated by the romantic mode, so as to bring about some reconciliation of this opposition.

A few qualifications must now be made. First, architecture of an 'independent' kind clearly continues to be produced even after the advent of classicism, and, of course, even after the emergence of the romantic mode, neo-classicism continues to flourish even down to the present day. What does Hegel make of these facts? Well, he would hold that independent and neo-classical architecture do indeed continue to be produced, but they have lost their spiritual vitality. The conceptions of humankind's relation to the Deity (and thence the Absolute) which informed the original epochs of independent architecture and classicism have now been superseded by more advanced spiritual awareness in the form of the Christian religion and Hegel's system of philosophy. To produce works of independent or classical architecture *now*, therefore, will be to offer up edifices with a spiritual content that is inert or fossilised. Even if such works are produced in the name of new sets of ideas or ideologies matters are actually little improved. For we must remember that in Hegel's terms art in general had had its day and been superseded. It can still play some role in life, but only as a perpetual variation of the romantic mode.

IV   First, a few boring points. Hegel's treatment of the whole sphere of art is an outgrowth of his overall philosophical position. But even if one broadly accepts that position there are still many problems – most notably in the way that Hegel makes art's dialectical development into the determinant of its chronological unfolding. If one does not accept Hegel's overall philosophical position the problems are infinitely worse. It might seem that the diversity and nuances of art and the aesthetic experience are being flattened out by a blunt metaphysical instrument. At best, it might be said that in the midst of Hegel's abstruse and implausible speculations, there is a wealth of rich concrete analysis of specific artworks. (This dimension of Hegel's thought it should be noted, is one which I have done *scant* justice to in this paper.)

However, these *are* boring points. A much more profitable way of engaging with Hegel is to tease out and critically develop plausible general insights and lines of argument. It is this task which I will now undertake at length, beginning with his notion of spirit. The great merit of this notion is that it *existentialises* self-consciousness and makes it something concrete. That is to say, instead of reconstructing human experience on the basis of some abstract and passive correlation between a thinking subject and given objects of experience, it focuses rather on the growth of human experience through its interaction with specific historical contents. Human experience *becomes,* through its unceasing striving to overcome or assimilate or be reconciled with that which is Other than it – be this nature, other people, or social institutions in the most general sense. This general schema is right. What is unacceptable in Hegel is the way he sees this as following a *necessary* course, determined by Absolute Spirit's striving for self-consciousness. Indeed, the very notion of the world as Absolute Spirit is itself hugely problematic in contemporary philosophical terms. However, it is possible to give this

notion an existential interpretation. On these terms, what is absolute or ultimate in human experience is 'being-in-the-world'; that is to say, the way in which finite thinking, feeling, embodied sensuous beings inhere in the natural and social world. To inhere in the fullest, most positive sense is *to achieve free belonging*. This means to attain a mode of self-consciousness wherein – through the recognition of *shared* problems and characteristics with nature and our fellow humans – we recognise the worth and possibilities of our own individuality. Such self-consciousness embodies, in other words, a profound complementarity of what is particular and what is general in being-in-the-world. More specifically, it integrates the two fundamental (and sometimes opposed) dimensions of such being, namely our sensuous existence as individual embodied creatures, and our existence as rational, acting beings.

Now to existentialise Hegel's notions of spirit and the Absolute, leads the way to an existential re-interpretation of his theory of art. Indeed it assigns a significance to art far in excess of that which Hegel himself allows. To show this, I will now expand and develop his two key insights about art, and will give particular attention to their relevance for architecture.

The first key insight is that art's central achievement is to bring about a reconciliation between spirit and nature. I shall start, however, with a critical point. We will recall that for Hegel artistic beauty consists of the shaping of natural sensuous material so that a spiritual content is explicitly set forth. This experience of beauty as a setting-forth is achieved through the artwork's illusionistic qualities and it is these which differentiate art from merely functional artifice. There are, however, at least two problems with this. The first is that whilst art may be illusionistic in some sense, not all illusionistic artifacts are necessarily beautiful. We may read some pointings, for example, *purely* in terms of the visual subject matter which they represent; and may pay no attention to the fact that this subject-matter has been set forth for us by human artifice. The second point is that, as the example of architecture shows, beauty is to be found in functional artifacts that may have little or only highly ambiguous illusionistic qualities. Hegel's own analysis of classical architecture, indeed, suggests that beauty should be linked, rather, to the notion of a 'self-contained totality'; that is to say one where all the parts are thoroughly permeated by the organisational principle or function of the whole. Hegel's difficulties here arise from the fact that he wishes to tie beauty to art's setting forth of a content; but as my objections show, beauty must surely be something wider than this. Hegel's point about classical architecture points us in the right direction. At its most *basic* level (and there are other levels besides) the experience of beauty is a function of our discrimination of harmonious relations between the parts in a phenomenal whole and the organisational principle which governs their distribution. Relations of this sort, of course, can be enjoyed in relation to nature, and the domain of artifice – be it functional or illusionistic. More specifically, what we are looking for here is not just a fit or cohesion between parts and whole, but one which invites and facilitates perceptual exploration of it. Hegel's analysis of romantic architecture is instructive here. For with, say, a Gothic cathedral, we have a building with a specific function, but one whose formal organisational principle encompasses an astonishingly diverse variety of parts and elements. Hegel unfortunately does not see the scope of this example. The diversity involved in the beautiful object need not simply be one of particularity and difference; it could also hinge upon multiplicity. The Egyptian pyramids, for example a multiplicity of uniform units, but their juxtaposition in the organisation logic of the pyramidal structure energises the multiplicity into relations of perceptually engrossing symmetry.

Now to experience beauty in these terms is not just to inhere in the world. It is to enjoy a felt and *free belonging* to it. There are many reasons for this. First, if the relation between some phenomenal configuration's parts and the organisational principle of the whole, is one that stimulates perceptual exploration and discrimination of the relation, then we can describe such a relation as free. The organisational principle unifies and directs but does not suppress our awareness of the parts. Indeed, it enriches our awareness of their individual identity and collective interplay. This is a kind of image of full and positive belonging – of 'being-in-the-world' in its highest sense. It is the echo of our aspirations to live a life with overall direction and organisation, but which harmonises with the needs and interests of the present – with, as it were, the texture of the immediate. It also echoes the fact that in our relation to human society we need to be part of a whole, but one that respects the integrity of the individual member. One might even say that this experience of beauty is an image of freedom in a rather more direct sense. For in it we exercise our cognitive capacities for an end – perceptual exploration, which is *not necessarily tied to the immediate gratification of some practical or physiological need.* We find in the beautiful object, in other words, a sensuous configuration which reflects the fact that whilst we are part of nature, and subject to natural needs and drives, our cognitive capacities also make us independent of this deterministic causal framework. Reason may indeed be the slave of the passions and instinct, but it also to some degree frees us from them. I am suggesting, then, that in the experience of beauty, spirit finds its own aspirations and characteristics reflected in the sensuous forms of natural material. It thus achieves consciousness of its free belonging to the world.

Now despite its phenomenological complexity, the enjoyment of beauty – whether in nature or artifacts – is only a crude form of aesthetic experience. The more subtle and far reaching varieties pertain primarily to the domain of art. I shall now explore some aspects of this issue by drawing on another of Hegel's key insights. This concerns the centrality of illusionism to art. Putting it broadly, for Hegel artworks are modes of representation which *qua* representation refer to some specific subject-matter or range of subject-matter. Reference is achieved by virtue of the medium being organised on the basis of some culturally conventionalised semantic and syntactic code, or combination of codes. The artist's particular mode of handling or articulating the codified medium serves (to use a crude but effective metaphor) to 'chew over' his or her subject-matter, so that it is presented in a new light, and in a way that manifests a conception of the Absolute. Art is thus a form of knowledge which is midway between the generality of ordinary or theoretical uses of language, and the concrete sensuous particularity of real material things. In broad outline, Hegel is right – if we continue the strategy of interpreting his insights in existential terms. One might proceed as follows. First, artworks do indeed refer to a specifiable subject-matter or range of subject-matter, by virtue of their articulation of codified media. Painting and sculptural representation works on the basis of visual resemblance projected from two or three dimensions. Poetry and storytelling imaginatively invoke their subject-matter by means of characteristic linguistic devices such as meter, rhyme, metaphor and narrative. Music operates with a tonal system of major and minor keys whose thematic and harmonic expositions are commonly regarded as structurally analogous to specific patterns of feeling, mood, and emotion. Now this grounding in a culturally accepted and rule-governed code enables the audience to grasp what kind of subject or character the work is 'about'. However, the artist's particular choice of medium and particular way of handling is governed by further sets of rules. Some of these are strictly technical; others – such as particular sorts of brushstroke or colours, or metrical schemes and metaphors, may be features which, in the terms of our shared cultural stock, carry quite specific symbolic connotations (This, of course, is of especial significance for abstract art). The following of rules also extends to questions of formal cohesion, and the adaptation of, or reaction against, idioms and models established in the tradition of the medium. What all this means is that when the subject-matter appears in the finished artwork, it has been thoroughly mediated by complex processes of socially intelligible signification – as well as by the personal and idiosyncratic stylistic traits of the artist. The subject-matter is, therefore, re-presented in a context of symbolic clarification and articulation which does not surround it in everyday life. Through this complex process, the artist is able to set forth his or her personal vision of those elements which make that subject-matter significant, but on a codified basis which can be grasped by the audience. This sharing of the artist's vision can take many forms. The audience might, for example, find a revelation of possibilities and truths which they had not thought of in relation to that kind of subject matter before. Or they might find that the artist's treatment of it clarified aspects of their own existential problems. Again they might simply marvel at the fact that the transience and complexities of some human experiences have been brought into the open, and welded into a lucid aesthetic object. Now what makes all this into more than simply a case of shared understanding is the fact that these dimensions of truth are embodied in sensuous media. Truth is a function of our cognitive faculties forming and applying concepts, but in existential terms this is not a purely 'mental' operation. It is a function of all the senses functioning in co-ordination as a unified field. Knowledge is *emergent* from this sensuous base. Since, therefore, in the artwork truth is encountered as a function of some organised sensuous configuration we find in the work an image or echo of what we ultimately are – embodied spirit. But there is more to this than a sense of mere belonging. *Qua* sensuous object, the artwork has a closeness to our immediate experience of the world which the ordinary uses of language do not. Indeed, because of the formats and the intelligible codes that the work embodies, we recognise that it is a sensuous configuration which has been created by a fellow human, and which sets forth a view of some aspect of our shared world. However, the artist is not literally present in the work. The work becomes physically discontinuous from him or her as soon as it is completed. This means that we can take the work very much on our own terms. Through its shareable vision, we recognise aspects of our own situation in the world, or the possibilities of new ones, reflected in the Other. But since the Other is here a sensuous embodiment of truth rather than a face to face engagement with another person or simply a report of truth, the inhibitions arising from direct confrontation, and the alienating distance arising from merely abstract communication, are, therefore removed. We are not bullied or pressurised by the artist's physical presence into sharing the vision on exactly his or her terms, but neither are we being offered something second-hand or remote from the immediacy of direct experience. In the experience of art, we recognise ourselves in and through the Other, with a degree of freedom that is foreign to all other modes of discourse. This is the *supreme* significance of Hegel's insight concerning art's midway position between pure thought and sensuous material things.

Now in the foregoing account, I have been following up some Hegelian themes that focus on the artwork's capacity to be 'about' some specifiable subject-matter or range of subject-matter. But where does this leave architecture? The immediate answer might *seem* to be 'in very much the place occupied by abstract painting and sculpture and non-tonal music'. This, however, is not strictly true. For these abstract tendencies rely substantially (for their cultural reception and survival) on being read in terms of the codes governing representational art. Abstract painting, for example, frequently uses organic imagery, or, in the way paint is applied or colours rendered and/or juxtaposed exploits familiar symbolic associations. Such works become representational by allusion and suggestion. This, indeed, is what makes them, at times, so powerfully affecting. Similar considerations apply in relation to non-tonal music. Even if, say, we can follow the structural development of a piece of serialist music, it has emotional overtones beyond the dry logic of its formal progression. On the basis of our common cultural stock, the audience will appropriate it as an image of fragmentation and chaos, or as an image of painfully achieved reconciliation with such phenomena. Now to some limited degree a similar approach can be taken with architecture. Hegel himself hints as much when he talks about the 'music' of architectural proportions. However, I would claim that the cultural stock of common symbolism, or association which gives subject-matter to ostensibly abstract art styles, cannot be applied with the same felicity to architecture. One reason for this is that, as already noted, abstract tendencies in the other art forms remain firmly embedded in traditions of reception determined by dominant representational tendencies. Architecture of course has no such representational matrix. Indeed, given the centrality of function in architecture, it might seem at best churlish, and, at worst, lunatic, not to make this central to its significance as an art form.

What I propose, then, is that we look to function as an analogue of subject-matter, so as to integrate architecture into the neo-Hegelian theory of art expounded earlier. Before this can be done, however, we must take full account of Hegel's points about the restricted referential possibilities of architecture. He holds, we will recall, that architecture has a fundamentally 'external' relation to spirit, because of the representational indeterminacy or ambiguity of its sensuous material and techniques of shaping, and because of the indeterminacy of its content. Let me deal with these two points in turn. First, the ambiguity of material and shaping. A great deal of modern and postmodern architecture feels it has a great deal to 'say' about architecture, the universe and everything. One of the most ambitious tendencies in this respect is the deconstructionist work (or plans) or architects such as Peter Eisenman and Bernard Tschumi. Now the problem with this as with theory-inflated modernist and postmodernist architecture in general, is that the audience does not have any culturally established code to decipher the works. They simply look in the catch-all sense 'modern'. Of course buildings often embody piecemeal references to other works, but ad hoc references are not sufficient to constitute a code. Hegel is right. The more an art form's embodiment is tied to real physical material ordered in terms of mechanical relations, the less scope it has for being unambiguously 'about' something. Now if the architect provides a text whereby his or her work can be decoded, this might seem to solve the problem. But again Hegel has a viable worry about this. It consists in the fact that if an artwork is dependent on some external element such as a text, in order for its content to be recognised, then this is a kind of sell-out of art's essential sensuousness. Here, embodiment in a sensuous medium would not 'chew over' a subject-matter so that it is known in a new way. Rather it would simply exist in order to illustrate something already known.

Let me now address the issue of indeterminacy of content, that is to say architecture's inability to articulate the Absolute in an adequate way. Reinterpreted in existential terms this might read as follows.

Many buildings are informed by, and meant to manifest, some more total vision of architecture, and, even, society. The rise of modernism, for example, is permeated by a tendency to link the individual building or project with some vision of a utopian society and environment. Here the problem of indeterminacy looms large. For what the architect is operating with is not a concrete projection, but rather – and literally – a *picture* of the future. Art, of course, involves picturing and images, but only on the understanding that these just *are* pictures and images. In the architect's case, however, the image functions as an exemplar of the real – in the sense of realisable possibility. It might genuinely have *something* of this character, but only if part of a more total project formulated with the participation of town-planners, economists, statisticians, sociologists, politicians, community councils, and one or two others. But (for the most part) architects are oriented fundamentally to how they imagine the future will look, or more commonly, how they imagine it *ought* to look. In its very visuality, such a vision is indeterminate. The fruits of this indeterminacy are, of course, often concretely manifest nowadays in the form of concrete being demolished ... (Hegel would doubtless point out to us here that that which is one-sided necessarily engenders its own negation).

This problem of indeterminacy is especially pronounced in relation to deconstruction. The discourse of deconstruction hinges on such things as the problematics of determinacy of presence, the incongruence of signifier and signified, the false rigidity of oppositions such as inner and outer, etc. etc. Now the fact that architecture here draws its text from philosophy should make us wary at the outset. The suspicion should grow when we realise that 'indeterminacy of presence' is here meant to be declared in a medium which involves the creation of determinate material presence, determined by, absolutely determinate mechanical laws. Charitably speaking this might appear to present a challenge; realistically speaking it is what it seems at first sight – a contradiction. Indeed it points towards the general untenability of *différance* and the deconstructive position. This position is an indeterminate abstraction – something arrived at through signifying practices being viewed outside the context of their concrete use. In theoretical terms the possibility of meaning and presence is determined by an item's location within an inexhaustible network of relations to other items. But in our direct experience this abstract structure is focused and fixed by our body's hold upon the world. Presence is paramount – despite its theoretical indeterminacy. The problem is that deconstruction does not simply posit a theory about indeterminacy, it does so in terms which *are themselves abstract and indeterminate* through their failure to deal adequately with the dimension of embodiment. This means that any attempt to instatiate the theory in terms of concrete material artifacts will be arbitrary – the creator will simply invent his or her own ad hoc code to tie object to theory. In the case of architecture, indeed, which is so preeminently bound to the reality and definiteness of material presence, the concreteness of the signifier will tend to contradict the indeterminacy of the signified.

Given, then, the clear restrictions upon architecture's capacity to refer, let us now return to the question of whether its functions can serve as an analogue to subject matter in the other art forms. Now Hegel himself is, in effect, *driven* to this position – at least in relation to classical and romantic architecture. But his reticence to make more of the analogy is understandable given his broader philosophical position. Those needs such as the provision of shelter and enclosure which define architecture in its most general sense, are not direct needs of the spirit. They are, rather, needs of the body, and are thence external to art. However, by re-interpreting Hegel in existential terms, the significance of this point is transformed. For I have suggested that what is ultimate in experience is being-in-the-world, that is to say, consciousness of self formed through reciprocal interaction *qua* embodied spirit, with nature and the human world. Given this ultimacy, the provision of enclosure and/or the emblematic setting forth of physical space – let us call these *the physical articulation of site* answer a *primal need*. Finite spirits must create such sites for their physical existence and social intercourse, not simply in order to survive, but also in order to *become* – to develop a fuller consciousness of what they and their fellows are, and their place in the scheme of things. This primal need for site gives the functionality of architecture a much more central role in the achievement of self-consciousness, than can be assigned to other functional practices. For, even though a specific building is normally addressed to a quite specific function, it is always one which calls forth and co-ordinates a host of human practices or activities in relation to that function. Think of the *enormity* implied in simple descriptions such as 'a house is a place to live in' or 'that building is where people work' or 'that one is where people worship'. Architecture, as the physical articulation of site, in other words, answers *complex* needs of spirit even when addressed to ostensibly simple functions. Indeed there is one other quite specific need of spirit which it answers. It consists in a kind of obverse to Hegel's whole position on architecture. We will recall that in existential terms cognition – knowledge - arises through the Other being probed and modified by all the senses acting as a unified field. Now precisely because of the greater physicality of its presence, we might reasonably expect the work of architecture to engage sight, sound, and touch in complex networks of judgement that are more total and more immediate than our engagement with the illusionism of the other art forms – where the physicality of the medium is less all-embracing. In engaging us primarily in terms of its real sensuous presence, the work of architecture opens up possibilities of direct perceptual exploration that more than compensate for its semantic restrictedness. It is an image of our total sensory immersion in the world.

I am suggesting then, that in architecture function acts as an analogue to subject-matter in the other art forms, and has a complex spiritual significance of its own. On these terms, the particular way in which a building embodies its function, serves to 'chew' that function over so that it is known in a new way. The embodiment of function (and more generally of sitea) provides a code whereby the work can be recognised and appraised. It may surprise us say, that a church can be 'done' on the basis of *this* relation between its parts and the organisational principle which governs the phenomenal structure as a whole. We may find that *this* way of physically articulating a site using *these* materials, creates a space in which we feel at ease. Its balance say, of heavy stable-looking elements with the play of light from the windows, seems to achieve an adventurous equilibrium – the kind of thing we yearn for in our own existence. Again we may vicariously

identify with the architect's achievement as such. But throughout all this, of course, the architect is not present in person. There is no pressure to identify with his or her articulation of site. The achievement of sensuous belonging here, is free.

One final general point of substance needs to be made. In Part Three, I noted that Hegel was rather uneasy about the role of rule-following in relation to beauty and the creation of art; and I asked why it is that beauty cannot be achieved simply by following rules. One answer is that since beauty and art are, by definition bound up with sensuous configurations, their embodiment is always *particular*. Hence, even if we hold that the beautiful object or artwork must satisfy certain rules – such as having a perceptually interesting relation between its formal organisational principle and its parts – we can only decide if this rule has been applied successfully by judging each case individually. That is to say, by having direct perceptual acquaintance with it. Now this dimension of particularity has a further complex twist to it. This is because the question of what things count as perceptually interesting is not a simple intuitive issue. It is historically and ideologically variable. Whether or not a sensuous configuration engages our attention in formal terms, and whether or not it is to be regarded as meritorious, always demands a comparative context of judgement. The key criterion operative in this context is that of *originality* – in the sense of either refining some familiar kind of configuration to an exemplary degree, or else in innovating and breaking with what we are accustomed to experiencing. The configuration, in other words, must be creatively different from what has gone before. There is a subjective and an objective dimension to this. The former consists in us responding to and learning from a configuration the likes of which we personally have not encountered before. The objective sense is when, say, in the case of art, our judgement is informed by a detailed comparative knowledge of the medium as a historically developing structure. Here we learn from the achievements of the particular work, through its qualities being defined and appraised in relation to a continuing tradition of creative endeavour. Now generally in our culture we know the worth of the individual in abstract terms. Original art, however, elucidates this in the most direct and concrete terms. It exemplifies its own individuality and the significance of the individual through creatively differing from tradition; but, in so doing, it at the same time affirms the worth and universal validity of the enterprise of which it is an instance. To experience art on these terms, in other words, involves a free and harmonious relation between elements of particularity and universality in experience; and since it is the relation between embodied particularity and the universality of rational projects which defines self-consciousness, we can conclude that art embodies it in the most *positive* way.

Notes

1 Hegel, *Logic*, trans A V Miller, Oxford University Press, 1978, p 41. 2 Hegel, *Aesthetics*, trans T.M. Knox, Oxford University Press, 1975, Vol I, p 31. 3 *Ibid*, Vol I, p 31. 4 *Ibid*, Vol I, pp 635. 5 *Ibid*, Vol I, pp 8-9. 6 *Ibid*, Vol I, p 16. 7 *Ibid*, Vol I, p 76. 8 *Ibid*, Vol I, p 78. 9 *Ibid*, Vol I, p 78. 10 *Ibid*, Vol I, p 85. 11 *Ibid*, Vol I, p 79. 12 *Ibid*, Vol I, p 87. 13 *Ibid*, Vol I, p 87. 14 *Ibid*, Vol I, p 89. 15 *Ibid*, Vol I, pp 83-4. 16 *Ibid*, Vol II, p 637. 17 *Ibid*, Vol II, p 640. 18 *Ibid*, Vol II, p 637 19 *Ibid*, Vol II, p 660. 20 *Ibid*, Vol II, p 660. 21 *Ibid*, Vol II, p 662. 22 *Ibid*, Vol II, p 663. 23 *Ibid*, Vol II, p 685.

GIANNI VATTIMO
THE END OF MODERNITY, THE END OF THE PROJECT?
On Architecture and Philosophy

The important thing to notice in the title of this essay is the question mark; one cannot insist on the equivalence of the 'end of modernity' and the 'end of the project'. I propose, therefore, to discuss the state of the project, and of the architectonic project in particular, in the light of a situation that in my view may be defined 'Post-Modern' – a term that is today still not in common usage, although this

varies according to geographical area. By 1987 J-F Lyotard had already declared the term 'Post-Modern' outworn, but listening to the topic of discussion in conferences and debates, there is reason enough not to consider the Post-Modern thematic obsolete, at least not in certain areas of *mittel-europaisch* culture. I believe, then, that one can still say in all seriousness that we shall – or do – find ourselves in a Post-Modern condition. Moreover, its character may be such as to give the impression that the very notion of a project has become problematic.

To begin a general definition of the Post-Modern condition, which I have already spoken about on many occasions in my books and essays, I would like to refer to two lines from Holderlin, often cited by Heidegger;

Voll Verdienst, doch dichterisch, wohnet
Der Mensch auf dieser Erde
(Full of merit, yet poetically, man
Dwells on this earth).

These lines from Hölderlin define the condition of man in the moment of transition to the Post-Modern; the *doch*, the 'yet', is what signals the turn. One can think of modernity, then, as defined by the idea of a dwelling *voll verdienst*, of a life 'full of merit' – which is to say, full of activity. The most conventional image of modernity is certainly that according to which modern man has taken his destiny into his own hands. He has abandoned the transcendence, superstition and faith of the past and has taken his own fate upon himself. One could indeed take this *voll verdienst* to be the most conventional – but perhaps also the truest – representation of modernity. A vast historical and philosophical tradition concurs in this vision of modernity as immanentism, laicization, secularization. As is well known, this tradition began with Kant and his definition of *Aufklarung*. The *doch*, then, altogether beyond Holderlin's intentions and perhaps those of Heidegger too, could mean the turn, the change in direction which brings us into the Post-Modern condition. Whereas, that is, modernity was characterized by an existence defined essentially in terms of projective activity and a drive towards the rationalization of reality by means of structures founded on thought and action, the Post-Modern would be the time when 'poetic' characteristics are rediscovered: 'doch dichterisch, wohnet/der Mensch auf dieser Erde' – yet poetically man/Dwells on this earth.

I would like to underline just one feature of the 'poetic', namely, its indefiniteness. To dwell poetically does not mean to dwell in such a way that one needs poetry, but to dwell with a sensitivity to the poetic, characterized by the impossibility, in a

sense, of defining clear cut boundaries between reality and imagination. If there is a passage from modernity to Post-Modernity, it seems to lie in a wearing away of the boundaries between the real and the unreal, or, at the very least, in a wearing away of the boundaries of the *real*. Without entering into a sociological analysis, we can nonetheless say that contemporary reality seems to exhibit a tendency to posit itself entirely at the level of simultaneity. Contemporary history is that phase of history in which everything tends to be presented in the form of simultaneity. For example, one could take the *terminus a quo* of the birth of contemporaneity to be the diffusion of the daily press, or, better still, the invention of media such as radio or television that are able to let us know what happens around the world 'in real time', as one might say. The 'reality' of real time, then, is given by the fact that there are technical means by which we can, so to speak, 'simultaneitize' events that take place all over the world. This 'simultaneitization' of history, of reality, is significant insofar as for apparently different reasons that may actually be the same – it occurs in a situation in which historicity as diachrony tends to waste away to nothing.

The 'mediatization' and 'simultaneitization' of our historicity take place in a world that is living through a crisis in the very notions of history and historicity. When we speak of History with a capital 'h', we assume that there is a single course along which we can place events that occur in America, in Africa or here at home. But this is no longer true. The historians were the first to lose faith in this schema: above all in recent decades, but actually ever since the expansion of schools like the French school of Annales, founded at the end of the twenties, the debates of historians have revolved around the problem of knowing whether there is a dominant history, a history that would be the basis for other different histories. For example, one speaks of the history of art, of micro-histories such as the history of kitchen utensils, the history of economy, as specialized histories that branch off from a principal history. Yet there always emerges an awareness that this principal history is not objective and external, but rather presupposes a subject with reasons for universalizing certain schemata. One of the most common realizations in contemporary historiography, then, is that history presupposes literary rhetorical schemata, different ways of telling stories. History, therefore, is not history, but histories, in the sense of stories that have been narrated and whose meaning depends on the perspective, the coordinates or the point of view adopted for their narration. We are witnessing a dissolution of historicity – in communal life, conditioned by technology, no less than in methodology, historical consciousness and philosophical reflection. Now, in the tradition of Western metaphysics, history is real to the extent that it is a realization and an articulation of a *Grund*, a foundation. This may be seen in the idea of 'revolution', a familiar concept in the Western tradition. But could revolution not also be called 'innovation'? A revolution is an innovation that leads that which happens – history back to its originary foundation: the Renaissance was a rebirth of Greece, in the same way as the French revolution, based on the thought of the *Aufklarung*, of the enlightenment, was itself set on returning to an original state, on regaining an authentic human condition etc. History, then, is affirmed as positively real to the degree that it realizes a foundation already present in an implicit form. But this conciliation between being and becoming presupposes the possibility of speaking of history as if it were a single course, in order that a rational schema may be identified within it. When it is no longer possible to speak of a single history, however, neither can there be any recourse to the rational schema. What is at stake in historicism is not merely establishing whether Hegel was right or wrong, but the fact that if one can no longer speak in terms of a single history, the only possibility of speaking of being as foundation is lost – as we see clearly in Nietzsche and Heidegger.

If these authors are read, that is, if Hegel, Nietzsche, Heidegger are read, one can no longer simply return to an earlier conception of the relation between the founded and the foundation. In our recent history, the development of the relation between founded and foundation has taken the form of historicism, which means that the rationality of reality is presented as the rational progress of events. Once it is no longer possible to speak of a rational progress of events because it is no longer possible to speak of progress (we are no longer imperial thinkers), then rationality as B*egrundung* (grounding) and as the substantial reality of that which is, is no longer given. What I mean to say, without insisting on further schematic philosophical detail, is that the 'simultaneitization' of reality in the contemporary world is, almost inevitably, also a 'simulacrization'. That which becomes simultaneous also becomes 'simulacral', in the sense that it concerns appearances that cannot be referred back to a basic rationality, to a true world – according to an expression Nietzsche uses in an aphorism from *Twighlight of the Idols* – since there is no longer the single thread of rationality that was found in historicism, and which served as the law of history.

In his *Zur Seinsfrage* (*The question of Being*), Heidegger writes the word *Sein* with a cross through it. Clearly, it was not a way of writing the word *Sein* in order to mean something else. Instead, it seems to me that this way of writing 'being' should be interpreted as having more or less the same meaning as the *doch* of the 'yet poetically man/Dwells . . .' Alternatively, perhaps it should be seen from the point of view of that which I have just described as 'simulacrization', or reality's turning into a simulacrum. In other words, in our present historical condition, we are witnessing a manifestation of being marked by disappearance, by becoming lighter, less cogent, less definite. Will the processing of the world into information not also serve to open a way of being of things in which it is no longer a simple matter to tell reality from the fictions of the imagination? In the end, what do we know of reality? Ours is a world where the channels by which our experience of reality is mediated have become increasingly explicit. To be sure, one can say that in medieval times too experience of external reality was mediated. For example, it was by the preacher, the priest, that people who spent almost their entire lives in a tiny village were told of the history of the world. But then the mediation was not visible: there was a form of mediation sufficiently unitary to blend with reality almost without trace. Today, the 'simulacrization' of reality is a combined effect of invention, innovation in information technology and a loss of centrality in the vision of history. It is not a case of saying that only today is the information we have of the world mediated; perhaps it has always been so. But in the past, in the time when mediation did not occur in situations of conflict between images of the world, it was not visible. We live in a situation where the mediation has become visible by virtue of the proliferation of perspectives with, say, social and political origins that make it difficult to identify the image with reality – about which, in turn, one no longer knows anything directly. We know only that if we want to produce an image of the world, we have to collect many different images. Yet even this does not absolutely guarantee that we that we shall be in a position to see the world as it 'truly' is, only that we shall no longer be conditioned by a single image, a single interpretation.

This is the framework within which, with particular attention to the theme of architecture, I shall try to redescribe the activity of the project.

Does planning a project in these conditions – those I have summarized with the notion of 'poetic dwelling' – open a way of being that is more free or less free? I don't know. But the task posed is to find legitimations for the project that no longer appeal to 'strong', natural, or even historical structures. For example, one can no longer say that there is a golden number, an ideal measure that can be used in the construction of buildings or the planning of cities, nor even that there are basic natural needs, since it is increasingly absurd to try to distinguish them from new needs induced by the market and therefore superfluous, not natural. It may be that as a philosopher I am particularly sensitive to this loss of 'foundation', but I believe that, at times, it may also be experienced by architects and planners as they reflect on their work. I know that often one receives a commission for a determinate project and then works from models. But even in this situation, it is increasingly difficult to find clear cut and convincing criteria to which one can refer. Those concerned with planning cities accept that planning does not appeal to ideal guidelines and work instead in the knowledge that it is a contractual matter. It is in all cases a question of social rhetoric, of exchanges, deals, the planning of what one is setting out to do and its conciliation with that which is already there, that is, of taking into account so many variables that one can no longer speak of a plan.

In keeping with this idea of planning, architecture is sometimes defined by 'strong' aesthetic criteria: it is a matter of creating a good project and a beautiful building. The notion of 'beautiful' in this instance cannot be referred back to Kant's aesthetics, inasmuch as beauty is not defined by objective criteria and there are no models one has to measure up to – as, for example, there are in classicism. What, then, is the criterion? How, in the situation described here in a philosophical-sociological manner that has hardly anything to do directly with the projective activity of architects and planners, can one imagine the activity of projecting, the working conditions of the architect or the planner? It seems to me that here, in analogy with philosophy, the only way of finding criteria consists in appealing to memory or, as Heidegger says, to *Ueberlieferung*, to handing down. We possess no criteria that may be traced back to the rational structure of man, the world, nature or anything else; not even to the inevitable, providential or rational, course of history. In philosophy as in architecture, we have nothing by which to orient ourselves but indications that we have inherited from the past. This view is not far removed from Wittgenstein's notion of language games, which are precisely domains of rationality in which the rules in force are given by the game itself. From Wittgenstein's, and to some extent Heidegger's, point of view, our existence is defined as a multiplicity of language games, or games in a broad sense, having an internal normative character that we have always to confront, and which says something to us, regardless of whether we modify, accept or reject the games themselves. The rationality we have at our disposal today, in the epoch of the end of metaphysics, is no longer like this, at least not if one accepts the presuppositions I have just described. There are rules of games in force or, in more Heideggerian terms, there is an *Ueberlieferung*, a handing down, that issues from the past, but not only from the past. It may also issue from other cultures, other communities in this multiplicity of communities of values that come to light in the world of the simulacrum. It is the proliferation of the simulacra that shows the simulacra for what they are, and their proliferation amounts to minorities, disparate and ethnic groups etc., having their say – which is precisely what occurs in the world of generalized information.

Does handing down, in this wide sense, offer up a meaning? Can it signify something more precise and detailed at the level of the project? In conclusion, I shall put forward, very briefly, three ideas that are really no more than consequences that may be drawn from these premises.

First and foremost, it should be underlined that the *Ueberlief-erung*, the handing down, does not issue only from the past, but from all the communities that have found a voice in, to use Ricoeur's expression, the conflict of interpretations in which we live. In this sense, moreover, the legitimation of the project – and I use the term legitimation not only in a critical sense, but also to mean that which can guide and orient the one who plans and carries out the project – issues not from a strong metaphysical 'foundation', but from the voices of different communities, speaking not only from the past, but from the present too. At this point the difference emerges between the viewpoint that I am putting forward and the criterion of the 'beautiful' work. The idea of an aesthetic value to the architectonic work as such, which can coexist with the conception of planning as contractual and mediatory, leads back to a choice, to an historically enrooted taste. In other words, to construct a good building, one has to refer to a determinate community amongst the multiplicity of communities that speak in our society, and one has to represent it in a definite way, for example, by building a beautiful mosque in Rome, recalling the Arab culture, whether the Arabs from Rome (of whom there are only a few), or the Arabs of the Arab world (who are more numerous), etc.. As a possible criterion, it derives from the metaphysical aesthetic tradition of the West, and in particular from Hegel, yet is applicable at the level of proliferation. In Hegel, the work of art represents absolute spirit in the form of the historical spirit of a people, which is to say, of an historical community. The work of art is classic – that is, valid – when it is an accomplished expression of the world-view of a community which recognizes itself in it. But would Hegel have said this if he had lived in a world of proliferating communities? At bottom, Hegel identified the most evolved human community with the community of XIX century Europe. The idea of a value, of a valid aesthetic linked to the complete representation of an historical community in a true or accomplished fashion, necessarily implies the idea that this historical community represents the highest point of evolutionary development. Hegel would never have maintained that a work of art could be perfect if it represented, for example, a bunch of criminals, in however accomplished a fashion it did so. He could not say this because a bunch of criminals does not have sufficient inner freedom to give themselves an accomplished representation. Hegel's judgment on the symbolic art of the Asiatic peoples reached the same diagnosis. The symbolic art of which Hegel speaks precedes classic art and is imperfect insofar as spirit's inner freedom has not reached a degree such that it could achieve adequate expression in an image. This means that the criterion of recog-

nizing aesthetic value in the ability to represent perfectly a living historical community necessarily implies a vision of history that comes back to historicism, or if one prefers, to an evolutionary view of history. In the context of the proliferation of communities, can we be satisfied with this criterion of representation typical of a world-view that lays out the other worldviews and considers them from an external and privileged point of view? In my opinion, this has become problematic. I believe, rather, that the criterion of aesthetic value, in this world of multiple models of existence, cannot be legitimated except via the multiplicity, a multiplicity lived explicitly as such, without any realist reservations. Nowadays, it could be said that what is *kitsch* is precisely the work presented as classic, which naively readvances a 'natural' or objective criterion; it has the look of certain very formal rules of dress that are only observed now in marginal communities. *Kitsch* is nothing but that which has pretensions to classic status in the context of a proliferation of voices and tastes. The problem, therefore, is one of seeing how to bring a conscious multiplicity into effect within the construction of the work. I cannot propose a definite solution to this problem. But it is not true that the classic view of the work gives criteria that are any clearer: they only appear to be so, but in fact one has always to appeal to the Kantian genius, or in the terms we are using here, to the artist as one aware of the multiplicity of voices and *Weltanschauungen* and capable of thematizing them whilst standing outside them. This is all as regards the first point of my conclusion.

The second point regards the concept of monumentality: the ability to listen to the *Ueberlieferung*, the handing down, from the past no less than from the present, may also be expressed in the forms of a new monumentality, or in less solemn terms, in the forms of a new ensemble of recognizable characteristics, of a 'recognizableness'. It is neither a response to a nostalgia for relocalization, nor a new offer to enroot our experience in some stable reality. It responds to a perhaps affinitive need for a symbolic and ornamental dimension. It is as if to say that the need for monumentality makes itself felt when architecture and planning, in their reciprocal relation, no longer respond clearly to immediate needs – shelter, clothing . . . – but are left in that indefinite state that derives from the principle of reality having been worn away. In this situation a need arises for ornamentation, for that ornament which has been the object of polemic between, for example, many functionalist and rationalist architects and which, in the present situation, seems to be widely and strongly reaffirmed. We have needs that are not immediate and vital but symbolic, and which emerge all the more when every deducible, metaphysical reason founded on the nature of man, the needs of life etc., is to some extent dissolved.

Viewed in this way, it is most instructive to consider what used to happen when the architects' clients were above all the monarch and the rich bourgoisie, in contrast to the current proliferation of communities and value-systems. The comparison suggests – and I come here to the third point in my conclusion – that the position of architect is increasingly less that of 'genius' and more that of a 'symbolic operator' with a clear awareness of what he is doing. I don't know if, for example, the court architects that built the hunting villa of the Dukes of Savoy in Turin were conscious of expressing in their work the aesthetic expectations of a monarch. They probably believed they were conforming to the classical models they had taken as guides for their activity. Today, this conception of architectonic creation, more even than poetic or literary creation, is no longer possible. The architect is no longer the functionary of humanity, just as the philosopher no longer thinks of him or herself as a functionary of humanity or interpreter of a common vision of the world, despite having more reason for doing so. The philosopher is always the interpreter of a community. Yet this does not mean referring back to an ethnicity, to groups or places. The real problem of the Post-Modern condition is that one can no longer make any appeal to these 'realities', in however naive a manner. Even when one is said to refer back to a community, one no longer does; the innocence is lost and one has to be able to work in an intermediary zone between an enrootedness in a place – in a community – and an explicit consciousness of multiplicity. This is what I mean by a 'new monumentality': building cities where one recognizes oneself, not only in the sense that there is a perception of shared values, but also in the sense that one recognizes where one is, that there are distinguishing 'marks'. We need to be able to build in such a way that these marks are there from the beginning, and do not become marks only subsequently, like the monuments of present cities that are, so to speak, 'reduced' to being territorial markers, whereas originally they were or wished to be the incarnation of the idea in the sensible, as Hegel would say. We are in a situation of conscious historicity that could even block creativity, as Nietzsche said in one of his essays the second *Untimely Meditations* – yet it is precisely this that we need. We need the ability to engage in building and in urban structure projects that satisfy these two 'conditions': an enrootedness in a place, and an explicit aware-ness of multiplicity.

I realize that these conclusions are not sufficient in them-selves, but they may open up discussion. Once the architect is no longer the functionary of humanity, nor the deductive rationalist, nor the gifted interpreter of a world-view, but the functionary of a society made up of communities, then projection must become something both more complex and more indefinite. This means, for example, that there is a rhetorical aspect to urban planning (and perhaps also to architectural projection) that is not merely a response to the need to provide persuasive justifications to the listening public. Instead, it reveals the problem of links with non-technical cultural traditions – in the city, the regions or the state – that must be heard and which condition the creation and development of the plan. In this sense a plan is a contract, not something that the city can simply apply straight away. It has the form of a utopia, so to speak, that guides the real future project, but which will itself never actually be realized as a project 'put into action' and 'applied' on the landscape. Gathered together in this statutory form of the project are all the conditions of rhetoric, persuasion and argumentation regarding the cultural traditions of the place in question, those different cultural traditions within the community that significantly modify and redefine the activity of the contemporary architect and planner.

MOSQUE, CAIRO

'I love beginnings. I marvel at beginnings. I think it is beginning that confirms continuation. If it did not, nothing could be or would be. I revere learning because it is a fundamental inspiration. It isn't just something which has to do with duty; it is born into us. The will to learn, the desire to learn, is one of the greatest of inspirations. I am not that impressed by education. Learning, yes; education is something which is always on trial because no system can ever capture the real meaning of learning.'
Louis Kahn

LOUIS KAHN, SKETCHES OF KARNAK

CHRISTIAN GIRARD
THE OCEANSHIP THEORY
Architectural Epistemology in Rough Waters

LOUIS KAHN, SKETCH OF DELPHI

Nowadays architecture is a very insecure discipline: its search for legitimacy is so compelling that it has brought it into the vicinity of philosophy.[1] The number of texts that have been published in this domain does not contradict the fact that a critical epistemology of architecture remains a task to be attempted. After two decades that have seen the architectural field crisscrossed by different socio-

logical, linguistic and semiological approaches, the eighties will be remembered as a period when some architects have turned towards Boulder, philosophy . Moreover, it is also a decade when at last philosophy came to put architecture under scrutiny wearing neither the lenses of traditional aesthetics nor art history.

For better or for worse, a specific philosophical body of work, namely 'deconstruction' has been willing and to some extent, able to establish a connection with the architectural realm. Or what could be taken as a junction if compared to the previous state of mutual ignorance in which the two practices carefully remained. A handful of architectural critics and historians did refer to philosophical works – C.Rowe, A. Colquhoun or M. Tafuri, to name only some of the foremost – but in doing so they never pretended to cross the borders and stayed in the known boundaries of the historiography, theory and criticism of architecture.

Even though I accept Richard Rorty's arguments concerning 'the demise of foundational epistemology'. A 'nonepistemological sort of philosophy' can be elaborated as Kuhn, Dewey, Sellars and Feyerabend have shown, 'one which gives up any hope of the 'transcendental'[2] it is none the less convenient to keep the notion of 'epistemology' for two reasons: in in the first place it prevents us from exploring the rather vague territory of

'philosophy and architecture' and secondly it is one of the most productive areas of thinking today, thanks to the development of what can be roughly labelled a post-structuralist epistemology or a non-positivist epistemology.

If the legitimacy of architecture is a question that arises with great regularity, it is only recently that architects and historians or critics have tried to answer by analysing concepts. The very idea of 'concept' has been fashionable in architecture ever since the end of the seventies. Today, every architect uses his or her own brand of conceptualization and there are very few who do not claim at least one concept behind their projects. There is a re-activation of the power of words which has little to do with the earlier practice in which architecture borrowed discourses from sociology, semiology, linguistics and psycho-analysis. The discourses now being held are no longer meant to give a *posteriori* explanations to the works of architecture: they support the design process from beginning to end. Or this is what we are told. However, it is true that more and more architects have conceptual pretensions out of keeping with the theoretical means they give themselves to achieve such conceptualization.

Architects have increasingly tended to believe that the more they would import concepts from other fields the more their practice would gain recognition. Such a quest is useless. Indeed, the types of relationship that architecture may develop with different branches of contemporary knowledge bear witness in their own way to the impossibility of a 'general epistemology'. Not only has the question of the capacity of architecture to reach an objective positive self-awareness become pointless, it should no longer be raised. The point is to have architectural theory released from positive schemata as well as from constantly calling upon or resorting to the ideology of reconciling art and science. What could a theory of architecture be when global knowledge together with a universal epistemology of knowledge has gone ?

It would be a discourse produced in such a way that it both takes into account the 'nomadic' character of the concept it uses and gives up any operational goal in the design process. In other words, a theory of architecture has nothing in common with what is meant by a science or by scientific knowledge. It cannot correspond to a scientific knowledge of the discipline nor can it claim architectural practice as its direct goal. This is why we prefer to speak of the 'indisciplined' nature of architecture .

What is to be understood by the idea of the 'nomadic' character of concepts ? Far from being able to constitute a closed conceptual system meeting the positivist criterions of scientificity, the conceptual entities developed by any theory – be it architectural or other – remain scattered and always liable to become metaphoric. They keep infringing on extra-linguistic grounds, getting entangled with affects, drives, materials which do not obey the so-called 'rules' of language and do not form a 'system'. In such conditions a theory of architecture can neither describe nor systematise, translate, reproduce or explain the architectural design process. Pure instrumentality becomes impossible.

From this standpoint, the only distinction that can be made between a theory of architecture and a doctrine would have to be found in its attitude towards its own object and its own tools. The theory (or rather, what would stand as a theory) would then be a recognition of metaphor-concepts,[3] of their autonomy from any ruling or organizing still grounded in the postulates of classical 'episteme' or those of modernity. As regards the corresponding doctrine, it would result from implementing these nomadic concepts, even consciously, without ever definitively accepting their incapacity to enter into a system or to be systematized. The theory would then have an ironic attitude and the doctrine would be tinged with blindness. In all cases, the difference would never lie in different degrees of scientificity.

By playing with 'nomadic concepts', architectural thinking succeeds in becoming autonomous while interpreting parts of disciplines or even whole disciplines as V. Gregotti did with the notion of geography .

The hypothesis of 'nomadic concepts' does not provide a reading grid for architecture and does not even offer a convenient tool for its analysis. On the contrary, it suggests that grids are of no avail. Architecture refuses to have such systems applied to it. All the efforts to promote a 'reading of architecture' or an 'architecture as text' are nothing more than the enactment of a grid fantasm. Any architectural design involves at times intense rationalization but it also needs to draw such a number of relationships and correspondences between heterogenous or definitively incongruous elements, that it eludes any attempt at imposing a systematic or structural hold on it. Contrarily to what can often be read, the design process cannot be compared to synthetizing elements of knowledge called upon by the architect: such an idealistic view is akin to a myth. Nomadic concepts do not produce a synthesis: they only make it possible, in a transient way, punctually, for heterogenous levels of reality to combine with each other, to conglomerate, into new dimensions or 'plateaux'[4] to use the terminology of Deleuze and Guattari. It is the case with the concept of type which during the

last two decades allowed a convergence of the socio-economic and formal aspects of architecture.

From a rational and, to some extent, operative concept, 'type' drifted towards less firm grounds: 'type became not merely a method of taxonomic analysis – no longer simply a continuation of nineteenth century natural science – but a poetic'.[5] With the notion of 'poetic' we enter a province foreign to epistemological enquiries.

There is another consequence to these propositions. The common analogy between architecture and language which has been condemned as unscientific, viewed from that new angle, seems quite 'innocent'. It must be exempted from any normative evaluation. The linguistic analogy can have its origin in local, punctual, infinitisimal movements, it can appear under the cover of nomadic concepts and, in that case, according to what we have just suggested, still be theoretically valid. In this respect, Charles Jencks' work, which has been generally overlooked by 'theoreticians' of architecture, could in fact be seen as one of the last possible forms of theoretical activity in architecture. This claim will work to distort the commonly accepted meaning of 'theoretical activity'.

Thanks to his constant production of labels, coined words, verbal creations, Jencks shows he has recognized the irretrievable nomadic character of concepts in architecture and the flexibility which belongs to them. In the last analysis, the idea of post-modernism can stand as a perfect prototype of a nomadic concept. It's a concept impossible to locate and this is why it succeeded so well, beyond the dreams of its promoter. Needless to say 'deconstruction' is another good example of nomadic concept.

There is a very special architectural criticism tool which is questioned by what is described under the name of nomadic concepts: the notion of metaphor. It seems that architectural historians and critics will never cease to use this concept without ever discussing it. There is no stronger example of its overwhelming strength than the way it has replaced, in the language of the critic, the banished notion of style as a stereotype, used and abused. On this matter, Jencks' approach has indeed been anything but rigourous: despite his long time interest in rhetorics and semiology, he has always kept a simplistic stand on metaphor.[6]

In the twenties, Le Corbusier drew a section of an ocean liner which happened to be the Titanic. Later he also drew the deck of the oceanship which was taking him to South-America and wrote on his perspective sketch: 'pour l'immeuble d'Alger = excellent/ rechercher les coupes du paquebot' ('for the Algiers building = excellent/find the section drawings of the oceanliner'). As is well known, Le Corbusier's designs were often given the taste or flavour of an ocean liner. For most of the critics up to now[7] this is nothing more than an another example of metaphoric elaboration in the architectural field. Not only this linguistic analogy has all the failures of any linguistic analogies and, at the same time, its sheer innocence; but it is of little help to grasp what was at stake in Le Corbusier's work. Incidentally, there are hardly any portholes to be found in his complete work. He has designed with naval vessels in mind, yet his projects never fell into the 'style paquebot', or into the 'streamlined' fashion .

What needs to be documented is the process by which something like an 'oceanlinerity' (to use a provisional and, it must be admitted, inelegant, coinage) acts upon Le Corbusier's mental universe. Memories, references, archetypes, sources of formal inspiration, can never be restricted to a simple linguistic analogy. Le Corbusier, but also Patout, Herbst, Mallet-Stevens in the thirties, or more recently Eisenman, Meier, Rogers, and a host of architects are undergoing a distinctly 'oceanship *drive*'. They seem to share some kind of deep move or affects with whatever is linked to oceanliners. Namely: the sea, the steam machines, the steel - its smoothness, its sound, its reflection - the bolts, the whole voyage mood, the idea of speed. All this combined in various ways represents the 'oceanlinerity' and accounts for much more than a spatial image or configuration to be 'metaphorically' transferred to architecture. The liner (the object) is not a mere model to be initiated – contrary to usual interpretations - the liner (the word) is not a mere concept to shift according to Colqhoun's argument, see note 7, nor is it simply a metaphor. The liner (the word, the object) is the addition of all these operations within and outside language: it is a concept and a metaphor. It is an ecstatic body, a feeling, an affect, an ordering of multiple facets.

Reading Le Corbusier gives some hints on how such a complex alchemy can pervade the architect's mental – and corporal – stock of references. It suffices to note how the mere word 'paquebot' ('oceanliner') is used, re-used and worked upon in Le Corbusier's discourse (written or spoken). Verbalisation is one very effective means of transferring, carrying, diffusing, global environmental images. Thus, at one point, there exists and continue to exist, an oceanliner sensibility, yet it is not really a *Zeitgeist*: it is less than that, but perhaps more precise. A fixation on a formal condition, a mind setter, a nondescript fusion device. But it is not a reminiscence, not a bow to the past.

A noun can be at the same time an ordinary everyday notion and an effective concept: through its different uses in architectural practice 'oceanship' becomes a remarkable . . . conceptual too.

The same indirect instrumental necessity leads architects like Louis Kahn to celebrate 'Silence' or 'a building's urge to come into being', Vittorio Gregotti to speak of 'geography' and 'territory' or to endlessly repeat the notion of 'discipline' in each of his *Casabella* editorials, as a refrain, and Peter Eisenman to comment, in his early works, upon the 'deep structure' and then to keep commenting from 1972 up to now on the 'architectural sign'.[8]

At the risk of being repetitive, further emphasis needs to be placed on the use and practice of metaphor. It is most intriguing, for example, to see Derrida, one of the foremost contemporary analysts of 'metaphor' write: 'Contrary to what it seems, 'deconstruction' is not an architectural metaphor. The word should, it will name an architectural thought, an on-going thought. First it is not a metaphor. We don't give any credit here to the concept of metaphor'.[9] If there were at least one single certainty about 'deconstruction', it would be that it is, in part, an architectural metaphor. More often than not, it is precisely nothing more than that: an architectural metaphor. No denial will do: no absolute purification of language from metaphors is possible. And, thanks to Derrida's decisive insights any will to oppose definitely metaphor and concept is just a step back into metaphysics. This is why the aphorism quoted above seems a serious discrepancy in Derrida's thought as Christopher Norris has rightly noted in his interview with him. Things become even more surprising if we quote a conference where Derrida himself comments on 'those typical moments when, using formulas one would be tempted to receive as metaphors, Heidegger points out that they are not'.[10] To negate any metaphorical presence in a text where metaphor remains evidently encapsulated is a ritual exercise continental philosophers often indulge in. For instance, the epistemological writings of Michel Serres are, to a certain point, made of this constant balance between a metaphorical discourse and a denial of any metaphor.[11] It is no wonder therefore that his work has been progressively absorbed by its writing style and acclaimed

as highly poetic. The problem is that as soon as a philosophy (or an epistemological endeavour) is accepted and treated in the poetical realm it often starts to loose much of its strength. The figure of denial has also become an easy cliche in architectural thinking. No one is fooled however, when reading, for example Mark Wrigley, on Deconstruction: 'The use of the formal vocabulary of Constructivism is therefore not a historical game . . .', 'deconstructivist architecture does not constitute an avant-garde.' and of course 'This is not a style'[12] to which we could oppose Magritte's famous 'This is not a pipe' painting. Philip Johnson sets the tone: 'however delicious it would be to declare again a new style, that is not the case today. Deconstructivist architecture is not a new style' . . .[13] but the very fact of writing 'deconstructivist architecture' is not altogether innocent. And if 'No generally persuasive '-ism' has appeared' what does an '-ist' stands for? The play on the postfix is in itself interesting: 'deconstructivist', 'deconstructivism', and 'deconstructionist architecture' have all been used here and there. We could add: have been phantasmed about and verbalised. To locate verbalisation within the architectural process as an element among others, side by side with the drafting activity, is far from enough. And sticking to the idea of an architectural 'text' does not, finally, really pay tribute to the complex role play which is at stake. The 'word-making machine' once evoked by Kisho Kurokawa[14] seldom stops. Logocentrism is the unescapable horizon on which things must be observed.

The 'architectural text' metaphor is indeed a reduction of the worst kind, for it represses all that would not fit in the flat unidimensional format. The concept (and, of course metaphor) of 'trace' has been exactly and rightly proposed to avoid such crude reduction. From words to project and project to words, the drawing and drafting activity sets itself as an autonomous world of exploration. The 'drawing as text' analogy raises more questions than it answers by reactivating a search for meaning when such a capture remains value-laden.

In this sense, Eisenman's harshest critic is without any doubt Daniel Libeskind. The author of Cham*ber Works* (1983) pushed the graphic experimentation to the point where he has no other comment than a: 'it is a Not-Architecture'.[15] Later on, Libeskind raised Eisenman textual phantasms far beyond its limits.. bringing us back to the surrealists' automatic writing: 'Ow*erp*. Ow erp, owerpower, pow er po werpower pow er' – and so on . . .[16] Libeskind throws architecture into language instead of simulating a convergence between them. Any speech-act, any discourse, any text struggles with the logocentric attraction. Put down a word on a sheet of paper, pronounce a word: it is always a metaphor and it is always a concept. It is a metaphor-concept.

Andrew Benjamin's[17] use of the concept of 'enactment' pertains to what we are trying to argue here. An enactment needs or postulates a language inscription. Action, movement, motion, process, dynamism are provoked, initiated from within the language region (the logo-centre) towards its externality. In several texts, Benjamin's writing firmly grasps its object of thought in terms of 'enactment'. What else allows enactment than the metaphor-concepts, the 'nomadic concepts', the perpetual language glissandos . . . towards a centre at the same time as towards a radical periphery?

In conclusion therefore it is the impossibility of writing outside the process of language – outside of language as a process – which entails that simple denial can never stem language power. Reworking architecture concepts as nomadism allows them to work outside the predetermined realm of metaphysics as well as the denial of that realm.

Notes

1 In this respect, the fact that the Library of Congress Cataloging-in-Publication Data classifies P. Eisensman's *Houses of cards*, Oxford University Press, 1987, first under the heading 'Philosophy' is a remarkable accomplishment.

2 R. Rorty, *Philosophy and the Mirror of Nature*, Princeton, Princeton University Press, 1979, p. 381.

3 C. Girard, *Architecture et Concepts Nomades. Traite d'Indiscipline*, P. Mardaga, Bruxelles, 1986. Since our essay was published, the idea of 'nomadic concepts' has been transferred to the epistemological realm in a collective work edited by I. Stengers *Science a l'autre Des concepts nomades*, Le Seuil, Paris, 1987, in this process, from architecture to epistemology, the very concept of 'nomadic concept' can be easily grasped.

4 G. Deleuze, F. Guattari, *Mille plateaux*, Les Editions de Minuit, Paris, 1980.

5 A. Vidler, 'On Type', in: *Skyline*, New York, January 1979, p. 2.

6 C. Jencks, *The Language of Post-Modern Architecture*, Academy Editions, London, 1977, see Part Two: The Modes of Architectural Communication.

7 Even A. Colquhoun in 'Displacements of Concepts' *Architectural Design*, No 4, 1 972, p. 236, sticks to the metaphorical analogy on the same topic of the ocean liner in Le Corbusier's work.

8 For further interpretation of Le Corbusier's 'oceanship' drive, see: C. Girard. 'L'imaginaire transatlantique de Le Corbusier' in: *Le Corbusier. Ie passé à réaction poétique*, Caisse nationale des Monuments historiques et des Sites, Paris, 1988, pp. 191-197 catalogue of the exhibit held at Hotel de Sully (9.12.1897-6.3.1988).

8 'Up to now' means at least up to *The House of Cards*, published in 1987 where we read: 'All building must support, shelter, enclose, allow access. Therefore in order to distinguish architecture from building there must be an intentional act. the form must evidence, or signify, an intention that is architectural. Therefore, at the most fundamental level, the distiction between building and architecture depends on the presence in the latter of a 'sign of architecture'. P. Eisenman, Misreading, in: *The House of Cards*. Albeit his derridian (mis)readings, a strong metaphysic of the sign still pervades Eisenman's thinking.

9 J. Derrida '52 aphorismes pour un avant-propos' in: *Mesure pour Mesure. Architecture & Philosophie*, Cahiers du CCl, Centre G.Pompidou, Paris, 1987, Aphorisme No 48, 1972. 'White Mythology: Metaphor in the Text of Philosophy', Margins of Philosophy, trans. A. Bass, Chicago: University of Chicago Press, 1982. See also Jacques Derrida In Discussion with Christopher Norris, retranscription of a march 1988 interview, *Deconstruction II*, Architectural Design, Vol 58, No 1/2, 1989, pp. 7-11, especially p. 6.

10 J. Derrida, Le retrait de la metaphore, *Psyche Inventions de l'autre*, Galilee, Paris, 1987, p. 82.

11 M. Serres, *Hermes I. II. III. IV*, Editions de Minuit, Paris, 1969, 1972, 1974, 1977, 1980. The conversion of the epistemological and metaphorical gamble into a pseudo-poetical writing starts with *Genese*, Grasset, Paris, 1982.

12 M. Wigley, Deconstructivist Architecture, in: *Deconstructivist Architecture*, MOMA, New York, 1988 pp.10-20.

13 P. Johnson, Preface, ibid. pp. 7-8.

14 All sorts of words tumble forth, as if ejected from a word-making machine (. . .)' K. Kurokawa, *Metabolism in Architecture*, Westview Press, Boulder, 1977.

15 D. Libeskind, *Chamber Works: Architectural Meditations on Themes from Heraclitus*, Folio 1, Architectural Association, 1983. With essays by P. Eisenman, K. Forster, J. Hejduk and A. Rossi. For an acurate review, see R. Evans: 'In front of lines that leave nothing behind', AA File No 6, May 1984, pp. 89-96. Evans gave also a seminal critique of Eisenman's work where he insisted on the more than ambivalent role he confers to words; see: 'Not for wrapping purposes' in AA File No 10, 1985, pp. 68-74.

16 D. Libeskind, Architecture 1, in: *Line of fire*, Electa Spa, Milan, 1988.

17 A. Benjamin, Eisenman and the Housing of Tradition, *Oxford Art Journal*, April 1989, and Deconstruction II, *Architectural Design*, Vol 58 No 1/2, 1989, pp. 63-66; The redemption of value: Laporte, writing as Abkurzung, *Paragraph*, Oxford University Press, Volume 12,1989, pp. 23-36.

———— * ————

MARK WIGLEY

ARCHITECTURE AFTER PHILOSOPHY:
Le Corbusier and the Emperor's New Paint

RIPOLIN POSTER, EUGENE VAVASSEUR, 1898

What is the place of architecture? How is it placed before it places? I mean what is it to write here, in the Journal of Philosophy and the Visual Arts, of 'Philosophy and Architecture'? What is the status of this familiar and that places architecture in the arts and after philosophy? But more than that, that places architecture in the visual. The and sustains an institutional history which prescribes where

this 'visual art' can be seen, from where it can be seen, what kind of vision is required and who sees. Of course, this history needs to be interrogated. But such questions of visuality must be, at least, doubled here because they are also architectural questions. To interrogate the institutional mechanisms that construct architecture as visible is to investigate the place of architecture, how it inhabits culture before culture inhabits it, how it is housed. Indeed, it is a question of its architecture. Architecture is involved in the construction of the visual before it is placed in the visual. It is this convolution that organises the domestic life of that old couple philosophy and architecture.

Some of the strange lines that bind visuality and architecture can be traced through Le Corbusier's lesser known 1925 text *The Decorative Art of Today,* which he describes, in a preface added in 1959, as the result of an extended inquiry which began with the question 'Where is architecture?'.[1]

The Look of Modernity
The Decorative Art of Today examines the objects of contemporary everyday life, condemning those that have ornate decoration and praising those without it. The lie of decoration is that it is added to objects as a kind of mask. It is a form of 'disguise', a representational layer inserted between the new reality of the modern object which results from modern techniques of produc-

tion and the new reality of modern life those techniques make possible. Misrepresenting both, it produces historical and spatial alienation by sustaining a nostalgic fantasy in the face of modernity. Like the everyday object, architecture has to discard the representational debris that clutters the surface of its structures and distracts the eye from modernity.

This erasure of decoration is seen as the necessary gesture of a civilised society true to itself. Civilisation is precisely defined as the elimination of the 'superfluous' in favour of the 'essential' and the paradigm of inessential surplus is decoration. Its removal liberates a new visual order as civilisation is a gradual passage from the sensual to the intellectual, from the tactile to the visual. Decoration's 'caresses of the senses' are abandoned in favour of the visual harmony of proportion. The materiality of representation is abandoned in favour of the immateriality of clear vision.

This erasure of decoration is a form of purification. The argument concludes with the chapter *A Coat of Whitewash: The Law of Ripolin* which advocates replacing the degenerate layer of decoration that lines buildings with a coat of whitewash. The whitewash is a form of architectural hygiene to be carried out in the name of visible truth: 'His *home is* made clean . There are no more dirty, dark corners. *Everything is shown as it is.*'[2] The true status of the object is exposed. Cleansed of its representational

84

masks, it is simply present in its pure state, transparent to the viewer: 'Law of Ripolin, Coat of Whitewash: Elimination of the equivocal. Concentration of intention on its proper object. Attention concentrated on the object. An object is held to be made only out of necessity, for a specific purpose, and to be made with perfection.'[3] The look of modernity is that of utility perfected, function without excess, the smooth naked object cleansed of all representational texture: the architectural machine.

The apparent consequence of this argument is rehearsed within the canonic interpretation of early Le Corbusier. The white villas are interpreted in terms of a visual logic of transparency to function – the machine aesthetic – understood as an architecture of abstraction emerging from the rationalism of modern technology. But surprisingly the striking whiteness of the villas is not examined as such. It is taken for granted. At the moment the modern movement is transformed into a cannon, the whiteness becomes inconspicuous, regardless of its undeniable dominance in practice. At most, it is referred to in passing as 'neutral', 'ground', 'pure', 'silent', 'degree-zero', 'reduction', 'essential'. This rhetoric is passed on uncritically into 'critical' language and disseminated.[4]

The buildings are understood as objects, machines to be looked at, inhabited by a viewer who is detached from them, inhabited precisely by being looked at, whether it be by the user, visitor, neighbour, critic, or reader of architectural publications. The whitewash is tacitly understood as part of the look, but its relationship to Le Corbusier's arguments about the status of architecture in industrialised society are not examined. The obvious tension between the opaqueness of the white surface and the transparency of 'modernism' is not problematised. Precisely by being made part of a look, the white wall is looked through. This privileging of the look seems to be supported by Le Corbusier's writing which everywhere appears to privilege the visual. But the nature of that look and that privilege is not examined. The theory of the white surface becomes as transparent to the critics as the white wall itself. It is the critics who have 'eyes that do not see'. But why is it necessary for the whiteness to be ignored by the canon? What is preserved by this blindness?

Clearly, Le Corbusier's argument has to be understood in terms of the central role of whiteness in the extended history of the concept of cleanliness which, as Vigarello argues, 'consists, in the last analysis, of one dominant theme: the establishment, in western society, of a self-sufficient physical sphere, its enlargement, and the reinforcement of its frontiers, to the point of excluding the gase of others.'[5] Whiteness plays a key role in the constitution of space understood in terms of an economy of vision. Some kind of displacement of that economy is integral to the construction of modern space. Le Corbusier's arguments about whitewash are arguments about visuality. What cannot be seen by the critics is a particular theory of looking that subverts their own institutional practices.

For Le Corbusier, the look of whitewash is not simply the look of modernity. While the text employs the white walls of a transatlantic liner as a model, whitewash is not the mark of the industrialised twentieth century but of civilisation as such.

> Whitewash exists wherever people have preserved intact the balanced structure of a harmonious culture. Once an extraneous element opposed to the harmony of the system has been introduced, whitewash disappears. . . Whitewash has been associated with human habitation since the birth of mankind. Stones are burnt, crushed and thinned with water – and the walls take on the purest white, an extraordinarily beautiful white.[6]

The collapse of authentic culture caused by the intrusion of otherness is identified with the loss of whitewash and degenera-

tion into the sensuous excesses of decoration. The white walls of the ocean liner mark the maturing of the very industrial culture responsible for 'brutally driving out' vernacular whitewash. It is the status of the object in the twentieth century that is new, not its coating with whitewash. The neutrality of whitewash is therefore more historical than formal.

But it is not a passive neutrality. The whitewash is not simply what is left behind after the removal of decoration. It is the active mechanism of erasure. More than a clean surface, it is a cleaning agent, cleaning the body in order to liberate the eye. The whitewash makes the objects of everyday life visible, as any impurity, any decorative excess would leave a 'stain' on its surface:

> On white ripolin walls these accretions of dead things from the past would be intolerable: they would leave a stain. Whereas the stains do not show on the medley of our damasks and patterned wallpapers . . . If the house is all white, the outline of things stands out from it without any possibility of transgression: their volume shows clearly; their colour is distinct.[7]

More than just the appropriate setting for the look, a neutral background, like a gallery wall, and even more than the active removal of distractions from the eye, the whitewash is itself an eye: 'Put on it anything dishonest or in bad taste – it hits you in the eye. It is rather like an X-ray of beauty. It is a court of assise in permanent session. It is the eye of truth.'[8] It is not simply the look of cleanliness but a cleaning of the look, a focusing of the eye. Not a machine for looking at but a machine for looking.

But does this viewing mechanism only focus on the supplements of building: objects placed inside, outside, or on its surfaces? What happens when it catches the building in its own look? What does it see in architecture?

The Clothing of Space

Le Corbusier's account of civilisation as progress from the sensuality of decoration to the abstraction of form through the progressive removal of ornament is, of course, taken from Adolf Loos' notorious criminalisation of ornament:

> 'The lower the culture, the more apparent the ornament. Ornament is something that must be overcome. The Papuan and the criminal ornament their skin. . . But the bicycle and the steam engine are free of ornament. The march of civilisation systematically liberates object after object from ornamentation.'[9]

Le Corbusier's text appropriates those of Loos much more than its two brief references to Loos indicate.[10] It is everywhere indebted to Loos.[11] In Loos' canonic essay 'Ornament and Crime', which Le Corbusier republished in the first issue of *L'Esprit Nouveau* in 1920, the removal of ornament is a process of purification which ends up with the whitewash: *The evolution of culture is synonymous with the removal of ornament from objects of daily use. . . We have outgrown ornament . . . Soon the streets of the cities will glow like white walls!*[12] This concern with whitewash can be traced throughout Loos's writing. The degeneration of contemporary architecture is repeatedly opposed to the construction of the vernacular house, which concludes when the peasant 'makes a large tub of distemper and paints the house a beautiful white'.[13] The aesthetic purity of this traditional gesture is now guaranteed by principles of modern hygiene. As with Corbusier, the whitewash is seen as at once the mark of modernity and tradition, the erasure of the historical and its restoration crucial role in Le Corbusier's thought seems to have been neglected by architectural discourse, should be understood in a context that precisely undermines that discourse .[14] The *Law of Ripolin is* a specific reference to Loos's, *Law of* Dressing (Bekleidung). [15] With this law, Loos legislates against any 'confusion' between a material and its dressing. The dressings must not simulate the material they cover. Rather, they must only 'reveal clearly their own meaning as dressing for the wall surface'[16], identifying their detachment from a structure without identifying that structure. It must be understood as accessory without revealing that to which it is added. Consequently, Loos does not simply advocate the removal of decoration in order to reveal the material condition of the building as an object. What is revealed is precisely the accessory as such, neither structure nor decoration. The perception of a building is the perception its accessories, its layer of cladding.

The idea of the whitewash is bound to this other perception in which structure is dissimulated by an added layer that can be as thin as a coat of paint. Indeed, for Loos the coat of paint is the paradigm. The *Law of Dressing* emerges from a reading of the traditional whitewashed wall. His argument turns on an anecdote about the perception of the difference between a window frame that has been stained and one that is painted white. The twentieth century invention of wood staining is opposed to the peasant tradition in which pure colors are set against the 'freshly whitewashed wall.' The transparency of the stain is dismissed in favour of the opaque mask of white paint: 'wood may be painted any colour except one – the colour of wood.'[17] Immediately, Le Corbusier has to be thought in terms of a nineteenth century logic of veiling rather than transparency.

The *Law of Dressing* is, in turn, a specific reference to Gottfried Semper's *Principle of Dressing* which precisely defines the essence of architecture to be its covering layer. Because of this privileging of the supplement, traditional criticism has always distanced Semper from modern architecture (and even from Loos).[18] Semper retells the story of the origin of architecture retold at least since Vitruvius. No longer does architecture originate in the construction of material protection, a simple wooden shelter, which is then supplemented and represented by successive ornamental traditions – such that ornament is always representative of, and subordinate to, the original structure (at once the first structure built by man and the structure that is built first in a contemporary building). The story of architecture is no longer one of naked structures gradually dressed with ornament: 'Rather, it was with all the simplicity of its basic forms highly decorated and glittering from the start, since its childhood.'[19]

For Semper, building begins with the use of woven fabrics to define social space. Specifically, the space of domesticity. The textile are not simply placed within space to define a certain interiority. Rather, they are the production of space itself. Weaving is used 'as a means to make the 'home', the *inner life* separated from the *outer life,* and as the formal creation of the idea of space.'[20] This primordial definition of inside and, therefore, for the first time, outside, with textiles not only precedes the construction of solid walls but continues to organise the building when such construction begins. Solid structure follows, and is subordinate to, what appear to be merely its accessories:

> Hanging carpets remained the true walls, the visible boundaries of space. The often solid walls behind them were necessary for reasons that had nothing to do with the creation of space; they were needed for security, for supporting a load, for their permanence and so on. Wherever the need for these secondary functions did not arise, the carpets remained the original means of separating space. Even where building solid walls became necessary, the latter were only the inner, invisible structure hidden behind the true and legitimate representatives of the wall, the colourful woven carpets.[21]

The textile is a mask which dissimulates rather than represents the structure. The material wall is no more than a prop, a contingent piece of 'scaffolding', 'foreign' to the production of the building, merely a supporting player, playing the role of support, supporting precisely because it does not play. Architecture is located within the play of signs. Space is produced within language. As its origin is dissimulation, its essence is no longer construction but the masking of construction. Just as the institution of the family is made possible through the production of domestic space with a mask, the larger community is made possible through the production of public space through masquerade. Public buildings, in the form of monumental architecture, are seen to derive from the fixing in one place of the once mobile 'improvised scaffolding' on which hung the patterned fabrics and decorations of the festivals that defined social life. The space of the public is that of those signs.

Semper identifies the textile essence of architecture, the dissimulating fabric, the fabrication of architecture, with the clothing of the body. He draws on the identity between the German words for wall (Wand) and dress (Gewand) to establish the *Principle of Dressing* as 'true essence' of architecture. The chapter *Correlation of Costume with Architecture* explains the 'intimate' relationship between clothing and the arts and demonstrates the 'direct influence' of developments in clothing on developments in the arts. But architecture does not follow or resemble clothing. On the contrary, clothing follows architecture.

The definition of domestic interiority precedes the definition of the interiority of the body.[22] The clothing of the individual follows the clothing of the family. The body is only defined by being covered in the face of language, the surrogate skin of the building. The evolution of skin, the surface with which spatiality is produced, is the evolution of the social.

In a footnote to his treatise, Semper inverts the ethnocentric teleology of social progress. Civilisation is no longer detachment from primitive material desire. Primitive desire is recast as dissimulation. Culture does not precede its masks. It is no more than masking. The highest art form is no longer that which is most distant from the material desires of the primitive but that which most successful develops the primitive dissimulation of materiality by dissimulating even the mechanisms of dissimulation:

> I think that the *dressing* and the *mask* are as old as human civilisation. . . The denial of reality, of material, is necessary if form is to emerge as a meaningful symbol, as an autonomous creation of man. Let us make forgotten the means that need be used for the desired artistic effect and not proclaim them too loudly, thus missing our part miserably. The untainted feeling led primitive man to the denial of reality in all early artistic endeavours; the great, true masters of art in every field returned to it – only these men in times of high artistic development also *masked the material of the mask.'*[23]

The subordination and dissimulation of material does not imply ignorance or disregard of material.[24] On the contrary, it is the 'mastery' of material. Materiality is hidden by being mastered. Only through a detailed understanding of the construction can it be effaced – reduced to an invisible prop.[25]

Repeatedly identifying architecture with clothing, Loos follows Semper's arguments closely.[26] This is nowhere more explicit than in his essay *The Principle of Dressing* in which architecture emerges from textiles and structure is but the scaffolding added to hold them up.

> The architect's general task is to provide a warm and livable space. Carpets are warm and livable. He decides for this reason to spread out one carpet on the floor and to hang up four to form the four walls. But you cannot build a house out of carpets. Both the carpet and the floor and the tapestry

on the wall require a structural frame to hold them in the correct place. To invent this frame is the architect's second task. This is the correct and logical path to be followed in architecture. It was in this sequence that mankind learned how to build. In the beginning was dressing.[27]

The textile masks the structure but does not misrepresent it. It hides the building but does not disguise it. Following Semper, Loos is against lying. The dressing dissimulates in the name of truth. It must register its independence without identifying that from which it is independent. Materials organise forms but the material of the dressing is different from that of construction, and the form of a building is only produced by its cladding. The structural prop is not revealed, even as prop.

Even in paying attention to the layer of paint, Loos follows Semper whose whole argument turns on the status of a coat of paint. Semper produces a history of paint within which the addition of a coat of paint to the surface of building is the way in which the original textile tradition was maintained in the age of solid construction. (In this way, architecture, the 'mother art', gives birth to the art of painting). This simulated textile, the painted text, becomes at once the new social language, the contemporary system of communication, and the new means by which space is constructed. Architecture is in the layer of paint. Paint sustains the masquerade in the face of the new solidity because it is 'the subtlest, most bodiless coating. It was the most perfect means to do away with reality, for while it dressed the material, it was itself immaterial.'[2]

Semper's argument was based on contemporary archeological evidence that the ancient buildings of antiquity only appeared to be naked white stone because the layers of coloured paint had been weathered off. This undermined the status of the materiality of the structures to that of a prop for a layer of paint. Semper argues that white marble was used precisely because it was a better 'base material' for painting on. It is transformed from the traditional paradigm of authentic materiality to but a 'natural stucco', a smooth surface on which to paint. Its smoothness is no longer identified with the purity of its material or of its forms, but as the possibility for a certain texture. Architecture is not the painted decoration of a naked structure. The sense of the naked is produced within the supplementary layer itself. The building never becomes visible, even where it coincides with the layer: the places 'where the monument was supposed to appear white were by no means left bare, but were covered with a white paint'[29].

Loos develops the *Principle of Dressing* into the *Law of Dressing* by prohibiting any such coincidence between the structure and its cladding. While this has the specific consequence of disassociating whiteness and structure, the general purpose of Loos' law is to keep the naked/clothed distinction within the textual economy sustained by the layer of paint rather than between the layer and its prop. It is this agenda that organises all of Loos's arguments. While his demands for the removal of ornament and the purification of the sensual in the name of whitewash appear to be a rejection of Semper's privileging of ornament, they are in fact the maintenance of it. The whitewash is the extreme condition, the test case, of Semper's argument. Loos is not simply arguing for the abolition of ornament but for collapsing the distinction between structure and ornament into the layer of cladding, a layer between structure and ornament within which difference is produced and can be inscribed.

Prosthetic Fabrications

But what of Le Corbusier's transformation of the *Law of Dressing* into the *Law of Ripolin*, in which there is no explicit rehearsal of Semper's argument? Indeed, it appears to be set up in direct opposition to Semper. The whitewash removes precisely those accessories that Semper identifies as the essence of architecture: 'Imagine the results of the Law of Ripolin. Every citizen is required to replace his hangings, his damasks, his wallpapers, his stencils, with a plain coat of white ripolin.[30] The textile tradition seems to be explicitly abandoned. Surface texture is erased. Indeed, decoration has to be removed because it 'clothes' the smooth modern object. Decoration is repeatedly described as clothing to be discarded in the name of the naked truth. Whitewash purifies by eliminating the 'superfluous' in favour of the 'essential'. The culture it sustains is one of 'rejection, pruning, cleansing; the clear and naked emergence of the Essential.'[31] In order for civilisation to progress from the sensual to the visual, the sensuality of clothes have to be removed in order to reveal the formal outline, the visual proportion, of the functional body.

But the body cannot be completely naked as that would be to return to the sensual. There is a need for some kind of screen, a veil neither of the sensuality of decoration nor of the sensuality of the body. A screen that remodels the body as formal proportion rather than sensual animal. The whitewash is inserted between two threats in order to transform body into form. The modern savage is not entirely naked. Purification results not in the naked body but the 'well-cut suit':

Decoration is of a sensorial and elementary order, as is colour, and is suited to simple races, peasants and savages. . . The peasant loves ornament and decorates his walls. The civilised man wears a well-cut suit and is the owner of easel pictures and books.

Decoration is the essential surplus, the quantum of the peasant; and proportion is the essential surplus, the quantum of the cultivated man.[32]

Here, as always, Le Corbusier identifies modernity with modern clothes. His lists of exemplary modern objects always include clothes. But it is not just that clothes form part of the list. Purification itself is explained in terms of the cut of a suit. *The Decorative Art of Today* begins by contrasting Louis XIV's 'coiffure of ostrich feathers, in red, canary, and pale blue; ermine, silk, brocade and lace; a can of gold, ebony, ivory, and diamonds' and Lenin's 'bowler hat and a smooth white collar'. His lists of modern objects always begin with clothes.[33] The first item in his 'museum of everything', the twentieth century archive, is 'a plain jacket, a bowler hat, a well-made shoe'. It is not accidental that the first thing we know of modern man, the first piece of evidence for his elevation from the degenerate realm of the senses into the realm of the visual, is his clothing. Indeed, Le Corbusier seems to suggest that clothes were the first objects of everyday life to lose their decoration:

But at the same time [that household objects were decorated] the railway engines, commerce, calculation, the struggle for precision, put his frills in question, and his clothing tended to become a plain black, or mottled; the bowler hat appeared on the horison.[34]

But clothing is even more than a historical precedent, Le Corbusier's whole thinking of modern objects is organised in terms of clothes. Objects are understood as 'auxiliary limbs', 'artificial limbs', prosthetic additions 'supplementing' the fixed structure of the body.[35] Diogenes' clothing of the naked body with a barrel is cited as 'the primordial cell of the house'. Diogenes serves a model of both purification and the identity between clothing and housing. The apparent rejection of decoration is therefore not a rejection of clothing. Architecture is clothing. Modern architecture, like all the many sciences of artificial limbs, is a form of tailoring:

He chucks up cornices and baldacchinos and makes himself more useful as a cutter in a tailor's shop. . . Decorative art becomes orthopaedic, an activity that appeals to the imagination, to invention, to skill, but a craft analogous to the tailor: the client is a man, familiar to us and precisely defined.[36]

Decorative art is the prosthetic 'art' of the tailor. It is a man centred art, but this is no humanism, this is a science of the artificial, centred the imperfect body, the 'inadequate', 'insufficient' body in need of protection by 'supporting limbs'. It is the prosthetic supplements that support the body not the body that supports the supplement.

For Le Corbusier, objects are clothes. The story of whitewash, as the endgame of the story of the modern obj ect, is a story of clothing. The coat of paint is, after all just that, a coat. It is still dressing. Even if it is the most simple dress . Semper's argument has not been abandoned. Even without texture, the smooth white surface remains a fabric.[37] We are still are in the domain of the text.[38] Le Corbusier makes a twentieth century reading of clothes, a displacement of what constitutes clothes rather than a displacement of clothing as such. Hence the central paradox of the text: '*Modern decorative art is not decorated*'.

It is symptomatic that the critics who neglect Le Corbusier's

losophy. It is philosophy's condition of possibility. Its not that rational theory's detachment of the superfluous from the essential leaves simple clothes, the 'essential surplus', but that the distinction between them is made possible by those clothes. Indeed, the distinction emerges in the text from a discussion of the simplicity of Diogenes' clothes. The high theory of philosophy is made possible by the low art of clothing, exceeded by that which it subordinates. In this sense, the look of the whitewash seems to be that of traditional metaphysics, the eye of reason. But Le Corbusier is not simply advocating a rational architecture. High theory is not the only institution to emerge from low art. Reason follows architecture but is not its endpoint. Architecture does not simply subordinate itself to the theoretical order it makes possible.

The whitewash makes possible the reason that may then be applied to the structure it covers. But it does not exhibit the rationality of that structure nor is it the result of that rationality. The truth made visible by the whitewash is not that of structural materials or construction technology but the truth of modern life. The layer of white paint exposes the 'structure' of the 'edifice' of modern culture rather than the structure of the building.[40] Le

L TO *R*: NEW CLOTHES, ILLUSTRATION FROM *THE DECORATIVE ART OF TODAY*; LOUIS XIV

arguments about whitewash systematically remove clothing from the list of everyday objects used as models by the Purist sensibility. Unlike the other objects, clothes can only be understood as supplements. They make explicit the Purist concern with the supplement which is at odds with the ideal of the authentic, irreducible object transparent to the gase which is sustained by traditional criticism as a model of both modern architecture and of sound historiography.

For Le Corbusier, it is precisely such a supplement, the simple fabric, that is the possibility of thought: 'The naked man does not wear an embroidered waistcoat; so the saying goes! . . . The naked man, once he is fed and housed...and clothed, sets his mind to work. . . The naked man does not wear an embroidered waistcoat; he wishes to think.'[39] Likewise, his original clothing, the house, is not embroidered. Its woven surface occupies the space between the new savage body of modern structure and the old seductive body of decoration. The thin opaque layer of whitewash masters the body in order to liberate the mind. The discretely clothed object makes pure thought possible by bracketing materiality.

Architecture is therefore more than simply an agent of phi-

Corbusier is concerned with the relationship between clothes and everyday life rather than that between the clothes and the body. He is opposed to the masking of cultural life but not the masking of the body. Structural conditions are never simply equated with those of everyday life. It is the prosthetic additions to the body that are the possibility of everyday life, not the body itself.

The decorative screen of folk–culture is 'the perfect mirror of its people' because it exposes what is in front of it rather than what is propping it up, the truth of culture rather than of material. Modern man can only exist in harmony with the realities of modern physical life by being isolated from them. The whitewash is a form of defence. It is not an extraordinary addition to everyday life but is the representation of the ordinary to a subject increasingly anxious in the face of modernity, dissimulating structure in order that people can feel.

Decoration is not removed in favour of pure structure. The expression of construction is precisely seen as but a temporary 'fashion' that followed the nineteenth century separation of decoration from structure and is succeeded by the truly modern concern for the straightforward, simple working clothes. For Le Corbusier, construction is mere reason, the rational tool by which man is set free. It is not a thing of interest in itself. It is masked with a coat of paint.[42] Structure can only be exposed when it has been rationalised to the minimum, so reduced that it can only be seen as a subordinate prop. Le Corbusier's central principles of the 'free plan' and the 'free facade' are precisely no more than the attempt to free the building from being 'the slave of the structural walls'. His buildings are multiple layers of screens suspended in the air. But even where the structure is apparently exposed it is clothed in a layer of paint, purified. Even the bones have skin, a self–denying skin. Following Loos, the object is, like all modern slaves, a 'self-effacing' prothesis, with an 'unassertive presence', marked only by the absence of decoration.[43] But this is not to say that the object is silent. The white is not neutral. The 'aesthetic of purity' speaks about silence. Purist rather than pure, the building exhibits the look of the naked, the clothing of nakedness, the clothes that say 'naked'. Nakedness is added and worn as a mask.

Construction technology does not simply produce new forms but lighter props for form. Technological progress is the increasing reduction of construction. Structure is but a frame for a skin, a cloth, the clothing of modernity. The house may be a machine

to sentiment in a variety of seemingly incontrovertible ways'[47] Theory is organised by and for art. The whitewash does not bracket materiality in order to simply construct a space of pure theory. It screens off the object in order to make a space for art which necessarily employs theory as a prop. It frees an eye for art. But what precisely is the status of this look which precedes that of theory? Is the 'detachment', 'disinterest' and 'distance' from materiality that the whitewash produces simply that of the traditional aesthetic?

Architecture after the Eye
It must recalled here that Semper's argument is explicitly set up in opposition to the account of architecture sustained by the philosophy of art. Aesthetics is seen to subordinate art by framing it: 'art appears isolated and shunted off to a field especially marked out for it.'[48] For Semper, art and philosophy belonged together in antiquity. Indeed 'philosophy was, as it were, an artist itself'[49] But it detaches itself from art by splitting art with alien categories which follow from an original split of the art object from its accessories.[50] This originary split is at once the possibility of the division of the arts and the detachment of

 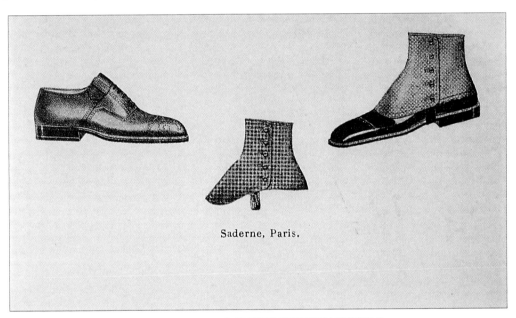

L TO R: M GASTON DOUMERGUE; NEW CLOTHES, ILLUSTRATION FROM *THE DECORATIVE ART OF TODAY*

but in as much as it is architecture, it does not look like one: 'Art has no business resembling a machine. But the means of art are set free. Illuminated with clarity'[44] The look of the machine is transformed into the look at art, a new look made possible by the machine. The white coat is a 'channelling of our attention only to those things worthy of it'[45] It is precisely a way of looking away from the structure towards art: 'In this mechanical, discreet, silent authentic comfort, there is a very fine painting on the wall.'[46] Suspended in the void between structure and decoration, the whitewash is a new, strange ground, a 'platform' on which objects 'stand out' either as artistic or as utilitarian. The look of the whitewash is split into the utilitarian look of rational theory and the aesthetic gaze.

Le Corbusier repeatedly separates utility from aesthetics and prohibits any 'confusion' between them by placing them in a vertical hierarchy in which art subordinates rational utility. Utilitarian objects are the 'platform of art' and reason is the 'support' of aesthetics but support in the Semperian sense, a supplementary prop that comes after, and is subordinate to, that which it holds up: 'Even before the formulation of a theory, the emotion leading to action can be felt: theory later gives support

philosophy from art. Art becomes an accessory to philosophy. The relationship between architecture and philosophy follows from its division into fundamental material structure and contingent accessories which entraps it:

In ancient and modern times the store of architectural forms has often been portrayed as mainly conditioned by and arising from the material, yet by regarding construction as the essence of architecture we, while believing to liberate it from false accessories, have thus placed it in fetters.[51]

Not only is architecture subordinated by being detached from its accessories and identified with its materiality, but it becomes the paradigm of materiality while the arts that emerged from it are elevated to high art. Hence architecture's 'organising and at the same time subordinate role' in the production of high art. Everywhere Semper opposes the placement of architecture through its division by a philosophical regime of distinctions that all turn on the originary distinction between essential object and inessential accessory, structure and decoration.

The operation of such a regime can be traced in the canonic text of aesthetics: Kant's *Critique of Judgement* which establishes an economy of the disinterested eye by splitting architecture in two. On the one hand, building is the paradigm of that which the aesthetic exceeds because it cannot be thought outside its utility.[52] As such, its beauty is merely 'appendant'. On the other hand, the decoration of building which can be considered as things in themselves: 'ornamental gardens', 'the decoration of rooms', 'wall hangings', 'wall-paper', 'ornamental accessories'– are elevated into 'free' beauty, free precisely from utility. The bracketing of material function liberates an economy of pure vision, the uncontaminated eye. Since the building is opposed to its decoration as the body is opposed to the eye, it is unsurprising that the decoration of a building is repeatedly identified with the decoration of the body which can be detached from it. Available for appropriation by the look, they constitute a 'picture':

> the decoration of rooms by means of hangings, ornamental accessories, and all beautiful furniture the sole function of which is *to be looked at,* and in the same way the art of tasteful dressing (with rings, snuff-boxes, etc). For a *parterre* of various flowers, a room with a variety of ornaments (including even the ladies attire) go to make at a festal gathering a sort of picture which, like pictures in the true sense of the word . . . has no business beyond appealing to the eye.[53]

The decoration of buildings is promoted into the highest form of art: painting. The functional body, whether that of a person or a building, on the other hand, cannot participate fully in this visual economy because it cannot escape its materiality. This gap between building and decoration is maintained by a number of prohibitions organised by race, gender and class discriminations which subordinate architecture by separating it from its accessories. The text seems to have no problem placing architecture.

But clearly it is not so simple. The question of architecture's place is complicated because Kant's argument is not simply applied to architecture. Rather, it is put in place in terms of architecture. The critique begins with two architectural examples with which it defines the fundamental disposition of aesthetic taste. The first separates the aesthetic eye from the eye of reason by opposing the rational cognition of a building to taking aesthetic delight in the building.[55] The aesthetic is detached from the rational knowledge it 'accompanies' and placed in a 'separate faculty'. The second employs the distinction between a decorated palace and functional buildings like simple huts and eating houses to establish aesthetic disinterest as a disinterest in the existence of an object, its purpose or utility.[56] Before we get the concepts, we get architecture, one of the arts to which the concepts are later to be applied. But why does architecture figure here so insistently? In both cases, the argument does not appear to depend on architecture. Any of the arts could be used as an example. Why is the aesthetic eye defined in terms of architecture?

The appropriation of architcture has already occurred in the preface in a more explicit form when it begins by describing metaphysics, the rationality from which aesthetics is detached, as an 'edifice'. Aesthetics is itself a decoration of the building of philosophy. A meta-metaphorics of architecture organises the text. Architecture passes between the preface, the introduction and the text they frame with ease.[57] It is not simply framed by philosophy. On the contrary, it frames philosophy. Exceeding its designated place, it at once subverts and organises Kant's project.

Reason is understood in terms of construction. Buildings necessarily engage the eye of reason and so compromise the detached aesthetic eye. But that detachment is itself precisely structural detachment, detachment from structure. It cannot be thought outside structure. It is itself structural. The structural art, architecture is therefore not just another example. Aesthetic detachment from reason and from utility are related through the figure of a building. Building is not simply an example of adherent beauty and the decoration of building an example of free beauty. The opposition is understood in terms of that between building and decoration.[58] The separation between adherent and free is itself understood as structural. Free beauty is detached from the reason and utility on which it is necessarily supported. Both reason and utility are identified with building. The text is organised around an opposition between building and its decoration whose influence can be traced everywhere.

In the text, architecture is the link between the aesthetic eye and the eye of reason. It both maintains the gap between them and makes the analogy between them, the contractual 'agreement' that is the basis of the third critique, possible. The visual is constructed. Structure cannot be separated from vision. Both the eye of reason and the aesthetic eye are understood in structural terms. Architecture is not simply placed in the visual, the visual is constructed on the basis of architecture. The economies of the visual are set up by a theory of architecture as decorated structure.

The critique attempts to control and exploit its architectural examples by oscillating between establishing an argument on the basis of architecture and applying that argument to architecture without producing a sense of circularity. Architecture undergoes a curious reversal. In metaphysics, building is the model of ideal structure and decoration is the model of gratuitous material seduction. In aesthetics, building is the model of inferior materiality and decoration the model of ideal detachment. This reversal is what allows the figure of architecture to pass between the different domains. Both domains attempt to maintain a gap between building and decoration. The architectural figure is reversed by turning on this 'axis'.

Kant maintains this gap by splitting ornament, that which lies between the grounding of structure and the detachment of decoration, between presence and representation. Ornament is 'only an adjunct and not an intrinsic constituent in the complete representation of the object' but, unlike decoration, it cannot be completely detached from the work and understood as an object in itself. It is split into formal 'beauty' and material 'charm' and can only 'augment' the work by means of its form.

Semper undermines this framing of architecture by inverting the distinction between high art and low art that follows from it.[59] He opposes 'the perversity of modern artistic conditions, according to which a wide gap, unknown to the Greeks, separates the so called small arts from the so-called high arts'.[6] This gap is based on the one between structure and decoration. Philosophy employs the traditional architectonic in subordinating craft as merely 'applied' but, for Semper, weaving, for example, is not an 'applied' art. It is neither applied to something – it precedes that on which it is propped – nor is it detached from something else – it does not precede the enclosure it establishes. Weaving simply originates as building.[61] Semper bases his theory of architecture on the low decorative arts rather than the monumental high arts.

In so doing, he inverts the traditional architectonic, subordinating structure to decoration by demonstrating that the 'false' accessories are the 'true' essence of architecture. This inversion necessarily distorts the economy of vision organised by the architectural trope in which what is seen on the outside articulates some inner unseeable truth.

> . . . even where solid walls become necessary they remain only the inner and unseen structure for the true and legitimate representatives of the spatial idea: namely, the more or less artificially woven and seamed-together, textile walls . . . the *visible* spatial enclosure.[62]

The truth of architecture is located in its visible outside. The Roman substitution of unpainted coloured materials for the Greek use of coloured paint, which lets the material 'speak for itself' is condemned as a loss of the greek conviction 'that inner content should conform to outer beauty.' The inside submits to the authority of the exterior. The 'true' wall is its visible 'artificial' surface. The 'invisible' structure is secondary. Everything is reversed to the extent that 'naked architecture', the absence of a coat of paint, is described as a 'disguise'.

Having inverted the architectonic, Semper then subverts the gap that divides ornament by undermining the distinction between form and colour. As part of the inversion, he privileges colour over form, by arguing that it came first[63], but then radically complicates the distinction between them. Since Kant splits ornament in order to sustain the account of architecture around which the pure vision of both philosophy and art are organised, Semper's frustration of the split necessarily promotes a different visuality. In countering the aestheticians who argue that applied colour 'must confuse the forms and pamper the eye' he argues that the 'visible wall'

> brings the eye back to the natural way of seeing, which it lost under the sway of that mode of abstraction that knows precisely how to separate the visible and inseparable qualities of bodies, the color from the form.[64]

Once form cannot be separated from colour, the figure of architecture is displaced. The visuality Semper describes is so entangled with a sensuality that cladding materials are analysed in terms of their feel, their tactility, and smell becomes part of the essence of a building.[65] The 'visible spatial enclosure', the surface texture that constitutes the architecture of the mask, is produced by this convolution of vision and sensuality.[66] Architecture no longer simply occupies the visual. Its sensuality is not screened off in the name of the uncontaminated eye. Visuality is a construction of necessarily sensuous social transactions.[67] The eye is impurity itself.

Occupation Strategies

It is in the context of this displacement of the visual that Le Corbusier's appropriation of low culture has to be rethought.[68] His convolution of the relationship between the everyday object and the art object disturbs the place of architecture and therefore its visuality. In the middle of *The Decorative Art of Today,* engineering is identified as the new decorative art and the original question 'where is architecture?' is reformulated: 'Can one then speak of the architecture of decorative art, and consider it of permanent value?' The text attempts to clarify the question by separating art from decorative art and placing them in a hierarchy.

> The Permanent value of decorative art? Let us say more exactly, of the *objects* that surround us . This is where we exercise our judgement: first of all the Sistine Chapel, afterwards chairs and filing cabinets; without doubt this is a question of the secondary level, just as the cut of a man's suit is of a secondary importance in his life. Hierarchy. First of all the Sistine Chapel, that is to say works truly etched with passion. Afterwards machines for sitting in, for filing, for lighting, type-machines, the problem of purification, of cleanliness, of precision, before the problem of poetry.[69]

As in the aesthetic tradition, art is supported on the utilitarian objects which come 'before' it but which are secondary to it. Art is a supplement, a form of decoration. But here the base object is itself decorative art. While the model of decorative art is yet again 'the cut of a man's jacket', the model for art, the Sistine Chapel, is precisely the paradigm of the painted surface, Semper's clothing of space. The opposition between them is between two forms of decoration, two forms of clothing of the object. In fact, the difference between them is social. It is a choice between the collective 'mirror' of decorative art or the individual 'mirror' of art.[70] Architecture cannot simply be placed in either domain.

Le Corbusier always identifies architecture with both: 'Architecture is there, concerned with our home, our comfort, and our heart. Comfort and proportion. Reason and aesthetics. Machine and plastic form. Calm and beauty.'[71] The question of architecture's place is not answered. The text is unable to simply place architecture within its own categories.

The same enigma can be found throughout Le Corbusier's writing. The opening of his most famous text: *Towards an Architecture,* for example attempts to place architecture by splitting it from engineering. But the division is immediately confused. On the one hand, architecture exceeds engineering: 'ARCHITECTURE is a thing of art, a phenomenon of the emotions lying outside questions of construction and beyond them'[72] but on the other hand, 'engineers produce architecture'. Nevertheless, it is precisely in the face of this displacement of the institutional practices of architectural discourse by engineering that the possibility of architecture, the 'essential surplus', is announced:

> Nevertheless, there does exist this thing called ARCHITECTURE . . . Architecture is in the telephone and in the Parthenon. How easily it could be at home in our houses![73]

These overlooked sentences from the beginning of the first chapter of probably the most influential text in twentieth century architectural discourse at once raise and complicate the question of the place of architecture. Architecture is itself housed. It has a home. But more than that, it houses itself. The new architecture of the telephone inhabits the old. The sentences involve more than just a juxtaposition of high and low art. Its not that the telephone is now to be thought of as a beautiful object available for appropriation by the detached eye. Rather, the Parthenon has to be thought of as a system of communication like the telephone. And the telephone has to be thought of as a means of production of space like the Parthenon. The telephone, like all systems of communication, defines a new spatiality and can be inhabited. It is the modern equivalent of the carpet. Like the coat of paint, it is a form of clothing that can be occupied. But not by some pre-existing culture. It is a new language that produces rather than represents modern culture. The telephone institutes a new community in the same way as the carpet instituted the family.

In Semper's model, the idea of the individual can only emerge within the institution of domesticity. The interior of the body is produced for the first time when its surface is marked in response to the definition of the interiority that is the family which is itself constituted by the construction of the textured surface that is the house. The idea of a speaker with an interior life only emerges within language. Interiority is not simply physical. It is a social effect marked on the newly constituted body of the individual.

Just as the language of the carpet produces the speaking subject in need of representation through clothing, the new means of communication produce a new individual in need of self-definition in art. Art being, for Le Corbusier, the mark of the individual. It is the systems of representation detached from the physical definition of interior that constitute shelter and make possible the 'inner life' he repeatedly identifies as the goal of architecture: 'the human spirit is more at home behind our foreheads than beneath gilt and carved baldacchios.'[74] Home is an effect of the appropriate decorative art, the art that is, by definition, 'something that only touches the surface'. Enclosure is a surface effect. While architecture is housing, the production of shelter, this is, for Le Corbusier, as it would later be for Heidegger, primarily a question of representation.

> The terminology employed today is no longer exact. The word 'architecture' is today more understandable as an idea than as a material fact; 'architecture': *to order, to put in order.*[75]

Architecture constructs through classification. The lines it draws are not simply material. Rather, they are the framing, the 'look' of different systems of representation. The whitewash is but one such system. It cannot simply be placed in either equipment or art because it is the mechanism for making the distinction between them. It is a system of classification defined in its intersection with other systems, each of which reframes the others. The traditional look of the whitewash, the limit condition of the painted wall, is transformed by its interaction with new systems.

The whitewash is inserted into the gap between the bodies of structure and decoration in order to construct a space for architecture which is neither simply bodily or theoretical. It occupies the gap in the architectural metaphor that organises traditional accounts of vision. An immaterial fabric which traces the convoluted lines stitching the tactile and the visual, its visuality is not that of either theory or aesthetics. The whitewash is produced where the visual cannot be simply detached from the sensual and each is transformed: 'Our hand reaches out to it [the modern object] and our sense of touch *looks* in its own way as out fingers close around it.'[76] Architecture is compacted into the

recording device on which other textualities are registered, and with which they are accommodated.

Architecture is to be found in these new textiles. It responds to transformations in the systems of communication – railway, automobile, aeroplane, radio, camera, cinema and telephone before it responds to the objects of industrialised everyday life.[78] Le Corbusier reinterprets the whitewash of vernacular culture in terms of these contemporary mechanisms, new languages that appear to operate increasingly independently of buildings. Le Corbusier places architecture within systems that do not require a structural prop. The whitewash dematerialises building in order to make a space for them, a space for new spacings, new sensualities. It is a double gesture. Architecture accommodates the new systems and is, at the same time, accommodated within them.

Because it is the gesture of placing, architecture has no intrinsic place: 'Where does architecture belong? In everything!'[79] It can only be placed by a specific architecture, an ensemble of representational techniques which preserve specific institutional agendas. Architecture's placement by philosophy involves such an architecture. Le Corbusier's arguments about

L TO *R*: PAGE FROM *THE DECORATIVE ART OF TODAY*; THE BARREL OF DIOGENES

thickness of the mask where this sensuous vision operates.

The eye of the whitewash, like the decorative art of the past, is a system of representation. Such systems change as technologies are transformed. Modernity is the production of new ways of looking before it is the production of new forms. Le Corbusier finds a 'new vision' in low art industrialised buildings which architecture, as a high art, a visual art in the traditional sense, resists. The new vision is sustained by the thickness of paint into which architecture is collapsed, Semper's 'non-bodily surface' between inside and outside. Flattened, it is pure image, a two dimensional projection of modern life. The white wall is a screen on which culture is projected: 'The white of whitewash is absolute: everything stands out from it and is recorded absolutely, black on white; it is honest and dependable.'[77] It is a

whitewash can be understood as a critique of that architecture which mobilises new techniques. They translate Semper's argument in the face of the emerging twentieth century systems of representation, displacing architecture by subverting the account of architecture with which philosophy organises visuality before it places architecture within the visual. Displacing the contractually bound visions of both high art and philosophy, Le Corbusier sketches not so much a new kind of object with a particular look, but an architecture by which the institution of architectural discourse can occupy the decorative art of today, the sensuous space of telecommunication – an architecture after philosophy and invisible to its art-historical servants.

But for the present we are most certainly not in the agora of the philosophers: we are only dealing with decorative art.[80]

The research for this paper was carried out under a fellowship at the Chicago Institute for Architecture and Urbanism.

1 Le Corbusier, *The Decorative Art of Today,* trans James Dunnet, MIT Press, Cambridge, 1987, p xix. [translations have been modified]
2 ibid, p 188.
3 ibid, p 192.
4 Most critics not only do not address Le Corbusier's theories about whiteness, but they do not even refer to the whiteness of the projects, even in the most exhaustive accounts of the early villas, such as Tim Benton's *The Villas of Le Corbusier.* Often elaborate arguments about Le Corbusier's use of colour are made but they ignore the status of white. The whitewash is so taken for granted that it usually only comes up by way of negation. Curtis, for example, discusses the way in which the later Le Corbusier left behind 'the image of the white, machine–age box' ('Le Corbusier: Nature and Tradition', in *Le Corbusier: Architect of the Century,* Arts Council, London, 1987, p 20.) and Frampton talks of the resistance to thinking of Le Corbusier outside the 'Purist–machinist vision' of 'the white modern whitewash from *L'Esprit Nouveau* that were reframed in *The Decorative Art of Today* to explain Le Corbusier's interest in the industrial vernacular but he goes on to dismiss *The Decorative Art of Today* as 'a polemical work of only local interest'(*Theory and Design in the First Machine Age,* MIT Press, Cambridge, 1960, p. 248).
5 Georges Vigarello, *Concepts of Cleanliness: Changing Attitudes in France since theMiddleAges,* trans Jean Birrell, Cambridge University Press, Cambridge, 1988, p 231.
6 Le Corbusier, op cit, p 189.
7 ibid, p 189.
8 ibid, p 190.
9 Adolf Loos, 'Ladies Fashion', in *Spoken into the Void: Collected Essays 1897-1900,* trans Jane O. Newman and John H . Smith, MIT Press, Cambridge, 1982, p.102. cf.'The lower the cultural level of people, the more extravagant it is with its ornament, its decoration. . . To seek beauty only in form and not in ornament is the goal toward which all humanity is striving.' Adolf Loos, 'The Luxury Vehicle', *Spoken into the Void: Collected Essays 1897–1900,* p 40.
10 'Decoration: baubles, charming entertainment for a savage. . . It

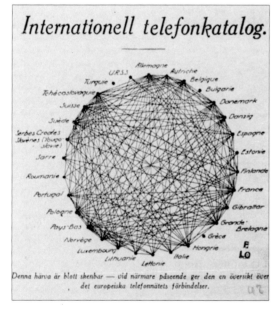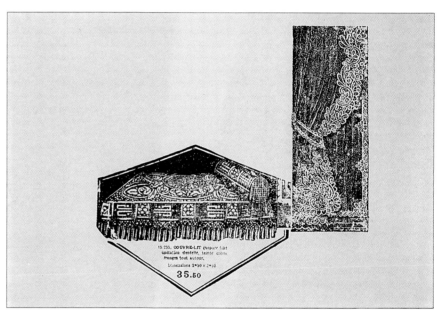

L TO R: INTERNATIONAL TELEPHONE NETWORK; OLD CLOTHES FROM *THE DECORATIVE ART OF TODAY*

architecture of the first half of the twentieth century' ('The Other Le Corbusier: Primitive Form and the Linear City 1929-52', in *Le Corbusier: Architect of the Century,* p 29.) Those who refer to the whiteness do so in passing, employing the unquestioned rhetoric of the neutral surface while making other points. Some briefly identify the whiteness with the mediterranean vernacular. Curtis, for example, refers to the 'stark white forms, a purist version of the vernacular' (William J. R. Curtis, *Le Corbusier: Ideas and Forms,* Rizzoli, New York, 1986, p 67.) It is in a series intended for readers outside architecture that this point assumes the most importance. Gardiner argues that Le Corbusier's white walls was as important as any other factor in making him the 'leader' of modern architecture. Quoting *The Decorative Art of Today* on the presence of whitewash in all mature vernacular culture, he compares the aesthetic links between the buildings in a mediteranean village to the links between the buildings of modern architecture: 'whitewash was also a visual bond between the buildings of the island villages; like the bare essentials that hold people together, whitewash was a bond that held aesthetics together... Thus white became the bond between Le Corbusier's early buildings. In consequence, it became the bond between all the European architectural modern movements of the 1920s and 1930s, white was the theme that held the total picture together.' (Stephen Gardiner, *Le Corbusier,* The Viking Press, New York, 1974, p 40.) Banham cites some passages of dealing with the

seems justified to affirm: *the more cultivated a people becomes, the more decoration disappears.* (surely it was Loos who put it so neatly).' Le Corbusier, ibid p 85. 'elsewhere, around 1912, Loos wrote that sensational article, *Ornament and Crime,. . .*', ibid, p134.
11 cf. Beatris Colomina, 'L'Esprit Nouveau, Architecture and Publicite', *Architecture production,* Princeton Architectural Press, 1988. p 77. Stanislaus von Moos, 'Le Corbusier and Loos', *Assemblage 4,* 1987, p 25-38.
12 Adolf Loos, 'Ornament and Crime', trans Wilfred Wang in *The Architecture of Adolf Loos,* Arts Council, 1985, p 100.
13 Adolf Loos, 'Architecture 1910', trans Wilfred Wang in *The Architecture of Adolf Loos,* p 104.
14 For explicit references to the *Law of Ripolin* in recent scholarship, see: Lion Murand and Patrick Sylberman's entry 'Decor (1925): Il s'agit d'une epaisseur de blanc' in *Le Corbusier, une encyclopedie,* Centre Georges Pompidou, 1987, 116-118; and Bruno Reichlin, 'La petite maison' a Corseaux. Une analyse structurale', in *Le Corbusier a Geneve 1922-1932: Projets et Realisations,* Payot, Lausanne, 1987, p 119-134.
15 *Bekleidung* is being rendered here as 'dressing' following Mallgrave and Herrmann's translation rather than Newman and Smith's translation as 'cladding'. For the respective notes on this issue, see Gottfried Semper, *The Four elements of Architecture and other Writings,* trans Harry Francis Mallgrave and Wolfgang Herrmann,

Cambridge University Press, Cambridge, 1989, p 293. and Adolf Loos, *Spoken into the Void*, p 139.

16 Adolf Loos, 'Principle of Dressing', *Spoken into the Void: Collected Essays 1897-1900*, p 67.

17 ibid, p 67.

18 Mullgrave and Herrmann use Peter Behrens' (for whom Le Corbusier initially worked) rejection of Semper in a 1910 essay as marking the detachment of twentieth century architectural discourse from Semper. This detachment followed the misreading of Semper by arthistorians, even though it had already been set up by Otto Wagner's displacement of Semper's concepts in *Modern Architecture*. Behrens cites Alois Riegel's reading of Semper to dismiss his thought. On the successive misreadings of Semper within architectural and arthistorical discourse, see: Magaret Ivenson, 'Riegel Versus Semper', *Daida70s 29*, 1988, 46-49; Michael Podro, *The Critical Historians of Art*, Yale University Press, New Haven, 1982, p 44-55; Rosemarie Haag Bletter, 'On Martin Frochlich's Gottfried Semper', *Oppositions 4*, 1974, p 146-153; and Wolfgang Herrmann, *Gottfried Semper: In Search of Architecture*, MIT Press, Cambridge, 1984.

19 Gottfried Semper, 'Preliminary Remarks on Polychrome Architecture', in *The four Elements of Architecture and other Writings*, p 52.

20 Gottfried Semper, 'Style: The Textile Art', in *The Four Elements of Architecture and other Writings*, p 254.

21 Gottfried Semper, 'The Four Elements of Architecture', in *The Four Elements of Architecture and other Writings*, p 104.

22 'The art of dressing the body's nakedness (if we do not count the ornamental painting of one's own skin discussed above) is probably a later invention than the use of covering for encampments and spatial enclosures.' 'Style: The Textile art', p 254. 'tribes in an early stage of their development apply their budding artistic instinct to the braiding and weaving of mats and covers (even when they still go around completely naked).' 'The Four Elements of Architecture', p 103.

23 Gottfried Semper, 'Style: the Textile Art', p 257.

24 The artist must not 'violate the material to meet halfway an artistic intent that demands the impossible from the material.' Gottfried Semper, 'Style: Prolegomenon', p 189.

25 'Masking does not help, however when *behind* the mask the thing is false or the mask is no good. In order that the material, the indispensable (in the usual sense of the expression) be completely denied in the artistic creation, its complete mastery is the imperative precondition. Only by complete technical perfection, by judicious and proper treatment of the material according to its properties, and by taking these properties into consideration while creating form can the material be forgotten,...' Gottfried Semper, 'Style: The Textile Art', p 257.

26 'But have you ever noticed the strange correspondence between the exterior dress of people and the exterior of buildings? ...But do our contemporary houses correspond with our clothes?' Adolf Loos, 'Architecture 1910'.

27 Adolf Loos, 'Principle of Dressing', p 66.

28 Gottfried Semper, 'Style: vol. 1', p. 445. cited by Henry Francis Mallgrave, 'Gottfried Semper: Architecture and the Primitive Hut', *Reflections 3(1)*, Fall 1985, p 65.

29 Gottfried Semper, 'Preliminary Remarks on Polychrome Architecture', p 59.

30 Le Corbusier, *The Decorative Art of Today*, p 188. cf. 'The time is past when we...can lounge on ottomans and divans among orchids in the scented atmosphere of a seraglio and behave like so many ornamental animals or humming-birds in impeccable evening dress, pinned through the trunk like a collection of butterflies to the swathes of gold, lacquer or brocade on our wall-panelling and hangings', ibid, p 192.

31 Le Corbusier, *Towards an Architecture*, trans Frederick Etchells, John Rodker, London, 1931, p 138. (translations have been modified)

32 ibid, p 143.

33 For example, Le Corbusier, *Towards an Architecture*, p 95.

34 Le Corbusier, *The Decorative Art of Today*, p 54.

35 cf Beatris Colomina, 'L 'Esprit Nouveau, Architecture and Pub7icite'.

36 Le Corbusier, *The Decorative Art of Today*, p 72.

37 cf. Osenfant, for whom white is the necessary frame against which

colour is seen: '*London requuires linen collars. The old London architects provided whites. Why have they been almost totally abandoned?*', 'Colour and Method', *Architectural Review*, vol 81, p 90.

The role of white linen is crucial to the concept of cleanliness. Viagarello traces how the wearing of white fabric constituted cleanliness before the body itself was cleaned. Georges Vigarello, *Concepts of Cleanliness: Changing Attitudes in France since the Middle Ages*.

38 Even his earliest readings of the vernacular whitewash understand it as decorative: 'its white arcades bring comfort, and the three great whitewashed walls, which are painted each spring, make a screen as decorative as the background of Persian ceramics.' Le Corbusier, *Journey to the East*, trans Ivan Saknic, MIT Press, Cambridge, 1987.

39 Le Corbusier, *The Decorative Art of Today*, p 23.

40 Gratuitous decoration not only covers over flaws in the structure of the object, it also covers over flaws in the structure of contemporary life: 'Then *background noise* to fill in the holes, the emptiness. Musical noise, embroidered noise or batiked noise.' ibid, p 30.

41 Architecture has another meaning and other ends to pursue than showing construction and responding to needs', *Towards an Architecture*, p 110 The Parthenon is seen as a climax of the gradual passage 'from construction to architecture', ibid, p 139.

42 This masking is often criticised as a departure from the rigorous theory of modern architecture in order to sustain the critical ideal of transparency to the essential status of an object. Kenneth Frampton describes the way the early villas 'masqueraded as white, homogenous, machine-made forms, whereas they were in fact built of concrete block-work held in place by a reinforced concrete frame. ' *Modern Architecture: A Critical History*, Thames and Hudson, London, 1985, 248. Here, the theory is understood to be precisely that of the necessity of such a masquerade. Likewise, John Winter argues that, in the early 'white stucco box tradition', 'the feel of the machine-made was more image than reality . . . all stuccoed and painted to try to give it the precision of machine products . . . traditional buildings decorated to look machine-made . . . the machine-age image.' in 'Le Corbusier's Technological Dilemma', in Russell Walden ed, *The Open Hand: Essays on Le Corbusier*, MIT Press, Cambridge, 1977, p 326. Here, the reality of the machine-age is understood to be image.

43 The human-limb object is a docile servant. A good servant is discreet and self–effacing in order to leave his master free.' Le Corbusier, *The Decorative Art of Today*, dec 79. cf. Adolf Loos: 'Rather, it is a question of being dressed in a way that stands out the least', 'Men's Fashion', in *Spoken into the Void: Collected Essays 1897–1900*, p. 11 'Primitive man had to differentiate themselves by various colours, modern man needs his clothes as a mask,' 'Ornament and Crime', p 102.

44 Le Corbusier, *The Decorative Art of Today*, p 114.

45 ibid, p 76.

46 ibid, p 77.

47 ibid, p 163. 'feeling dominates. . . Reason gives feeling the purified means it needs to express itself' ibid, p 168.

48 Gottfried Semper, 'Style: Prolegomenon', p 194.

49 ibid, p 194.

50 'What is the purpose of this constant separation and differentiation that characterises our present theory of art? Would it not be better and more useful to stress the ascending and descending integration of a work into its surroundings and with its accessories, rather than always to distinguish and divide? . . . must we again rob it of its accessories?' Gottfried Semper, 'The Four Elements of Architecture', p 89.

51 ibid, p 102.

52 'In architecture the chief point is a certain use of the artistic object to which, as the condition, the aesthetic ideas are limited. . . adaption of the product to a particular use is the essential element in a work of architecture.' Immanuel Kant, *Critique of Judgement*, trans James Creed Meredith, Oxford University Press, London, 1952, p 183.

53 ibid, p 188.

54 'Much might be added to a building that would immediately please the eye, were it not intended for a church. A figure might be identified with all manner of flourishes and light but regular lines, as

is done by the New Sealanders with their tattooing, were we dealing with anything but the figure of a human being. And here is one whose rugged features might be softened and given a more pleasing aspect, only he has got to be a man, or is, perhaps, a warrior that has to have a warlike appearance.', ibid, p 73.

55 'To apprehend a regular and appropriate building with one's cognitive faculties, be the mode of representation clear or confused, is quite a different thing from being conscious of this representation with an accompanying sensation of delight.' ibid, p 42.

56 'If any one asks me whether the palace I see before me is beautiful, I may, perhaps, reply that I do not care for things of that sort that are merely made to be gaped at. Or I may reply in the same strain as that Iroquois *Sachem* who said that nothing in Paris pleased him better than the eating-houses. I may go a step further and inveigh with the vigour of a *Rousseau* against the vanity of the great who spend the sweat of the people on such superfluous things. Or, in fine, I may quite easily persuade myself that if I found myself on an uninhabited island, without hope of ever again coming among men, and could conjure such a palace into existence by a mere wish, I should still not trouble to do so, so long as I had a hut there that was comfortable enough for me. All this may be admitted and approved; only it is not the point now at issue. All one wants to know is whether the mere representation of the object is to my liking, no matter how indifferent I may be to the real existence of the object of this representation.' ibid, p 43.

57 Bearing in mind the entanglement of architecture, institution, and preface: 'There has never been an architecture without preface'

'The preface is not an institutional phenomenon amongst others. It presents itself as an institution through and through; the institution par excellence.' Jacques Derrida, '52 Aphorisms for a foreword', trans Andrew Benjamin, *Deconstruction: Omnibus Volume,* Academy Editions, London, 1989, 67-69. See Derrida's reading of the thrid critique: 'The Parergon', in *The Truth in Painting,* trans Geoff Bennington and Ian McCleod, University of Chicago, Chicago, 1988, p 37-82.

58 The opening opposition between the functional hut and the decorated palace which establishes aesthetic disinterest punctuates the body of the text: 'With a thing that owes its possibility to a purpose, a building or even an animal, its regularity, which consists in symmetry, must express the unity of the intuition accompanying the concept of its end, and belongs with it to cognition. But where all that is intended is the maintenance of a free play of the powers of representation...in ornamental gardens, in the decoration of rooms, in all kinds of furniture that shows good taste, etc, regularity in the shape of constraint is to be avoided as far as possible . . . All stiff regularity . . . is inherently repugnant to taste.' Immanuel Kant, *Critique of Judgement,* p 88.

59 'Before this separation our grandmothers were indeed not members of the academy of fine arts or album collectors or an audience for aesthetic lectures, but they knew what to do when it came to designing an embroidery. There's the rub!', Gottfried Semper, 'Style: The Textile Art', p 234.

60 Gottfried Semper, 'Style: Prolegomenon', p 184.

61 'It remains certain *that the origin of building coincides with the beginning of textiles.*' Gottfried Semper, 'Style: The Textile Art', p 254.

62 ibid, p 255.

63 '. . . it ranks among the earliest of all inventions because the instinct for pleasure, as it were, inspired man. Delight in color was developed earlier than delight in form. . .', ibid, p 234.

64 Gottfried Semper, 'Preliminary Remarks on Polychrome Architecture', p 61.

65 'To complete the image of an oriental residence one has to imagine the costly furnishings of gold-plated couches and chairs, divans, candelabras, all kinds of vases, carpets, and the fragrance of incense.' Gottfried Semper, 'Structural Elements of Assyrian-Chaldean Architecture', trans Wolfgang Herrmann, *Gottfried Semper: In Search of Architecture,* 216. Semper cites Bruno Kaiser on speculative aesthetics: 'If form, colour, and quantity can only be properly appreciated after they have been sublimated in a test tube of categories, if the sensual no longer makes sense, if the body (as in this aesthetics) must first commit suicide to reveal its treasures - does this not deprive art of the basis for its independent existence?', 'Style: Prolegomenon', p 194.

66 In the play between the visual and the tactile in Adolf Loos, see Beatris Colomina, 'Intimacy and Spectacle: Constructions of the Modern Subject' a paper presented at the Chicago Institute for Architecture and Urbanism conference on architectural theory in 1988, forthcoming in *AA Files 19,* Spring 1990.

67 Semper recovers the sensuality of the sign rejected by Kant. For Kant, clothing and the decoration of buildings are become language. With the passage of civilisation, this 'work of communication' becomes independent of the body of the building and the body of man. While the aesthetic interest in the decorative depends on this independence, it is precisely not an interest in decoration as conventional language as, for Kant, language is itself utilitarian. The social reappropriates the decorative (that which is detached from purpose) as purposive. Semper describes architecture as language and embraces the social as sensual.

68 On Le Corbusier's transformation of the status of the artwork in mass culture, see: Beatris Colomina, '*L'Esprit Nouveau,* Architecture and *Publicite.';* and Stanislaus von Moos, *Le Corbusier: Elements of a Synthesis,* trans James Dunnett, Cambridge, 1979.

69 Le Corbusier, *The Decorative Art of Today,* p 76.

70 'The work of art, the living double' of a being, whether still present, or departed, or unknown; that faithful mirror of an individual passion' ibid, p 118. versus the decorative art 'in which particular is absorbed in the general', ibid, p 121.

71 ibid, p 137.

72 Le Corbusier, *Towards an Architecture, p 19.*

73 ibid, p 15.

74 Le Corbusier, *The Decorative Art of Today,* p 117.

75 Le Corbusier, *When the Cathedrals Were White,* trans Francis E . Hyslop, Reynal and Hitchcock, 1947, p 202.

76 Le Corbusier, *The Decorative Art of Today,* p 112.

77 ibid, p 190.

78 see Beatris Colomina, 'Le Corbusier and Photography', *Assemblage* 4, 1987, 7-24.

79 Le Corbusier, *When the Cathedrals were White, p 118.*

80 Le Corbusier, *The Decorative Art of Today,* p 170.

———— * ————

PETER EISENMAN
THE ARCHITECTURAL PHILOSOPHY

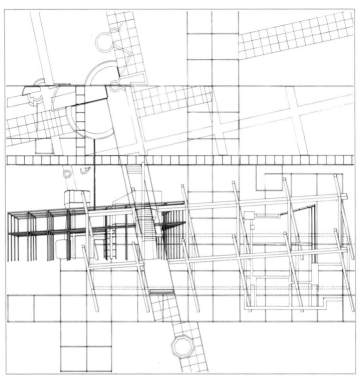

PETER EISENMAN, THE WEXNER CENTER, ASSORTED ELEMENTS

'In the sense of the pragmatic mind Wexner is not clear. The grid is very clear. But take away the rest of it – the student housing, the towers and you having nothing but this grid. Then it is back to a purist thing. It is the displacement of the grid, basically. What is interesting about the grid at the Wexner is that it is pulled away from the object itself. Don't forget the houses were grids, and the spaces within the grid. Here at Wexner, it is like the grid cover has been pulled away from the object, because it pulls away. The object isn't any longer just a grid. And the grid is something that pulls away and then this other thing sort of seeps into the stone, cuts into the stone, cuts into the brick. It is not the grid that cuts into these things, it is the other thing, the grid protected materials and materiality was the core of an abstract grid. Now if the core, this abstraction, is taken away, and it is the exposed core, and then you feel this exposed core, and then you fel this meltdown of the core, this displacement of the core. And I think that this grid is the displaced and then the core becomes displaced as well. That is metaphorically what happens at the Wexner'   *Peter Eisenman*

'The Wexner Center represents the first realisation of Eisenman's architecture in the United States, and it makes a powerful counter-statement to the current crop of massive cultural institutions which have begun to rear their blind heads from Washington, D.C. to Dallas to Orange County. These projects tend to result in monoliths whose volumes have all the subtlety of a giant wedge of cheese, and whose urban presence depends on a *cordon sanitaire* of irrigated lawn and vacant granite plazas. But there are signs of other approaches; Richard Meier's master plan for the new Getty Center in Brentwood, Frank Gehry's Disney Concert Hall in Los Angeles – if the project can be realised as Gehry originally conceived it – and now, for all to see, Eisenman's Wexner Center. However remote Eisenman's work may stand from either of these other two examples, it shares ideas with Gehry's recent thinking about the place of the 'new' within its context, and about the capabilities of architectural imagination. In sharp contrast to the encroaching extremes of programmatic determination, Gehry and Eisenman bring programmatic flexibility into a raport with architectural indeterminacy. In obvious ways, both of them let certain architectural events occur at the same time as they allow for elements that are not of the same origin as the design itself.'   *Kurt Forster*